Once Upon a Time in Italy

Once Upon a Time in Italy

The Vita Italiana
of an American Journalist

Jack Casserly

ROBERTS RINEHART PUBLISHERS

To my wife, Joy, and our beloved Mafia —
Kevin, Terry, Jeffrey, and Larry

Contents

Foreword

By Bob Considine

(Considine was, by the consensus of his peers, one of the great-est reporters in American history and perhaps its most prolific. In addition to his career as a reporter and columnist, Considine wrote many books and screenplays, hosted radio and TV shows, and was one of the most humorous after-dinner speakers of his time. Considine and Casserly covered many stories together and became close friends. Considine wrote this Foreword shortly before his untimely death in 1975.)

JOHN CASSERLY AND his treasured brood fell under the spell of Italy, once upon a time, and they will never recover. Italians, notably Romans, bewitched the lot of them. This book by my friend Jack, one of the ablest newsmen of my time, is a delightful account of their experience.

It is as fragrant as a freshly done bowl of minestrone liberally endowed with dated Parmesan. It is as sad as the sight of Pius XII lying on his death bed, and as hilarious as the struggle to tear down the language barriers. It is, in short, Italy as seen through the eyes of an American reporter assigned to go there, stay there, and live off the land.

The typical visitor to Italy finds himself restricted to a narrow corridor. He eats too much in Naples, drinks too much in Rome, gets pushed around at the Pope's general audience, develops bunions during the catacomb tours, and spends more money than necessary. The only Italians he meets are prime examples of venality: waiters, captains, cabbies, and guides.

He never gets to know, say Bagnoli . . . who made Joy Casserly (who couldn't speak a word to him) know that Italy was ready to embrace her.

He never knows the thrill of combat in the grocery market, or the struggle to get a telephone or a toilet seat. And he (or she) never knows what it means to be pinched on the rear.

Jack and Joy, and later the boys, fitted themselves into the fabric of this ancient land and learned to live with some of the most wonderfully exasperating people on earth. There was never a dull moment, never a day that did not confront them with a challenge—whether it was an empty water spigot or the coverage of a Communist strike.

You'll enjoy apartment-hunting with Jack and Joy, Roman-style. You'll experience with them the rigors of finding, placating, feeding, and watering Italian maids until Providence intervened and Elena came to live with them for six blessed years, tending to their every need, guarding the three little boys "like a lioness."

You'll be taken to places you couldn't conceivably know about, unless the Casserlys led you! The tiny pensione off St. Mark's Square in Venice that a jolly cardinal named Angelo Giuseppe Roncalli used to frequent for a nip of wine; a wood-carver's shop in Assisi, where an old man who carves only the image of St. Francis confided, "St. Francis travels from our workshop all over the world. His birds sing. His voice whispers again: 'Lord, make me an instrument of Your peace . . . where there is hatred, let me sow love. . . .'"

Jack Casserly served as bureau chief for the International News Service in Rome, then after the collapse of the INS was head of the American Broadcasting Company's bureau. In those capacities it was inevitable that he would meet such interesting people. A splendid parade of characters marches through his book. My favorite among them is Franco Bucarelli, a passionate volcano of a man. In applying to Casserly for a job with ABC, Franco disdained handing him a neatly typed resumé of his credentials—instead, he made a speech!

"The name is Franco Bucarelli! Citizen of Naples. Lawyer, newspaper reporter, radio sportscaster, movie actor, poet, sometime songwriter, and bachelor. . . . For references in Naples, I got the chief of police, Lucky Luciano, the cardinal, and Franco Bucarelli. That is, I am my own lawyer!"

Jack Casserly has written a long love letter to Italy, blown a kiss to a dream.

It is generous of him to share his rare memories.

Bob Considine

Introduction

I HAVE THOUGHT about this book for 30 years, ever since my wife, Joy, our three children and I left Italy in 1964. We lived in Rome for seven years and had three sons born there—Kevin, Terence and Jeffrey. They became "Romans of Rome," not only born in the Eternal City but baptized under the dome of St. Peter's Basilica.

Joy and I arrived in Rome in the spring of 1957—she from New York by ocean liner, and I by plane from Yugoslavia, where I had gone on a month's assignment reporting the differences between the Soviet and Tito's brands of communism. The long-time Yugoslav dictator argued against many Moscow doctrines and faced the threat of Soviet military intervention.

I was the new bureau chief of the International News Service. The INS merged a year later with United Press and I became bureau chief of the new Hearst Headline Service. In 1961, I joined ABC News and became its Mediterranean bureau chief in Rome. It was a dream assignment and I was walking on air. In addition to Italy and the Vatican, I covered other parts of Europe, Greece and Turkey, North Africa, the Middle East, and parts of Africa.

Rome was home, however, and every day away from it was like losing part of my life. It was *our* apartment, *our* piazza, *our* pasta, *our* sun on the beaches and, *our* Mediterranean sea.

A century ago, Austria's diplomat and statesman, Prince Metternich called Italy a "geographic expression" — as if nothing unified it. He was wrong. Italians are unique in living, eating, loving, opera, singing old songs, and making what they call *bel' confusione* (beautiful confusion).

I began chronicling our *Vita Italiana* only a few months after we came home to Washington, DC. Later, I divided the events and escapades into chapters. I would sit before my typewriter in the basement and chuckle. Sometimes cry.

Our boys would see me and they would say, "Papa, are you writing about our life in Italy again? When are you going to finish the book?"

I would say, "Soon, boys, very soon."

The months lengthened into years. I was assigned to cover the White House for ABC News after months on the 1964 political campaign trail with New York Governor Nelson Rockefeller, GOP vice presidential candidate William E. Miller, President Lyndon Johnson, and Republican candidate for president Senator Barry Goldwater. In 1965, I spent six months covering the revolution in the Dominican Republic. Then, in 1966, I was sent to report the war in Vietnam and spent most of the following year covering Dr. Martin Luther King and the civil rights movement throughout the country. In 1968, I was assigned to report the presidential campaign of Senator Eugene McCarthy.

During those and subsequent years, I was rarely home or worked long hours, and the manuscript gathered dust on a basement shelf. But the boys did not forget. They would often ask, "Papa, when are you going to finish the book?"

My answer slackened. "Well, I'm going to get around to it one of these days. For sure. You can bet on it." From time to time, I would descend to the basement to type and retype the manuscript. There were no speedy computers then.

Our three boys were joined by a fourth, Lawrence, in 1967.

It was impossible to forget Italy. For example, our son, Kevin, came in crying one afternoon and told his mother in Italian: "Mamma, those kids across the street called us a bunch of Greeks. Mamma, we're Italians!"

Eventually our boys no longer spoke to one another in Italian. Indeed, they forgot most of the language in time. Yet, in our mind's eye, each of us returned again and again to Rome, Naples, Florence, Venice, Sicily, and other places and people in *bella Italia*.

Through the years, on gray or melancholy days, I would think of Italy and return to the manuscript again. Joy and I often spoke of returning to Italy. As 1991 began, we told one another, "Perhaps this is the year." Inspired, the rhythm of Italian life returned to my soul, and I began to write more regularly. After a few weeks, people and places rose out of the past as if by magic. I was back in Italy again. One scene played over and over in my head and heart:

It was a late summer afternoon. I was walking in swimsuit and bare feet with our little boys along the beach near Anzio, south of Rome, in search of seashells. We would sift the shells from the sand and wash them in the Mediterreanean. Sometimes, the shells were strikingly beautiful, a crisscross of sea-blue and starry silver. Other times, they were as harsh brown as sun-scorched earth, or as gray as clouds in a threatening sky.

We learned that the brilliance or haze of the shell never told us anything of the faithfulness or beauty of its echo. We would cup the shell to an ear and listen. The most brilliant would sometimes waver in trying to capture the cry of a child along the beach. Yet the sea would sometimes become a symphony in the drabest shell of the shore.

This book is an attempt to recall those color-splashed shells and their sea of sounds, faces, and places that surrounded our homes for so long. These pages are echo chambers, recalling castles on the beach that crumpled into grains of sand, and heavenly Gregorian chants that lofted from the magnificent basilicas of Rome. And the people who shared our lives—from maids and plumbers to reporters and *papparazzi*, from gangsters and a gun moll to an opera diva and her retinue, and on to famous actors and a pop singer who also sang opera and, finally, three popes—Pius XII, John XXIII, Paul VI—and a string of cardinals and other prelates.

For all those unforgettable years, we sought the magic of the moment. A turn in the roads from Sicily to the Alps that brought us new friends and fortune. A toss of a coin in an old fountain where a palace had no prince and the vineyards no grapes.

Wherever the path or people, there was mostly joy in the journey. It was the call that mattered, the sounds of new seashells.

In October and November of 1991, Joy and I returned to Rome for the first time since we left in 1964. We visited old friends, homes, streets, piazzas, churches, and other long-ago haunts. Some friends and acquaintances had died or we could not find. Others greeted us with smiles and tears. Most landmarks remained but some had disappeared amid new construction. We walked Rome's hills and piazzas, and that which remained reminded us that it was still the Eternal City. That return is recounted in an epilogue to this work.

We were only a brief echo in the long history of Italy. Yet, to those we met along the journey, we kiss your hands. That beautiful expression of respect is our common bond of life and love—a love that has endured the test of time. *Viva Italia!*

Joy and Jack Casserly
Prescott, Arizona
1994

Chapter 1

Benvenuto

THE NOONDAY SUN blazed across the city as my plane touched down at Rome's old Ciampino Airport on May 10, 1957. I had just spent a month touring Yugoslavia, writing a series of stories for International News Service about how Tito's brand of communism differed from the Soviets'.

As the Yugoslav airliner approached Rome, I saw the outlines of the Eternal City and the Vatican for the first time. In those days, passenger planes flew across the Italian capital to Ciampino instead of today's Leonard da Vinci Airport on the Mediterranean. I was happy to see Rome. My high school Latin classes flooded back to mind. Hail, Caesar! I salute you, Cicero! Long live the Latin poets!

I arrived at the Massimo D'Azelio Hotel in bright spirits. Joy didn't know I had arrived. I phoned her room from the lobby. Almost before one could invoke the name of Enrico Caruso, she was down spilling tears on the concierge's desk. The gentleman smiled, perhaps in relief, because Joy had told him her husband would pay the mounting bill when he arrived. With a gesture of blessing, the concierge waved us into the parlor and sent in cof-

1

fee on the house. The full bill, to the day, was underneath the sugar bowl.

I kissed Joy, told her how much I missed her during the month, and held her hand. A tear of gladness slipped down her cheek, and we enjoyed just looking at one another. Then, as if fired by a Ferrari engine, Joy described the past four weeks in rapid bursts.

There had been announcements in the papers that I was the new INS bureau chief. She had some leads on apartments. Her Italian was *forte* (strong). Rome was *calda* (hot). Food was *meraviglioso* (marvelous). People were *amichevole* (friendly). And Rome was *grande, veramente grande!* (big, really big!)

"Well, is there anything wrong in paradise?" I asked. Joy answered in one word—"Men."

"Men?" I inquired.

They followed her everywhere. From 16 to 60. Short and tall. Fat and skinny. In bankers' vests and carpenters' overalls—*Cherchez la femme!*

"That's French," I told her.

"I'm becoming international," she said and wouldn't stop. "That's what these Italian men do all day long. Follow the woman!"

I was baffled. Joy added. "They seem to prefer blonde foreigners—*all* blonde foreigners."

She had been courted in English, German, French, Spanish, and several Scandinavian languages. Even, she thought, some Russian. They all had the same line: "How about a coffee? An ice cream? A glass of wine?"

Joy continued to pour it out. "Some of these Romeos look over seventy. I swear the old geezer who tried to pick me up outside a glove store the other day was at least seventy-five. And when I waved him off, he began following a young girl no more than eighteen."

An Italian woman, who spoke English and had watched the street scene, consoled Joy. "They think they can completely disrobe a woman with their eyes. I tell them that I'd kick them out of bed. That usually lets the air out of their balloons. It does no good to call the police. They just shrug their shoulders and look at you the same way."

Joy knew the woman was right. Italian men did try to disrobe women with their eyes. With calculated deliberateness, they started from a woman's ankles and went upward muscle by muscle—legs, hips, bosom, and face. To inexperienced foreigners, it could be quite unnerving.

With her tales of battle over for the moment, I turned to Joy and said sheepishly, "I have two suitcases full of dirty laundry."

She looked at me and declared with finality. "Men!"

I threw my arms around her again. After all, I was her best pal—and a man. The concierge watched us with restrained pleasure. He knew we had finished our coffee and I would soon turn my attention to the bill.

A few moments later, I paid our account in travelers' checks, tipped the concierge ten thousand lire ($16) for looking after Joy, and carried my baggage upstairs to our room. No sooner had I hung up my clothes than Joy sat on the large sofa and motioned me next to her. I thought she wanted to smooch but she was fired up and stepped on the gas pedal of her Ferrari again.

"Let me tell you about my arrival in Naples. The *Queen Frederica* was delayed because of fierce storms at sea. We arrived 18 hours late at 3:00 a.m. I knew nothing of a welcoming committee except that Ida (Ida Bernardini, an Italian friend in Manhattan) had told me that her uncle, a Signor Bagnoli, would meet me with family greetings in Naples. She said nothing about a parade."

As the Greek liner docked, Joy saw four men carrying large signs on the dock that read: BAGNOLI IS HERE. DON'T WORRY, JOY. THIS WAY TO BAGNOLI.

The fourth and last sign beckoning her along the docks was held by a tall, well-dressed, handsome figure with a large, dark mustache. In big, black letters, it proclaimed: I AM BAGNOLI!

Bagnoli wore a brave but tired smile. He had taken the train from Rome and had been waiting more than 20 hours for the ship to arrive. Not knowing of the delay caused by the storm at sea, he had hired the three-man crew to carry the signs. Bagnoli's only source of information was a letter from his niece, Ida. She told him Joy's name, the name of the ship, its approximate arrival time, and that her friend was a five-foot, four-inch blonde. Joy spoke no Italian. Bagnoli spoke not a word of English.

The young, blonde American in her early twenties, followed by 14 pieces of baggage, marched up to Bagnoli and announced, "I am Joy!"

With the aplomb of an accomplished actor—he was, in fact, a temporarily unemployed movie director—Bagnoli lowered his sign and identified himself in a flurry of Italian. He bowed politely and kissed the hand of the wide-eyed Joy. It was almost 4:00 a.m. An American woman passenger scoffed, "Oh, these Neopolitans!" As a matter of record, Bagnoli was a Roman.

At that moment, the other three sign bearers presented themselves for honors. They were Neapolitan. Bagnoli, with an air of grateful artistry, slipped each his pay, but not before much head- and hand-waving. Then, in virtually the same breath, Joy and Bagnoli began to have a happy, little cry. That was their one common language.

Bagnoli and Joy marched off to customs where he insisted that one of the agents immediately become his interpreter. The film director began with a flourish describing the beautiful bouquet of flowers he had bought the day before. A Neapolitan, he said with the superior air of a Roman, doubtlessly stole the flowers after he had fallen asleep on a waiting bench. (Here the Neapolitan customs agent gave him the glass eye of disbelief.) Bagnoli froze the eye with the wave of a hand which, apparently, had oratorical meaning. The Neapolitan agent, frowning on the late Cicero, waved the baggage through customs.

The two were off by taxi with 14 pieces of luggage swaying defiantly on the taxi roof, as the cab bounced over the cobblestones to the Mergellina railway station. Bagnoli would accompany Joy to Rome where, eventually, the entire Bernardini family would greet her. The American and the movie director spoke in smiles—large and small.

Day was beginning to dawn as the pair boarded the train for Rome. Bagnoli's black beard was now two days old and his hair was as wild as an Italian symphony conductor's. His head bobbed wearily, and he mumbled to himself while stealing glances in various directions. At this waking hour, every Italian worthy of the name thinks one thing—strong, black, and sweet. There was no time to explain to a foreigner. Bagnoli bowed briefly, then bolted for the door of the coach. Joy's only acquaintance in Italy had vanished in the middle of their train trip. Bagnoli had made a sign with his hands before leaving, however, which Joy interpreted as meaning he would return.

Joy looked lonesomely out the window of the speeding passenger train. The sun blinked on the fields and farmhouses. She wondered about the people out there, what they might have in common with an American, and what they were having for breakfast.

"Caffé Napoletano!" boomed a familiar voice. Bagnoli returned in triumph. He delicately balanced two full cups of black coffee on a piece of cardboard. He whistled over his cup, cooling it, happy as a bird at sunrise. Neapolitan coffee is as black as tar and some unaccustomed Americans say it tastes about the same. Joy bolted down a slug.

"Wow!" she fairly screamed.

"Buono!" Bagnoli beamed. "Buono!"

Joy fished her abbreviated English-language dictionary from her purse. She was surprised when Bagnoli pulled an English-Italian phrase book from his jacket pocket. Word by word, the two began to build a bridge between the distant worlds of America and Italy. It took Joy ten minutes to explain that her husband, a reporter, had gone to Yugoslavia on a news assignment and would arrive later. She also described her long friendship with

Bagnoli's niece, Ida, in New York. Bagnoli told of Ida's letter, asking her relatives to take Joy under their wings.

The two exchanged names, phone numbers, and other necessities during the two-hour-plus ride to Rome. The city came upon them in large streaks of sun that leaped from between the buildings. The seven hills rose and fell in timeless obedience to the *Senatus Populusque Romanorum*—the Senate and People of Rome.

On arriving at the Massimo D'Azelio Hotel near the central railroad station, Bagnoli again kissed Joy's hand as the concierge watched with nonchalant blessing. The film director would phone her later. He wasn't sure when. There was time for everything in Rome. *Domani. Dopo domani.* (Tomorrow. After tomorrow.) An appointment was only a business or social approximation.

Joy crawled into the largest bed she had ever seen and dreamed, *Roma . . . bella . . . grande.*

The room phone range at 7:30 p.m. The voice was fairly singing. "Bagnoli, signora. Eeenglish, signora . . . Eeeat spaghetti."

"Grazie," Joy chirped. "Grazie."

The starving duo ate in a nearby trattoria. Between spaghetti and chicken, they poured down a liter of white Frascati wine. Bagnoli explained that the town of Frascati was only an hour by car from where they were sitting.

Bagnoli politely dipped his fingers in a water bowl and wiped them with the care of a sculptor. There was a certain sadness in his smile. Tomorrow, Ida's sister Livia was coming. Other relatives would follow from breakfast to bedtime for several days. Both understood. His mission was completed. The women of the family were taking over.

Bagnoli, unnoticed by Joy, had already paid the check. She protested, but he ignored the plea, took her hand and kissed it. The film director stood stiff and straight. For the first time, Joy noticed that he was a man in his mid-fifties, with a light gray streak through his wild crop of dark hair. Then with a slight bow, he turned swiftly and was gone. Joy never saw him again.

She remembered the face, the smile, and the sudden discovery that beneath Bagnoli's expansive warmth and welcome there were deep lines of his own cares. It was a much older face than first appearances indicated. Was this, Joy wondered, perhaps the face of Rome?

Ida's sister arrived at eight o'clock the next morning. Livia, who spoke no English, had been forewarned by Bagnoli that Joy's Italian was no better. The good lady carried a big, new, brightly colored Italian-English dictionary.

Livia was a full-blown woman with a ringing voice and rolling laughter. She was all Roman. For her the Coliseum and Roman Forum were merely old markers along a bus route. They also could be pillars of contemplation, depending on traffic delays. In passing them, Joy heard Livia say several times to herself, "Quanto sei bello!" (How beautiful you are!)

Livia breathed tradition. Cultural beauty sprang from old ways and long-ago times. She would walk out to fetch a jug of fresh spring water from a public fount every evening because her father did it years before. To her, the perfect spouse was a man who wore his wedding tie every anniversary. She agreed with those who never bet on the national soccer pool unless it was Friday the thirteenth, considered lucky by most Romans. Livia viewed sentiment as important as a scholar's logic. Sometimes, even more significant.

Joy was having breakfast at the hotel when Livia arrived. A waiter introduced them. Livia later wrote Ida that the gastronomic habits of Americans at breakfast were indeed something to behold. Spread before the 105-pound American was a complete morning banquet that included coffee with enough milk to drown several Italian espressos—a Roman milk bath, as Livia described it—scrambled eggs with bacon, two slices of toast with butter and jelly, fresh fruit, and a croissant. Why the croissant? It remained a complete mystery to Livia.

Livia wasn't hungry and the two strode downtown in the warm, spring sun. Near the Grand Hotel, Livia bolted from her young new friend and rushed to a corner flower vendor. She exchanged a hard-earned 500 lire (80 cents) for a bright bouquet, and returned to Joy's side without a word. Then, she stopped at a niche in a thick brick wall where a weatherbeaten Madonna stood forlornly. Livia arranged the flowers around the Madonna's head, fastening them with string from her purse. Unmindful of Joy or the passing people, Livia knelt and prayed. All without a word.

Up from her knees, Livia's countenance changed. Her chin thrust out, she was now ready for combat. She led Joy to an open-air market in a small piazza near the U.S. embassy (where Joy was about to have her first Italian shopping experience). This was business and Livia's Roman nose rose high and proud. She was going to buy two apples. Her voice assumed an impatient edge. Her dark eyes widened as they darted along the apple stall, ignoring the vendor's smiling welcome.

The haggling voices of women rose and fell in mixed cadences. Their questioning tones implied they considered the vendors gentle grafters. A few fenced with charm but most adopted the role of cynics. It was the ordinary give-and-take of daily life. What diligent housewife would submit to the first price of a vendor—even in the most celebrated shops and snobbish stores? There was always *uno sconto* (a discount) and, if that failed, *un' piccolo sconto* (a small discount).

With dictionary and determination, Livia explained to Joy that Roman life would not be the same without open markets. Livia didn't like the new supermarkets. As she put it, "You can't discuss the merits of meat with a cash register. And everything is frozen!"

Livia purchased two apples. Joy's big breakfast had whetted the Roman's appetite. She crunched into her apple and handed Joy the other. A few steps away, inside a shoemaker's shop, a housewife told the cobbler that he was charging bandit prices. Livia described the exchange to Joy, pointing to the owner, "Al Capone!" The American burst into laughter and the pair moved on.

Joy reflected as the two sauntered along the crowded streets. Italian men and women talked with their hands, even their shoulders and heads. The din and waving seemed like public theater. Church bells pealed the hours but no one seemed to notice, much less say a brief prayer.

A middle-aged man bolted out of his upholstery shop. With fingers in his ears, he bellowed, "Basta! Basta!" (Enough! Enough!) An irate customer followed the shopowner into the street, hollering and waving his arms. The customer threw up both hands as high as he could, swept the scene with angry eyes, and screamed, "Cornuuuuto! Cornuuuuto a tutti!"

It was a most indelicate remark. Livia explained that *Cornuto* literally meant "horned"—your better half was sleeping with someone else. The gentleman obviously thought he was being cheated by the shop owner, and wished the same on everyone else.

But why the shouting, screaming, and waving, Joy wanted to know? Livia said it was the driving urge of every Italian—communication. Expressive, individual, unique communication. It was not only a national characteristic but a national sport. She added, "These explosions and hand gestures represent the Italian character—open, independent, free. Individual expression is our heartbeat. We're also actors."

Livia then took Joy on her first Roman streetcar ride. It was going part of the way to St. Peter's Square. The sights and sounds of the city rushed at Joy more quickly as the tram barreled along in the midday traffic. As the two began to make their way off the streetcar to change to a bus, Livia called out Rome's most common public contradiction, "Permesso!"

The word is shouted from dawn to dusk in every aspect of Italian life. It's difficult to translate aptly. Politely, it's a request for those blocking your way—on a tram or anywhere else— for permission to pass and proceed on your way. Depending on the inflection of the voice, it can mean: "Would you be so kind as to let me pass (politeness) . . . Getting off, I'm in a hurry and you're holding me up (urgency) . . . Move over, you jerk (disgust) . . . Get the hell out of the way, you damn fool! (desperation)."

One of the arts practiced by male tram and bus riders was pinching women on the thighs and behinds. Joy still insists she was pinched by a middle-aged Italian man on her first ride to St. Peter's. She was twenty-two at the time. Furthermore, she says the man was impeccably dressed and carried a briefcase. He appeared to be a lawyer, accountant, or some civilian executive at the Vatican. The gentleman was the only person close enough to pinch her—on the right thigh. Some gentleman! Her only solace was the tram driver's sanctified announcement, "San Pietro! San Pietro!"

Joy asked Livia about pinching. The Roman said it began during World War II when few buses ran and all were crowded. Pinching continued after the war and, at first, girls made scenes on trams and buses. But they quickly learned it rarely helped to make a public fuss. Men would snicker, even the old, and the accuser would be embarrassed. Other women would stare at the girl or woman, especially if she could afford new-style clothes, an indication she was trying to attract men. There was only one answer to pinching, Livia declared. That was to kick the pincher in the shins as you got off the tram. Joy asked why men pinched. Livia concluded, "Male ego." No further explanation was offered.

Since Joy often traveled by public transportation in Rome, she was to be pinched again and again. It became less of a surprise as the years passed. And she did kick the shins of a number of well-dressed gentlemen as she left the bus.

Joy and Livia finally reached their destination. The great, heavy doors of St. Peter's Basilica offered Joy her first close sight of the magnificent seat of the Roman Catholic Church. Joy later told me that St. Peter's was what St. Thomas Aquinas called "the essence of being." It was absolute totality—the complete union of God and man. That was how she felt as the Basilica's vast interior swept before her eyes for the first time. She not only saw

Michelangelo's *Pieta* and other major sculptures but walked in the footsteps of St. Peter and other early fathers of the Church. "It was the perfect union of religious mysticism and the jaded fortunes of human history represented by Rome," she added.

A general audience was taking place in the Basilica the day of Joy and Livia's visit. Some 25,000 pilgrims awaited the appearance of Pope Pius XII. Joy was almost breathless with anticipation. The Pope appeared suddenly, as if from nowhere, and was carried through the crowd to the front of the main altar on a portable throne, all the time blessing the throng. Men shouted and tossed their hats in the air. Women waved and, in a score of languages, called out to His Holiness to bless their rosaries and prayer books. Others closed their eyes and held up their arms in a kind of spiritual ecstasy. Some of them appeared completely transfixed.

The deafening babble appeared scandalous to Joy. This was the Church of churches and it seemed incomprehensible that it would burst with loud cries like those in a sports stadium. Joy asked why so many people talked and shouted in the Basilica. Livia answered, "The Church, any church, is our house." Livia then joined the thunder. She was shouting with thousands of other Italians, "Viva il Papa! Evviva il Papa!"

As Pius descended from his portable throne near the altar, an elderly woman in black rushed up to him. The Swiss Guards and plainclothes gendarmarie were too late to stop her. There was a hush when those in the audience saw the woman had handed His Holiness a live lamb. For a moment, the Pontiff stood dumbstruck holding the lamb in his arms. Joy smiled. Who said the Pope is infallible? she asked herself.

A papal chamberlain rushed up to Pius and took the lamb from his grasp. The young animal was passed down the line of papal attendants until it landed in the arms of a startled young priest. It later turned out that he was a visiting pilgrim!

After speaking in some half dozen languages, the Pope disappeared almost as suddenly as he arrived. He was already in the papal elevator and on the way to his third-floor Vatican apartment by the time Joy realized the audience had ended. Livia, who always seemed in common touch with events, whispered to Joy, "He has gone to lunch."

She smiled and asked Livia, "I wonder if he has a glass of wine?"

"Of course," Livia replied, "he's a Roman!"

As the two sauntered into the sunlight of St. Peter's Square, Livia spoke simply but elegantly of the man they had just seen. "He knows the family secrets. Our weaknesses and strengths. The little scandals in the back alleys of Rome. He walked there as a boy and later as a priest. He knows that we are cynical about some of the men and ways of the Church. Yet we're certain of one thing: He's part of our family—a father, brother, cousin, even friend. Family is everything. We may argue, fight, even hate. But we are of the same history and blood. We understand one another."

The two walked down the Via della Conciliazione for some time without speaking. The broad avenue, leading to and from the Basilica, was once the heart of a Roman slum. Mussolini rebuilt the area and named the street the "Way of Conciliation", following the Lateran Pacts of 1927. This series of agreements between Italy and the Holy See guaranteed the inviolate rights of the Vatican as a separate state. The 108 acres have been an independent state ever since. Livia knew it all.

Joy understood Livia, despite the fact that both were using dictionaries, because she constantly pointed to things—like the lamb, the dome, the streetcar—and gave the Italian word. Livia's vivid expressions showed her horror, surprise or affection at the happenings around them. Joy guessed the rest. Dripping perspiration in the warm sun, Joy wondered when she would speak fairly good Italian. (It took a year. In seven years, she spoke it like a Roman housewife—grimaces, gestures, shin-kicking and all.)

Livia accompanied Joy to the hotel but had to rush home for an appointment. She told Joy to be ready at 4:30 p.m. She would arrive to take her to tea at her mother's house on Monte Mario.

The Bernardini home was bursting with ladies when Joy arrived. There were aunts, sisters, sisters-in-law, cousins of all degrees, other full- and part-time relatives, and a flock of friends. All had come to look the American over.

In keeping with Roman tradition, the first guests arrived a half hour late. Joy and Livia showed up about the same time, just right for the guest of honor. The 26 ladies quickly descended on Joy—hand kissing, cheek kissing, and chattering about eighty kilometers an hour (fifty miles) between each embrace. Words and phrases flew from chandelier to candelabra and rattled crystal in a clinking symphony. It was high-voltage social shock. It was a Roman tea party!

From time to time, the group of ladies would stop talking, turn to glance at the guest with a smile, and turn on the vocal gas again. Joy had no time to use her dictionary. She smiled, even with a cookie in her mouth, nodded and sipped more tea to wash down the cookie. The ladies patted Joy's cheeks, held her hands and tugged at her arms, marveled at her small nose (the Roman nose is notably prominent), and offered her cigarettes.

Suddenly, virtually without warning, the tea was over. The ladies seemed to stand in a body, and they embraced all over again. Joy was hugged breathless, kissed and rekissed, and one of the departing guests sallied forth in English, "Good-bye, dear!"

Mamma Bernardini embraced Joy, who understood this was her signal to leave. Livia was quickly at Joy's side. The two left to catch the bus. As they walked down the hill, a cross fire of voices followed them: *Arrivederci! Arrivederci!* (Goodbye!)

Joy collapsed on a seat of the bus. She knew the way to the hotel so Livia wouldn't need to accompany her. The last thing she saw was Mamma Bernardini waving wildly to her from the family balcony. In her other hand, Mamma delicately balanced a cup of tea.

That was Joy's first full day in Rome. As she wrote in her diary that evening, it was only the beginning.

Chapter 2

The Baroness

JOY REPORTED SHE had found an apartment. It belonged, she said breathlessly, to an Italian baroness. The place was furnished and available for the summer months. We had to hurry. Royalty awaited us.

We met the baroness in a penthouse apartment on the Via Flaminia. The street had been made famous by Alberto Moravia's novel, *The Girl on the Via Flaminia*. She didn't sell flowers.

The baroness greeted us amid various nude paintings of herself. They covered much of the living and dining room walls. The baroness explained, since our eyes were popping out of our heads, that she preferred originals. In demure but understandable English, she explained, "Art has become so commercial, so copycat. Originals are so individualistic, so personal."

Both of us glanced at a rather revealing pose, framed on a living room wall. The baroness was wearing a knowing smile and that was about it. She said the painting was an artist's latest conception of her. A bit flattering, the baroness said, fluttering her thick, dark, false eyelashes.

She was about 40 years old, not tall, dark hair pulled back in

15

a pony tail, large hips, muscular legs, and a more than ample bosom. At first and later blushes, I thought the nudes celebrated her far beyond reality but restrained my gaze since Joy was watching me out of the corner of her eye.

The baron was gone. Just where remained a mystery. The baroness took a deep breath in his memory and immediately exhaled that she preferred taking her vacations in Spain. Apparently, that's where she was now headed.

It wasn't easy being alone in life, the baroness confided. As an afterthought, she mentioned the baron had left her with a young daughter. Then, she put on a warm, motherly smile and got down to business. "Now, about the rental contract . . ."

We would sign a two-month agreement that would include an assessment of the worth of her furnishings in the event anything was damaged, including the original paintings.

At no time did the baroness indicate to us that she was anything but the complete owner and mistress of the apartment, nor that she was anything but of the purest Italian stock. She mused softly that the baron was a very important Italian leader. Again, we were left to guess whether he had passed to greater rewards or was still nobly carrying on—somewhere. All we knew was that she had inherited his title and was gracefully carrying on his noble tradition.

After viewing the penthouse and telling the baroness of our approval, she immediately telephoned her lawyer. We were to meet him in 15 minutes at a notary public a few blocks away. The contract would be signed and registered with the government. The baroness casually mentioned the agreement would call for two months' deposit—one for rent and a second to cover possible damages. On preparing to leave, I noticed she was wearing slippers.

"I will not be going. My attorney handles my affairs," the baroness announced.

The formal document gave us the impression that we were renting a Roman palazzo. The sentences flourished with colons, semicolons, commas, hyphens, and various dashes, and sometimes 150 words before a period. The rent was 100,000 lire ($160.00) per month, a lot of money in Rome at the time. I finally signed the agreement, noting the baroness had previously written her name. The notary pasted a half dozen state stamps around each signature. The contract looked like a treaty between states.

I shuddered at what I had just signed. There seemed to be so many "howevers" (the accord was translated verbally to me in English) that anyone could interpret it any number of ways. Little did I know. We were responsible not only for the baroness's originals but her potted plants on the terrace, several valuable vases, a cabinet full of venerable glassware, and a live turtle. I estimated all the household effects to be worth no more than 1.5 million lire ($2,400). The baroness valued them at ten million lire ($16,000). I reneged on a live chicken. This prompted a temporary crisis. The lawyer hurriedly phoned the baroness and received her permission to leave the chicken out of the deal. I later learned the deletion provided the baroness with a tasty dinner.

Yes, we had found a place to hang our hats and coats. Hopefully, we would keep our necks out of all those nooses—the commas, semicolons, and dashes.

We signed three more apartment rental contracts in Rome with the same wariness as the first. Our most dramatic legal squabble wound up in court, and we lost. The details of that battle isn't a mere digression. The trials and troubles of apartment rental contracts were one of the most discussed—and cussed— subjects among the foreign colony of Rome.

I signed a contract to rent an unfurnished place over near the Tiber River. The landlord was in the process of painting and fixing up the place. The day before we were to move in, I took the bus to look at the shape of things. Some shape! Workmen had split the bathtub in four pieces. The kitchen sink was cracked in half. The kitchen faucet was broken, and paint trailed through various rooms.

I phoned the owner, a lawyer, who happened to be out of town on vacation. However, he called me back that evening, saying he would meet me at the apartment the following noon. The place was still the same huge mess.

In addition, the phone wasn't hooked up as promised and I would have to wait at least a month. That was an impossible condition for a reporter. One final discovery proved even more impossible: the building elevator went down but not up. Joy was pregnant and couldn't walk up six flights. The lawyer had led me to believe on previous visits that the elevator was under temporary repair. No such luck.

I told the landlord we weren't moving in under such conditions. He smiled and said he would sue me. I told him to go ahead. He did. Since the landlord was a lawyer, he managed to get the case on a city court docket after only a brief wait. These were some of the damages asked: the cost of pulling the owner off vacation; his anguish and loss of sleep; and an attempt to besmirch his dignity and honor. I had committed the cardinal sin in Italy—a crime of honor! In a long dissertation, the lawyer reminded the judge just how valuable his time and honor were.

I had a Sicilian lawyer, Antonio Corrao. Any Sicilian is a formidable opponent and Corrao was brilliant. With one move after another, he kept the case in court for more than three years. The landlord thought I was crazy running up all those legal expenses. However, Corrao, one of our company lawyers, took the case for nothing. He said to Joy and me, " I want you to know that all Italians are not Romans."

I was to hear that phrase a thousand times before leaving Italy. Many other Italians viewed Romans as social parasites, if not crooks. They despised the stealing, graft, and other corruption that percolated just below the surface of national government offices and Roman life.

Finally, the judge awarded the landlord 500,000 lire ($800) in damages. The verdict was pure larceny. But, perhaps to ease his conscience, the judge said I would not have to pay the apartment owner's legal fees. Of course, the landlord was his own lawyer.

The tales of many other rental lawsuits were related to us over the years. They ranged from a damaging chip in a family heirloom (cheap vases are sometimes family heirlooms of great sentimental value) to flower losses in a garden (often near collapse before the tenant arrived) and the most frequent of all, failure of the landlord to return a renter's deposit. The trick was to let foreigners take the owner to court and outwait them (cases sometimes took from two to four years to appear on the docket and longer on appeal). The foreign diplomat or businessman had, meanwhile, been transferred to Afghanistan and simply swallowed the loss.

On the day we were scheduled to move into the baroness's apartment, Joy awoke with acute appendicitis and was operated on later that morning at Salvator Mundi Hospital. After the surgery, I returned to the office to find a note asking me to phone the baroness. Her voice soft and purring. "It's all terribly unexpected. My daughter has scarlet fever. Five days quarantine, the doctor says. We're quite upset about it—the delay for Spain. My maid has everything packed. How inconvenient for all of us!"

Inconvenient! I had already checked out of our hotel. Our luggage was at the news bureau. This was the tourist season with few and costly hotel rooms. And Saturday to boot!

The baroness's tone spread sweetly and soothingly. "Naturally, you can still move in. You won't be breaking the quarantine. We'll divide the house in half—you'll have your own room and private bath. I'll leave the key under the doormat."

She was purring again. "Sorry to hear about your wife in the hospital. But my maid and I will look after you. Do give me a call and let me know your decision."

All this was really going to sound "original" to Joy, especially my opening line, "I'm moving in with the baroness."

There was, Joy concluded between gas pains, nothing to do

but move in with the "original." With INS no longer paying our hotel bill, plus the unexpected doctor and hospital bills, we had little choice. I moved in but the baroness was absent. The maid told me she had gone to the pharmacy for medicine. Later, the baroness said she had gone for a ride with "the baron"—not the original but a suitable replacement.

I lived with the baroness, her child, and maid for six days. In this time, I discovered a few subplots. The baroness tiptoed out every evening for dinner and returned late with the same gentleman whom she always referred to as "Baron." The pair was always in high spirits and invariably had a cognac in the kitchen. I finally understood their game. The child had no scarlet fever. The baron had planned to leave with the trio for Spain but unexpected business delayed him for a week.

I hadn't been eavesdropping. They would bellow their daily fortunes after the second or third cognac. I soon started to doubt not only the baroness's title but also her ancestry.

Frills flying, she finally made a grand exit out the front door to the baron and a waiting taxi. The child followed with the maid carrying most of the luggage. The baroness waved a ceremonial goodbye, apparently to any neighbors who might be watching, and flew off to her holiday in Spain.

Several days after Joy arrived from the hospital, there was a gentle knock on our apartment door. Little, unexpected knocks occurred a lot in Italian life. A tiny, well-dressed lady, who spoke a bit of English, stood at the door and introduced herself as the owner of the apartment. Joy invited her in and, no sooner had the good woman seated herself on the living room couch, than she asked Joy if we would like to rent the apartment from her.

Joy phoned me in the office and said the kettle was boiling in the apartment, and I had better get home, pronto. Meanwhile, she made tea for our unexpected guest.

Upon arrival, I immediately explained to the lady that the baroness had told us this was her apartment and furnishings. With a knowing nod, the woman advised us that we had signed a sublet agreement. She confirmed that the baroness owned most of the furnishings, sniffing dourly at them, but she held title to the apartment.

I had a terrible vision of setting up housckeeping in the office. The woman explained the baroness was always behind in her rent. She was presently two months behind in payment. The lady told us that we shouldn't worry. She would collect all the rent. The baroness's contract would be up about the time she returned from Spain. The owner assured us the baroness was virtually out the door—including her originals. Did we want to rent the apartment?

I needed time to think. The woman was clearly determined. The baroness was out. The neighbors were complaining she and her barons were making too much noise at night. Some of the housewives in the building also accused the baroness of flirting with their husbands at the postbox downstairs. And, apparently the ultimate seduction, she even gave them a welcome eye on the elevator.

The owner then denied that the baroness was Italian. She described the baroness as an untitled "South American nobody" who lived off some nondescript pension and the tidings of male acquaintances. I didn't pursue the subject.

I asked the owner how she knew so much since she visited the building only infrequently to collect her rent. She smiled and gave me just what I deserved. There are no secrets in Rome, the lady explained. She knew, for example, that I was the director of an American news office on the Via del Corso, 476 to be exact. I had the reputation of being an engaging young fellow but very American (I wasn't sure what that meant). Joy recently had an appendectomy. I waved my hand to indicate that was enough, and the woman sat back in triumph.

I was to recall that scene as long as we lived in Italy. The landlady was manifestly correct. The news chain began with the first link—*il portiere* (the porter) at the door of many Roman apartment buildings. It moved to the plumber, carpenter, electrician, wine merchant, and most everyone else along one's daily route.

I explained we had to turn down her apartment offer. Our furniture was coming by ship from America and we planned to rent an unfurnished place. I told her we would move at the close of two months in the apartment.

When we finally did vacate, the baroness had not returned from Spain. Her lawyer kept demanding a second month's rent, but I told him he could collect if there were any damages.

We eventually found a ground-floor apartment on Via Adelaide Ristori, about a mile from Piazza Ungheria. Again, we dealt with a landlady. Her name was Angelica. She was anything but angelic—another "original" in her own right.

Chapter 3

Pipes and Policarpo

UNFURNISHED APARTMENTS IN Rome mean exactly that. We found no light fixtures or sockets in any unfurnished apartments or houses, only bare wires. If that wasn't ludicrous enough to us innocents from abroad, we had to go out and buy our own toilet seat—*and* install it.

We had no closets in our old-style, first apartment and even in a later new one. I had to go out and buy *armadios*, as the Italians term them. We described these as off-the-shelf or on-the-hoof closets.

We found that even buying an armadio can be quite a trick. I had to measure a specific wall space and then try to find one that fit the measurement. Of course, the few standard sizes sold in Italian department stores rarely, if ever, fit precisely into our spaces. If I made the slightest error, the mistake was my headache. So I always bought an armadio with a width and height that were several inches short.

Many tenants called on a carpenter to build one or several armadios. But there was a catch even there—would they fit somewhere in the next apartment? Also the cost was always higher than standard models in a store.

Telephone service was one of the great barriers to family survival in Italy. We purchased our telephone at an electrical store only after we had been assigned a calling number by the Italian phone company. That was because the normal wait for a phone was a year or longer. The long odyssey is no longer true but there's still a wait. In my case, as a foreign reporter, the red tape took only a month—with the help of the Italian Foreign Ministry. Some newsmen, however, were delayed much longer. Hence, nobody bought a phone until being officially informed that a calling number had been issued. That meant the company installer would arrive in several days—hopefully. I was lucky.

I engaged in one battle or another with the phone company for as long as we lived in Italy. This was my biggest: To make long distance calls on the Italian system, it was necessary to place a deposit with the company. Bills were due every three months. Therefore, my deposit had to cover what I anticipated spending on long-distance calls over that period. My estimate was about $500 for three months since I had to call our news bureaus in London or New York on big, fast-breaking stories. The office paid for these calls from my home.

A famous phrase—it became infamous with me—employed by the phone company in referring to these deposits was *Fondi Perduti* (Lost Funds). This money was originally called a "deposit" when the procedure was instituted shortly after World War II. Only later was the money referred to as "Lost Funds." The phone company said the deposit was needed for two reasons—to help get the firm off the ground financially and to discourage gabbers from running up big bills and then taking the proverbial powder. I was later told the firm confiscated the original deposits, never returning a lira to customers.

I attempted to regain 300,000 lire ($480) that our news organization had deposited with the company in 1945 to obtain service. Everywhere I went in the firm, I was given the busy signal.

Finally, after considerable cajoling, I was ushered in to see a vice president. The gentleman thought he had the perfect pronouncement to shut me up. It was, "You Americans simply don't understand Italian business procedure."

Despite my brief history of dealing with Italian bureaucracy, I felt somewhat ready for the gentleman. "Sir, I never desired to see you in the first place. There's only one section of any Italian business that understands normal business procedure—the legal department. I want to see your lawyers!"

Over the years, that line worked wonders. Knock them off the chair with an implied threat. Challenge their best. Not bad for an American abroad. The vice president's face was dumbstruck. Actually, while protecting company money, I was gaining invaluable experience for our private life. It seemed like an intelligent risk.

Several days later, I met with a battery of phone company lawyers, four fencers who operated on the quick-thrust theory. One would stick me, followed by the next before I could answer. And on down the line. It was like four consecutive machine-gun bursts.

The action exploded on a Saturday morning (Italy was then on the six-day work week) at the company's central headquarters just off Piazza Argentina. (Not far from the Vatican, by the way. I acknowledged the proximity of the Holy See with a wry smile to myself.)

The four fired at me from all directions, one thrusting forward as the other withdrew: Could anything possibly be clearer? Do we have to spell it out for you? Lost Funds! How do we know where the money went? Have you ever tried to trace thirty 10,000-lire notes back through a dozen years of books and banks?

What do you mean that Americans do it all the time? This is Italy, not America. You had better get used to that. You're in Italy now, dealing with Italian law!

That was, of course, the ultimate threat. They were telling me to my face what I already knew: an American would have a very tough time winning in an Italian court.

Nevertheless, I persisted. I had a receipt for our deposit but they clearly indicated the note wasn't worth the paper it was printed on. Lost Funds! Got it? Get lost!

I never collected. Over the years, I would send them a telegram. A letter. A phone call. To the president. To the director of claims. Even back to the legal department. It became a hobby. They never forgot me because I never forgot—or forgave—them. However, perhaps out of Italian familial reverence, the telephone company did return the deposit I gave them for our home phone.

As we were about to leave Italy for our new assignment in Washington, DC, an Italian lawyer told me the phone company had finally instituted a policy of routinely returning deposits. I like to believe, even to this day, that my long crusade was one reason for this bureaucratic advancement.

The need for water was on a par with the phone in an Italian household. I place the phone in such high regard because Italians like to talk a lot. And they prefer wine to water—except for brushing their teeth and bathing.

Each apartment had two kinds of water—running, supplied by the city, and stored water in a reservoir on the roof. The reservoirs had tanks, allotted to each apartment. Each held an equal amount of water, thus guaranteeing the various occupants a fair shake. Like a good number of Italian guarantees, this was true only in a manner of speaking.

I discovered that little fix-it known as the *registratore*. The "register" could be purchased in many stores and easily installed. Actually, the mechanical device did no registering at all. It was a tiny do-it-yourself gadget that siphoned water from the other tanks to one's own.

The practice was, of course, unethical. But on those hot summer nights, someone in a nearby apartment invariably needed a shower or bath. It was your neighbor or you—sometimes your neighbor's dog.

When an American lady friend of ours resorted to the register, her hired handyman reported, "Yes, I put it in there for you. You were the last to install it. Now everyone is stealing equally from everybody else!"

I never put in a register despite our band of three kids. I thought it bad sport. The Italians blew it off as part of Roman life. To this day, I'm not certain how Joy managed to do our laundry, bathe the boys, and still have enough water for us to shower.

House painting was also a problem. Furnished places were normally fairly well-painted because the landlord didn't want cheap stuff chipping and falling on his rugs, drapes, or furniture. But getting paint for an unfurnished place was usually a roll of the dice.

I took a close look at the paint job before we moved into Signora Angelica's apartment. It was little more than whitewash and I told her so. She brushed off the complaint. Angelica said it was the best that money could buy in 1950s Italy. She would hear no more.

She did, of course. In the four years that we lived in Angelica's place, anyone who leaned against a wall walked away whitewashed. As the whitewash disappeared, another problem appeared. Names, phone numbers, unprintable graffiti, even a valentine stared out at us in deep dark ink. It was a genealogy lesson on previous tenants.

We and our guests brushed off the whitewash through the years, and Angelica heard about it every time we paid our rent. I played my broken record that she repaint the apartment with good paint, and on each occasion Angelica replied: *Non e niente.* (The double negative, but perfect Italian meaning, "It's not nothing.")

It meant nothing to Angelica.

In this dashing game of hide-and-seek, I began to understand Angelica. Like most apartment owners, she was still paying on the place and hoped the rent would cover not only the annual principal and interest payments but also a small profit for herself. Therefore, Angelica viewed any money spent on the apartment as robbing herself. As she put it, "I'm just a poor widow with a small government pension. You are an American!"

That was it. No argument. She was poor and we were rich. That was her law of social justice and Italian economics. The Americans must pay—to help the poor, support the Christian Democrats and block the Communists from power, keep the Vatican and the Pope afloat, and defend Italy with America's military might, but never to defend the Italians from themselves.

Angelica was telling me in effect: You don't have to be smart to understand that Mr. George Marshall's Plan was the building block of the new Europe. Italy floated no Marshall Plan. You can't count on the Italian government because we, the citizens, can't! Look what a mess Mussolini made!

This was made clear in one of the dictator's laws. Many Italian tenants lived under what was called *fitto blocatto* (fixed rent), established by the beneficent Benito to help him rise to greater power. Legally, no one was allowed to increase payment under fixed rent. In the immediate postwar period, some apartments were easily worth the equivalent of $150 rent per month, but tenants were sometimes paying as little as $40 monthly for them. Many of the same apartments now rent from $1,000 to $1,500 per month, depending on improvements. In those days, however, no landlord did much of anything to keep his place up because there were no incentives. Many apartments in Italy were close to ruin. The same is true today in New York City under rent control.

We realized most Italians were homemade lawyers and also soon understood the owner-tenant relationship. Indeed, this tug-of-war represented our early schooling in jurisprudence, but it never prepared us for our ultimate battle with Angelica.

Within two months of having moved into her apartment, tiny water leaks began to appear in various rooms. Spots on a bedroom ceiling . . . a few telltale signs in the kitchen . . . an ever-widening circle across a bathroom wall . . . and drips from different faucets.

We regularly reported all this to Angelica and she always replied with the perfectly respectable Italian double negative, "It's not nothing."

Meanwhile, Angelica began sending her son to collect the rent. The young man would always arrive without notice on the morning that the rent was due. He continually said, "Don't worry. I'll be sure to report the leaks to Mamma." Nothing ever came of it.

One morning I awoke and noticed a large, Ferris wheel–shaped circle on the bedroom ceiling. This was definitely water, I told myself, and walked down the street to speak with the neighborhood handyman, a gentleman by the name of Policarpo. He was a Turk. Polly, as we called him, took one look at the ceiling and reported, "Funeral bells, folks. A pipe must be broken inside the walls of the apartment upstairs. I'll probably have to rip down a wall up there and maybe here. Yes, indeed, funeral bells!"

I telephoned Angelica with this household flash. She couldn't have been less concerned. "Domani," she said with a yawn, "I'll be over sometime tomorrow." Just before putting her phone down, she fired four words of warning, "Don't touch the walls!"

I asked Polly to explain the legal ramifications of what Angelica had said. Polly responded without hesitation. According to Italian law, everything inside the walls was the responsibility of the owner. Everything outside was that of the tenant. Responsibility began at the point of penetration. He offered an example: The tenant should replace the washer on a leaky faucet since it's outside the wall, but the owner must pay to tear down a wall if there's leak inside it.

From that day forward, Polly became my household legal adviser, including dealing with Angelica. He advised, "For the moment, don't say or do nothing!" This time, I appreciated the double negative.

One day passed. Two days. The Ferris wheel in our bedroom was taking on passengers. The circle now covered more than half the ceiling and was still spreading.

On the third day, Angelica arrived. Her entrance could not have been more resplendent. Her natural red hair shone brilliantly in the morning sun. She wore a bright blue dress and carefully avoided the whitewash on the walls. The good lady, large with a booming voice, fairly sang, "My dear dears! How are you? So wonderful to see you! Nothing should excite us. Nothing on such a splendid day! La vita! Oggi! La gioia di Roma!" (Life! Today! The joy of Rome!)

Angelica exuded existence. The sweetness of life. She was like an accomplished actress on stage—her stage. She marched into the bedroom, looked at the ceiling, and announced, "The pipes are perspiring. It's the humidity!"

I hit the roof. "Perspiring? Signora, this is the start of a flood!"

Angelica would not be moved. Even after touring the house and seeing a half dozen other developing floods on ceilings and walls, she brushed it all off in two words, "Perspiration. Humidity."

With that, she fluttered off to meet friends, joyously waving a final farewell. Her magnificent hair flamed in the sun but she didn't perspire a drop.

We knew that our apartment building had four floors, but were unaware that anyone slept in the basement directly below us. The discovery came with one of those famous little knocks at our front door. Tommasina introduced herself. The elderly woman rented one room in the basement and was presently being washed out of her tiny space. We rushed downstairs.

Atop the bed, in the center of the room, Tommasina had placed an umbrella. The steadily dripping water came from a spot directly below the washbasin in our bathroom. Joy rushed upstairs and phoned Policarpo. He soon arrived with his usual appraisal. "Funeral bells, folks. That's it. I'll plaster it up—for now. Maybe it'll hold back the water for a week. But it's funeral bells. I gotta get inside that ceiling to find the leak."

About 4:30 the following morning, the plaster on our bedroom ceiling—the Ferris wheel—fell and hit me on the head. Just as I had told Angelica, the plaster had been loosening for weeks. Finally, the great white splotch opened and I was hit with a blockbuster. I let out a terrifying yell when the bomb hit. Wet plaster covered my pillow and sheet and a red circle throbbed in the middle of my forehead.

I woke Angelica with a blast on the phone at 7:00 a.m. She knew I was sore—inside and out. This, I declared, was Judgment Day. I was going to knock down at least two walls with my old baseball bat. With the first hint of concern in her voice, she promised to be at the apartment by 9:00 a.m.

Angelica arrived, viewed the plaster and the ceiling, and assumed a role of righteous indignation, "They'll have to pay. And pay. It's their fault—upstairs!"

She was about to march to the upstairs tenant, but we diverted her downstairs to Tommasina's. Policarpo's temporary plastering job was clearly visible. Tommasina opened her umbrella above the bed for dramatic effect. The landlady's double chin dropped and she surrendered. "Call Policarpo."

Polly arrived and was with us, off and on, for six weeks. He tore into four different walls—two in the kitchen, one in the bedroom, and another in the bathroom. As Angelica knew, this was her show, her day to come up with a check, since all the work was inside the walls. Polly found leaky and broken water pipes everywhere. He whistled while he worked. I never knew that anyone could whistle Chopin's Requiem and still retain its funereal quality.

The tenant upstairs, Jerry Chercchio, matched our wall pounding with his. We boomed and he bammed. It was like the lefts and rights against a big bass drum. A plumber ripped into his bathroom wall and found a broken pipe that led to another above our bedroom. Jerry, a gregarious American who owned Jerry's restaurant on the Via Veneto, told me that he hung a sign above his bathroom entrance that read "Noah's Ark."

During these weeks, we got to know Polly quite well. I referred to him privately as the town crier. He knew everything about everyone and concealed nothing. Polly was a Muslim. He neither drank nor smoked. However, he admitted liking the ladies and told me he had his eye on a few in the neighborhood. He was still a Fascist and said so, "These pipes and walls would have been fixed long ago under Mussolini."

Angelica, however, had the last words, "All right, I paid for the pipes inside the walls. But you must pay to fix the leaking faucets outside."

Like any good Italian, I didn't accept her argument. I maintained the broken pipes inside put pressure on the faucets and caused them to leak. It was no use. Angelica wouldn't budge. I paid.

Polly was in and out of our three homes for the entire seven years that we lived in Rome. He became a quasi-member of the family and would regularly help himself to Coca-Cola in the refrigerator. He liked Coke and credited it as the reason that Americans didn't drink wine at meals.

We fought various household legal battles until leaving Italy. Polly remained my lawyer. We lost most of the time, but that was not Polly's fault. I always caved in, knowing that if we went to court, the Italian was certain to win. But no claim, no incident, no misfortune ever surprised Polly. He merely said, "This would never have happened under Mussolini."

Chapter 4

The Office

THE PHRASE CHE bel'confusione has described many peoples. However, it may be truest of the Italians. Wherever two of them are gathered together, there will be three opinions. We had 17 Italians on the staff of our INS news bureau. I never figured out how many opinions they represented, but they were a mouthful. As one staffer described the place, "The organization is American, but the beauty of working here is Italian. This is organized confusion." *Che bel' confusione* (What beautiful confusion!)

Most of the staff worked full-time but some were only part-timers. After a while, I expressed this in my own way—some worked fully on part-time while others worked partly on full-time. I believed most Italians worked to live—not lived to work!

Our office was located at 476 Via del Corso. We shared celebrity status in the building with Pietro Nenni, head of the Italian Socialist Party, and his fellow travelers. I saw the gentleman frequently in the lobby, and we had a nodding acquaintanceship. Of all the politicians in Italy, I understood Nenni least. He was an intelligent, serious man, but his parroting of the

Communist party line caused me to question his genuine political independence from the Reds.

Our office wasn't far from Piazza del Popolo where Palmiro Togliatti, chief of the Communist party, addressed his comrades in a tumultuous rally every May Day. Later, on joining ABC News, I set up our office in Piazza di Spagna where the Pope came to pray each December 8 on the feast of the Immaculate Conception. Between the Pope and Palmiro, we had our moments.

The comrades were bused and trucked to the piazza from all parts of Italy, and were usually more than 100,000 strong. They brought lunches and waved red hammer-and-sickle flags. I always brought my own lunch and a portable chair because Togliatti was as long-winded as most Italian politicians. It was a roaring, daylong show of power.

Three Catholic churches faced the Communist throng in the square. Another three religious sanctuaries huddled out of sight on nearby side streets. Sometimes, the bells of all six would peal at the height of Togliatti's revolutionary oratory. The party chief would halt, look heavenward, and say that God agreed with him. That always brought a long roll of laughter from the crowd.

Hundreds of riot police were gathered on side streets in the event of trouble. Devout, old Italian women told me they represented the legions of the Lord against the masses of Marx. The women would go into the churches and pray for the souls of Togliatti and his followers. It was a toss-up. No side ever won.

The show at Piazza di Spagna, where I later opened a news office for ABC, was much different. Our second-floor office looked almost directly at the Spanish Steps and had a commanding view of the entire square. During their office, Popes Pius XIII, John XXIII, and Paul VI each knelt and prayed beneath a towering brick spire in the center of the piazza, surrounded by children's religious banners. A magnificent statue of the Madonna rested atop the spire.

At the climactic moment, Roman firemen climbed to the top of the spire on their long ladders and crowned Mary with a colorful wreath of flowers. The crowd would always jump and shout wildly. The Communists and Catholics were a photo finish in their tributes to motherhood, justice, and mercy toward the young. Neither religion nor revolution ever completely won the Italian soul. I swore that some of the people I saw with Togliatti also came to cheer the Pope.

As I came to learn with the years, many Italians carried both their party card and a picture of the Madonna in their wallets. Some had several party registrations in their bedsprings. That's what thousands of years of history teaches a people.

Via del Corso was a street of confusion and contradiction. It was Rome's longest north-south avenue with massive traffic, yet one of the city's narrowest thoroughfares. Some of the largest department stores in Rome were located in this suffocatingly humid snarl. So were many of the big banks and business offices. The Italian parliament also was nearby. This was civilized chaos, especially in the summer months when waves of tourists added to the melee, splashing across street and sidewalk.

Hundreds of thousands of people crossed and crisscrossed Via del Corso every business day in cars, buses, and on foot. It was an avenue of shouting masses, screeching brakes, smoke, fumes, and often scorching sun. The heat and traffic fumes were so intense on summer days that I often put wet, cold towels around my head. That blast-furnace regalia shocked more than one visiting fireman but it eased the sweat pouring down my neck.

Our news empire extended beyond our office with various stringers. These part-timers considered themselves "specialists" and made it known they wished to be treated accordingly.

We had our Vatican tipster, Dr. Cesare Lolli, reporting Church tidbits, who had to be handled with papal gloves. Then, there were our parliament stringers, who called in blow-by-blow accounts of legislative fights between the Communists and other parties. And, of course, there was Felici, the official Vatican photographer who took daily pictures of the Pope and sold the exact, same copies to every news organization in the world. Felici received nothing but white-glove treatment. We also had a stringer in Naples, an elderly gentleman who had worked part-time for us over many years. I was on the job only a few weeks when I received this letter from him: "INS owes me three months' wages. I am an old man and no longer work for glory. Please send the money."

I promptly paid him. It may have been the shock caused by payment, but the good man passed away shortly thereafter.

I was beginning to feel that even the office boy had to be handled with kid gloves. Only, Alberto was no kid. He had once driven a truck in Mussolini's Afrika Corps. The whim of time and place brought Alberto to us. Alberto wasn't the brightest of our office stars, but he had a sense of order and social decorum that brought notable respectability to our amiable, but apparently aimless, American manner of doing business.

In Alberto's realm, he was our "head usher," although we had no other ushers. His actual duties consisted of cleaning the office and delivering news packets and messages around town. He went to the airport twice a day to pick up news photos coming in from abroad and shipped our photos out to New York and overseas clients.

Often, we wouldn't see Alberto for long periods of time. Upon return, he always had the same excuse—the company motor scooter had broken down. The scooter was about three years old and everyone knew Alberto wanted a new one. But the lack of flair in his excuses underlined what other office staffers thought of him, that Alberto's best days were behind the wheel of that truck in the Afrika Corps.

In reality, Alberto spent most of his time outside the office drinking coffee and talking with pals. His chatter was more than a gift; it was a passion rivaling Italy's greatest quest, *L'amore*. That is, crimes or conquests of the heart.

The only time Alberto ever moved hurriedly was to sweep the office. Obviously, he considered his usher duties paramount.

Alberto always thoroughly washed his hands after cleaning, replaced the red tie he had removed (he always wore a red tie),
and sat behind a large, old desk in the corridor just inside the office entrance. My office was about twenty steps beyond. To see
me, or enter our newsroom, the visitor was forced to face Alberto,
who often had his head buried in the sports pages.

When a visitor entered, Alberto rarely put his paper aside
completely, never rose, and he always coughed. I once asked
him about the cough. Alberto confided it forced the visitor to
speak first, putting him or her on the defensive. He considered
that wise. The visitor should be made to feel ill at ease. Alberto
said that made the newcomer more pliant.

The head usher had his rules. He always asked the visitor for
a calling card. Then, he would ask questions: Why do you wish
to visit so and so? What do you mean a private visit? What's the
difference between a private and personal visit? Precisely what
business do you wish to discuss?

When convinced he had learned all he could about the gentleman, Alberto asked the newcomer to take a seat and wait. He
then came to me or whoever the visitor requested to see and laid
out the scene. Often, he would raise his right hand, point the
thumb and index finger upward and twist his hand. This was his
signal that he thought the matter was dicey and didn't like it.
Sometimes, he meant the person was crazy. I came to believe
Alberto would have made a top detective in the robbery detail at
police headquarters downtown.

I mention Alberto in some detail because it took me a long
time to understand why he wished to be our head usher. And
when he told me, I was truly humbled. He said the best offices
in Rome always had an usher at the door. True, the usher was
often a mantelpiece, but his presence was a symbol of decorum
and, indeed, distinction. High-class establishments added paintings of 18th-century bearded scholars, as if they were founders
of the firm, and other indications that the firm was notable
and noble.

Alberto was right to insist on a head usher and to assume that role. We were, after all, a large American corporation and it would have been embarrassing for an important foreign company not to have an usher. No matter that he often left his chair vacant to spend time gabbing with Italian customs officials at the airport or with his pals in coffee bars. Our dignity—and his—demanded an usher.

I have often looked back on those years. How so many firms and government offices padded their payrolls with relatives and friends in meaningless jobs. I recall running their gauntlets to see one of their directors only to discover he was the only jackass in the place. What unpardonable arrogance on my part. Nobility. Professional distinction. These were the keys to high acceptance.

I can still see Alberto . . . the bright red tie dazzling above the worn, blue workshirt; brushing back his curly brown hair and laughing with his large stomach bouncing up and down. Talking, talking, talking. Coffee and more coffee. And twisting those two fingers upward!

I can see him Up There with St. Peter, ushering souls left and right. Picking up the calling cards. Asking many to take a seat. I see a large sign. It says: Alberto, Head Usher.

There are still such ceremonial posts in Italy, especially among government ministries and the Vatican. Perhaps, as Alberto maintained, they do hold the keys to the kingdom.

The office staff addressed me as *Dottore*, which in America signifies a Ph.D., but in Italy generally indicates one was graduated from college. It can also mean a person holds a decent job, earns a good living, or just looks clever and dresses well. Italians used a long array of other titles. I viewed such pretense as a form of everyday snobbery.

I had several chats with the husband of Italian movie actress, Gina Lollobrigida, who was a stickler about being called *Dottore*. We met to settle a difference over who owned the rights to certain photos that INS had taken of her. He wanted payment for the photos. I maintained they were in the public domain since she was an actress, and would pay him nothing. Seeing he was backing a losing horse, he switched arguments indicating I had not been properly respectful to him. He demanded I call him *Dottore* and implied he was a medical doctor. Both of us knew his job was to manage Gina's career, and it wasn't much of a post. She simply showed up for a film, wore vamp clothes, whispered her dialogue in a sultry voice, took deep breaths to bare her bosom, and he picked up the check. The hard-eyed, sharp-tongued gentleman was a Yugoslav—the Italians weren't the only ones who played the title game.

I always insisted on being called Mister or Jack, although big cheeses in business, government, and the Vatican often addressed me as Doctor Casserly.

Despite some of their old-world hangups, the Italians could be ultramodern in some of their speech; for example, *fare lo snob* (to act like a snob) or *Lei e una ragazza di oomph!* (She's an oomph girl!) But in the late 1950s and early sixties, the archaic past usually dominated modern life.

We photographed the Italian *carabinieri* (federal police) and army officers in action. I sometimes accompanied the photographer. These troopers loved parading and saluting one another in all their finery. Had American police or army officers worn the same feathers and given the same exaggerated salutes, they would have been laughed off their parade grounds. The Italians loved it. As an American general observed privately, "The Italian army in attack looked like shit running through a goose."

In reflecting on all this, I came to two conclusions—Italians had an obsessive desire for public recognition, and their major weakness was flattery. Ingratiating apple-polishing was often practiced by the poor or the working masses. For example, the waiter who hoped for a large tip would call out to the kitchen throughout a meal: "Is the professor's first plate ready yet? Did you snap [your fingers] for more wine, Professor? Do we have the professor's desert ready? Coffee, Professor?"

Parking attendants called most male customers *Dottore* and most women *Dottoressa*. From the butcher to the hairdresser, the more modest constantly saluted the rich—or those believed to be rich—for business, tips, future assistance, or as a safety net in case of trouble.

This title-tilting was brought into American public view when President Dwight D. Eisenhower visited Italy in the late 1950s. Italian President Giovanni Gronchi gave a state dinner for Ike at the Quirinale Palace. My wife and I were invited. At various times, Eisenhower was addressed by Italian dignitaries as Mister President, General, Mister Eisenhower, and the Honorable President. Gronchi topped Ike. He was referred to only as Your Excellency. In talking with some of Ike's staff later, they roared with laughter about how the Italians addressed one another as Attorney, Engineer, Commended One, and other titles.

Slowly but surely, I was being introduced by the Italians into their world of traps and trappings. Truth was often covered with tinsel. Italy was a stage and Italians some of the world's great actors. Before we left Italy, I began to appreciate some of these artful dodgers. Unlike the French, Germans, and other peoples of Europe, the Italians avoided much of the meanness of life. They would rather outfox you with charm and a smile than a stern lecture or outright argument. I concluded that, while their title games were vain showmanship, the Italians offered no offense. As a people, they were not petty like many French and Germans. The Italians had a magnanimity of spirit matched by no other people in Europe, and I traveled extensively throughout the continent.

The finest gentleman I ever met worked in our INS office. His name was GianCarlo Govoni. He was in his sixties and had been a newsman throughout his long career, much of it in England and France. Govoni was both a realist and a proud Italian.

The white-haired gentleman with the thick spectacles carried himself with an extraordinarily gentle bearing and manner. He also had a great common touch. Govoni laughed at the playboy princes and nightclub contessas of Italy. Yet, as he reminded me, their parents, grandparents, and lineage for hundreds of years helped create Italy's great art, other notable craftsmanship, saints and popes, banking leaders, and indeed Italian reunification under Garibaldi. At the same time, in soft, intimate tones, he derided Italy's decaying aristocracy while still hoping some would become the backbone of the country's new middle class. Govoni never looked for heroes. He searched for hard-working men with a cultivated sense of social and moral justice.

Govoni would stand at his desk in the early morning, his black-framed glasses on his thin face, and plead for the unification of Europe. He was a passionate follower of Jean Monnet, a French economist and political figure who became the father of the European Common Market. Govoni would say, commenting ironically on Italy's *La Dolce Vita* (The Sweet Life), that Europe needed a common market, not a common mistress. "The siren call of Charles de Gaulle and old glories is dead," he insisted. "Only the new Europe counts."

Yet, Govoni could be sentimental and often reached out and touched the past. "Can you imagine sitting down to the same table and bottle of wine with Michelangelo, the Medicis, da Vinci, Raphael, and the Berninis? God, we have a great history!"

Govoni never touched me more deeply than the morning he came to me privately and said, "Please don't call me 'Doctor'. I know you do it because the other Italians do it. You think I ask for recognition. I don't. Please call me Mister."

Govoni passed away about five years after we left Italy. He wrote various articles to the end, encouraging, pleading with his countrymen to create a new Italy with greater social, economic, and moral integrity. Perhaps, in the public mind, he failed. Italy has had more than 50 governments since the war and most of them loaded with corruption. The financial kickbacks and other scandals involving hundreds of government and business leaders are still exploding in the Italian media. Amid all the titles and false faces of these Italian nobles and other leaders, Govoni is still a beacon of light to those who knew him. I want to say to him now, *Ti voglio bene, GianCarlo. Ti voglio bene.* (I love you, John Charles. I love you.)

My worst assignment in Italy came one summer when New York asked me to go to Venice and work with Elsa Maxwell, the gossip columnist. I had read her society drivel in the *New York Journal-American.* My editors said I was to make sure her column was written and cabled to New York on time. Luciano Mellace, one of our photographers, accompanied me on the train trip to Venice. Elsa had just dropped anchor in the lagoons of the city and was holding court at the Venice Film Festival.

We arrived mid-evening only to learn it was then impossible to have an audience with Miss Maxwell. Her social secretary informed me by phone she was dressing in preparation for dinner and a gala party that night. We were given an appointment for ten the following morning.

Elsa Maxwell was one of the queens of cafe society. She brought together the ne'er-do-wells of Europe's old nobility with the rich new jet set. Some of these movie, stage, and other stars wanted to exchange their fast bucks for a quick title. Maxwell was paid by film moguls to throw parties inviting the languishing dukes and countesses to meet the moneyed movie class.

We were ushered in to see Miss Maxwell a few minutes after ten. I was startled to discover Mellace and I were standing in the gossip's bedroom, and she was still beached between the sheets. She was a short, heavy, grumpy woman who apparently turned on her charm only when a party began or some prince or actor kissed her hand. Miss Maxwell immediately told me to take notes on the "sensational" party of the previous night. She began with this sentence: "Everybody—just everybody in Venice—was there."

I winced.

Maxwell dictated in bursts and pauses. She was reading from notes she apparently made during the party. She, and the editors in New York, expected me to write her column. She proceeded to rattle off the titles of various princes and counts whose names I couldn't pronounce, much less spell. I said so. Miss Maxwell reproached me, concluding, "Young man, you are not on the march!"

Her secretary shot me a knowing glance, indicating she would help me with the spelling later. It would be sufficient if I captured Miss Maxwell's various tidbits. The columnist gabbed for 45 minutes.

Mellace followed Miss Maxwell around at each of the parties and took the photos she requested. He got the names of those photographed from her social secretary who watched from a vantage point. We developed the photos, wrote cut lines for them, and sent the pictures to New York for distribution.

These audiences went on for three days with Miss Maxwell propped up by pillows in bed. Her dictatorial manner and re-proachment about the spelling of noble names continued. Somehow, with her secretary's help, I managed to make some sense of her bad grammar and flights of fancy. I rushed to the cable office before noon each day to meet New York's deadline.

Mellace considered Maxwell a mad hatter. The photographer told me he could not swallow the woman much longer. He detested taking her phony, posed pictures. Fortunately, a cable arrived from New York saying we should return to Rome for another assignment. However, Mellace was ordered to remain one more day. I broke the news to him gently. Mellace, a gregarious young fellow with a friendly smile, pleaded to return with me. I told him New York's orders were final. Miffed, he said I had deserted him. I left Miss Maxwell's social secretary a note saying I had been ordered back to Rome and caught the train.

Mellace showed up in the office two days later. He refused to speak to me, sending me his latest photos and asking me in a note to write the cut lines. He wanted several days off to recover. I agreed.

On returning from his brief vacation, Mellace came into my office and said, "You say you don't understand the Italians. Well,

I don't understand the Americans. You know what that woman told me after all my work? She said I wasn't on the march!"

If Elsa Maxwell was our low, Pope Pius XII was our high. INS merged with United Press in May of 1958 to become UPI. We were actually swallowed, the INS staff disbanded, and the office closed. However, the Pope agreed to see us in private audience and wished to say farewell. He had been reading our Vatican and other dispatches throughout his entire papacy and knew our names. We and our wives dressed in our Sunday best and met him face-to-face.

I shall never forget that day. Everyone was nervous. I had practiced about five different speeches. Eugenio Pacelli, a tall and noble prince of the Roman Catholic Church, appeared from his photos to be an austere man, but he was actually gentle and warm with soft brown eyes. He blessed our rosaries, medals, and us. He made small talk with us remembering, for example, the time when the Americans liberated Rome and U.S. General Mark Clark told him, "Your Holiness, I hope our tanks didn't make too much noise." The Pope replied, "General, anytime you liberate Rome, you can make as much noise as you like."

As the audience ended, the Pope came to me and said, "Please tell your management in New York that I hope they will help find a job for every member of your staff."

I cabled his words to New York but never received a reply.

Events in the office rose and fell like the Mediterranean tide. When INS finally closed down, each of our 17 full- and part-time employees sued the company. Most phoned me to say it was nothing personal. Mussolini had written most of the country's labor laws, and severence pay and other legalities were strict.

Buon Uscita (A Good Exit) meant large amounts of good-bye pay, from vacation and old-age pension payments to a host of other requirements. Staffers had already signed for and received such payments but then claimed to be entitled to more. It all came down to this: The Americans had money and the employees would win most of their demands in an Italian court.

I was to change jobs twice in Rome. When INS closed, I became bureau chief of Hearst Headline Service. In 1961, I joined ABC News as their Mediterranean bureau chief.

I met new Albertos and other Italian characters. Italy always held me in its spell. Every day was a new adventure.

Chapter 5

Mamma Mia!

"MAMMA MIA," JOY announced, "I'm pregnant!" The good news came a few months after we had arrived in Rome.

We celebrated by seeing a movie, an American Western made in the 1930s, starring John Wayne and Glenn Ford who hollered their whoops and commands in dubbed-in Italian. Admission was 100 lire (16 cents).

We laughed at some of the translation. Some of the other moviegoers wondered why we had burst out. When Ford said, "Stick 'em up!," the translation came out *Attenzione!* (Attention!) And as Wayne rode away into the twilight, he waved and shouted *Adios* which came out *Ciao* in Italian.

The best line of the day, however, came from Joy's gynecologist. He announced with the definitude of a pope, "Signora, lei sta interessante!" which translated literally means, "Madame, you are in an interesting state!"

It seemed much more acceptable than the French version—"Madame, you are in an embarrassing state!"

It didn't take long for the good tidings to spread through the neighborhood. Joy merely asked Giulia, the house porter and expert in administering hypodermic injections, whether she would be willing to shoot her up with high-powered vitamins. Giulia agreed with a knowing smile. That could mean only one thing: the American signora was building herself up for the Big Event. Giulia immediately confided to neighbors that the Americans expected a little GI Joe. Italians liked to slip their familiarity with U.S. lingo into conversations with and about Americans.

Professor Mario Mittiga had advised Joy to take the vitamin injections. Mittiga, our gynecologist, was a genuine professor, teaching at the University of Rome medical school. He was also a superb gentleman with an ironic lament. He had a houseful of girls—no son.

None of those vitamin *pills* for Mittiga or other Italian physicians. It was enough to see how small they were. But injections! Whammo! A real blast!

Home injections were not so simple as we thought. Joy had to buy a syringe and needles, a water pan in which to heat them, and packets of cotton and gauze to hold and clean them. The pharmacist instructed us to heat and clean the syringe and needle in hot water before and after use for complete sterilization.

Italians gave injections for just about everything and, if necessary, anyone could get a shot right in the pharmacy. Bring your own medicine or buy it there. Then, go to the curtained room in the rear, drop your pants and shorts, and pay the pharmacist—often a woman—300 lire (48 cents).

Then, there were the normal visits to the doctor's office. Your appointment was for 6:30 p.m. but you rarely, if ever, saw the physician at that time. There might be an emergency. He could be delivering. Or he was simply stuck in traffic like thousands of other Romans. Mittiga's nurse rarely notified anyone of emergencies. Her attitude was: He will arrive.

We faced many crashers, not only at Mittiga's office but elsewhere. They had many excuses, from meeting a grandmother at the airport to just plain self-importance. "I am Lorelai Longlegs, the singer, and am due on stage in 30 minutes." However, these crashers seemed more numerous in doctors' offices than any-where else. I never figured out why.

One lady swept into Mittiga's office regularly. She was fol-lowed by her husband, one or two of her children, and some-times a friend. "Gangway!" the expectant mother seemed to say, "I'm about to make history. Little Pietro is coming!" The unspo-ken answer from the nurse was always the same: Yes, Pietro is due in about six months. You're number seven in line. But a number of crashers did succeed.

This particular lady, with the loud voice, usually got ahead. She would barge into the doctor's office at the moment when an-other patient left. The woman would loudly announce, as she rushed forward, "Sono Io! Sono Io!" (It's I! It's I!) It was as if the nurse had called her name. Because of various crashers, our 6:30 p.m. appointment would sometimes slip to 8:00 p.m. or later.

The husband accompanied the wife to the doctor's office on these visits. It was an Italian ritual devised and supported by doc-tors. They felt it important to explain to both father and mother just what was happening at any particular stage of pregnancy. That is, the party of the first part was equally responsible for the child as party of the second part. Each, therefore, should take due note of his place and need—especially in case of fire, pre-mature birth, or some other insurance policy emergency. Even though childbirth was an act of God, no insurance firm dared exclude it from coverage. The only thing I ever got from these visits was a prescription blank.

These sojourns allowed me to examine another interesting slice of Italian life. There was a little fellow with a mustache who I saw regularly in Professor Mittiga's office over the years. I judged him to be a veteran because, instead of nervous glances around the room at other couples, he catnapped. His wife, a good fifty pounds heavier than he, would elbow the gentleman from time to time to keep him from sliding off the couch to slumber on the floor.

When awake, the little guy would steal glances at other men

waiting with their wives. His eyes betrayed a bored cynicism, as if to ask: Why are all of you so excited about this "miracle of life?" Get in line! It's been going on for thousands of years!

The more important and hurried patients acted, the more he closed his eyes and shut them out of his daydreams. His expression said: None of you knows what you've gotten into. You're prisoners for the next twenty-two years. I know!

I asked myself many times if this man's attitude was a particularly Italian quality. Would an American also see this as some kind of stage play and try to dissect the characters one by one like a center-aisle critic on Broadway?

I finally came to the conclusion this man considered himself a veteran of the wars of fatherhood and thus an expert. I also became convinced he probably considered himself wounded in the conflict—he had too many kids—and fate had made him a social victim. In response, he refused to bear guilt. Rather, he quietly chuckled to himself at life's vagaries. The trials and troubles of others. He judged them by the cynical whims with which life had treated him. The gentleman was, I judged, a soul worthy of contemplation.

When fully awake, the man spoke with his eyes. After many hours together in the doctor's waiting room over the years, he noticed I was a silent witness of his judgments about those who came and went. That didn't cause him to become more circumspect. On the contrary, he merely shrugged and carried on, offering me arched eyebrows or a knowing smile now and then.

The gentleman's greatest disdain was reserved for the man and wife who had been through parenthood before, and announced it in their conversations so everyone else knew. He would look at these strutting know-it-alls while rubbing his hands through his thinning dark hair as if trying to dismiss them.

Whenever his wife shoved an elbow in his ribs to keep him awake, he seemed to communicate with me most poignantly: I'm underweight. I can't sleep. I go to work and return to a housefull of wails and get a lecture about the cost of living.

Every night at dinner, she tells me to get a raise. *Magari!* (If only it would be!) He would slink in the couch and brood.

I remember the last time I saw the gentleman. He smiled sadly, as if to say: Another miracle. I'm tired of heavenly blessings. I need a rest. Have mercy, Lord! *Basta!* (Enough!) I shall never forget his quiet gallantry. He was a chivalrous victim. A wounded knight.

The good man wasn't typical of the thousands of fathers I met in Italy. Children are more important to many Italian men than position or wealth. Of course, they would like to have all three. But when push came to shove, Italians would mostly choose children. It was like wearing an earthly crown, like a prince of the neighborhood or village. Italian men glory in the masculine power of parenthood. My friend in the doctor's office was, however, a reluctant hero.

* * *

Kevin John Casserly was born at Salvator Mundi Hospital, overlooking Cleopatra's Gardens, on May 10, 1958, about 11:00 a.m. Joy was fine. I was so excited I ran up to a nun and asked what the child looked like. She joyously announced, "Enrico Caruso!"

Enrico Caruso? Since I had never heard or seen the great Italian tenor, except in some worn photos, this came as a bit of a shock. What about Dwight D. Eisenhower or Ted Williams of the Boston Red Sox? Nevertheless, I bounced around the waiting room as if I had just won the Italian national lottery. *Grazie mille!* A thousand thanks! I told the sister.

Italians feted the father as much as the mother, especially when a son was born. The centuries-old importance of carrying on the family name was paramount. More important than receiving a papal blessing. Yet, did we dare take up the challenge of the good nun? Would we name him Enrico Caruso Casserly?

All the neighbors as well as the mailman, garbage collectors, milkman, and others came to see the little *Americano*. Young children came, freshly scrubbed, in a group. They wanted to see if the American had the same number of toes as they, to look at the shape of his ears. One even asked if Kevin's nose would grow to the size of Pinocchio's if he ever told a lie. They never heard the name Kevin so they called him Nino, as close an Italian name as they could find. I heard one of them say, "The Americans are no different at all. Their babies are just the same as ours. I told you so!"

Italian law required all births be registered with the state within ten days of taking place. Thus began my odyssey at Rome's City Hall.

Two witnesses were required to sign the documents. Alberto, our head usher, and Alfredo Miccoli, a photographer, volunteered. As we arrived at the entrance, a man approached us and asked, "Testimonio? Testimonio?" (Testimony?)

I asked what that was all about. With a sheepish grin, Miccoli said, "He wants to know whether we need a witness."

I wanted to know how he could witness anything since he had never seen us before. As Miccoli explained, "He's created his own job. You hire him for 1,000 lire ($1.60) and he'll swear to anything. He also has friends inside who, with a tip, will move you to the head of the line. You pay for saving time."

I was to discover over the years that "making testimony" was a widespread occupation in Italy. Like selling ice cream or hot chestnuts on a street corner.

I should have hired the guy. We spent two days trying to register Kevin. This merry-go-round involved two problems. First, Rome's City Hall registered only the name of the father on the birth certificate (friends said this was to protect unwed mothers and their illegitimate children). However, the American embassy required the names of both parents on the same document if we were to register the child as an American citizen.

Second, city hall officials had some doubt as to whether Kevin was an Italian or an American—or both.

"Look," I insisted to the little man with the glasses behind the clerk's window bars, "I'm trying to explain to you for the ninth time, to wit: The United States embassy here in Rome demands the name of the mother on an official Italian document showing birth. Otherwise, the child cannot be registed as an American. *Capisce?* Do you understand?"

The man squinted and looked pained, as if I were squeezing the last drop of patience from his veins, "You look, sir, I'm telling you for the sake of the historical present that Italian law clearly states the name of the mother is never registered."

I fired back, "Well, then, how come Italy and America have apparently solved this problem for years. There must be an answer."

The man shook his head. "I don't know. I never registered an American—or Italo-American—before in my career and I've been here nine years."

I shoved the debate into another gear. "Let's pose a question. Forget about who the mother is for a moment. Give her any name. Cleopatra is as good as any. [He didn't smile, just buried his forehead in both hands.] Suppose I want to take my son to America with me. He needs a passport. Perhaps I can't take him on my passport. What do I do? Sir, the time and place for action is now—at birth."

The man cleaned his glasses with a large, blue handkerchief. Then carefully he twirled a pen in his right hand without looking up at me. He took a deep breath and blew the air out slowly before saying, "You have a problem. I agree. But I also have a problem. Let's go even further. I believe the boy is Italian. Let the Americans make him an American if they want. That's only to begin with. If you want to make him an American, talk to the U.S. embassy. Write to your president. But leave me in *santa pace* (holy peace)."

The gentleman lit a cigarette. He looked at Alberto and Miccoli as if to ask where they found this crazy guy. Nevertheless, he cautiously spoke again. "No society is perfect. We all make legal mistakes and human errors. In this case, we face a human error that happens to involve the law. A benign dilemma, sir. Should the innocent be blamed? I am innocent of all this. All I'm trying to tell you is Italian law says, protect the weak!"

I nodded agreement. For the first time, he leaned back in his chair with an air of accomplishment. I told him I would return tomorrow. He raised both hands in exasperation, nodded, and wished me a good day.

The American embassy was adamant. The mother's name must appear on the Italian document. I returned to the gentleman and simply said, "The American embassy insists."

He raised both hands again, this time only as high as his throat. He gave himself the old choke hold, then looked away and shook his head. Out of the blue, a compromise hit me.

"Why not make two copies, one for the American embassy and another for Italy? Isn't that the human way? Think about it. I only ask you to think about it."

"Va bene!" he announced. "VA BENE!" (Okay!) The man beamed. He wrote furiously, making one copy for each country. "Finito!" (Finished!) he pronounced with a flourish. "But may I add a few final words of caution. The boy was born in Italy. He can obtain an Italian passport to go to America, even if you get him an American one. If he still lives in Italy at the age of eighteen, it is he who decides — the American or the Italian army. That will decide his citizenship as far as we are concerned."

With that, the gentleman shook my hand and spoke these memorable words, "My congratulations to the lady!" It was a kind of gesture of conciliation. We both smiled and parted as two tired but victorious friends.

Somehow, despite the country's mountainous bureaucracy, Italians are born, marry, bear children, and die as people everywhere. There is a stamp, seal, or official signature for almost every milestone. But in Italy, it is easiest to die. You know you won't have to fill out another form.

Chapter 6

Strikes and Soda

ROME'S LOW-PAID TRANSPORT workers always seemed to be threatening a strike. Bus and streetcar drivers were paid about $120 per month. There were no boisterous picket lines that tied up traffic for a month or more. The walkouts lasted only a day or two with the strikers staying home to read the paper. Few unions had a strike fund and workers could afford few days without pay. This kept these strikes short.

The psychological warfare with management flared constantly—a strike threat, then pulling back; a quick two-hour stoppage; or simply running late and getting the passengers upset. These protests kept the riding public in nervous jitters about getting to and from work. A jumpy public made for a shaky management.

One fine day, however, Rome's bus and streetcar drivers walked out American style. They weren't coming back. The announcement stunned management. The strikers had planned the stoppage for some time. Many had lined up jobs driving the very trucks and other vehicles that the government pressed into service to carry the public. They could thus withstand a prolonged walkout.

I had walked up to Piazza Ungheria on the morning the strike was called. The *carabinieri* (federal police) and army troops had lined up vehicles of all types to carry passengers: vegetable trucks, animal carriers, lumber haulers, and even moving vans. The walkout proved to be an education about Italian life on the hoof.

For starters, the government charged double the normal fare. You got on most of the trucks by climbing a shaky wooden ladder. This was not difficult for most men but it proved tricky for many women, especially those with high heels, who did a precarious balancing act until they were safely aboard. Getting off was a lot tougher. Some gentleman would usually wait at the bottom and help those who needed it, but there were times when all the men walked away. Crowds of males would stand on street corners to watch women try to navigate the ladder alone. This always produced wolf calls—whistles were a form of derision in Italy—and some embarrassed ladies said they would never take what they called the cattle car again.

The ride was a dilly. There were no seats and, for those who couldn't lean against a wall or hold onto a rail of some kind, the only thing they could grab for balance was a neighbor. Of course, the Romeos loved these quick embraces. But the women were wary. The drivers, of course, wheeled around corners like they were Mario Andretti. All of this made for wild—and romantic—adventure.

One day, I rode in a truck that had been a former pigpen. The vehicle got overcrowded and many of the men, to relieve the strain with ironic humor, began to holler: *Porca Madonna!* I knew it meant something about pigs and the Madonna. A friend translated it as, "Mother of God, you pigs!" The phrase could have referred to the riders, who were often packed like pigs, or the striking drivers, or management. I never figured out whom.

On this particular day, a man and his son ran the show. They apparently had a pig farm some distance from Rome. The two were authorized to make a certain run after renting the vehicle to the state.

We were about halfway to Piazza del Popolo when the vehicle filled up with riders. Passengers, particularly those against the inside cabin, began shouting to take the canvas cover off the back. They were suffocating from heat and the smell of pigs. The father, who was driving, refused. That would take time and he apparently was paid more to make additional runs.

In a peace gesture, the son came back and, while the truck was still moving, tied a rope across the end of the vehicle. This further tightened the back canvas but was plainly a sign the truck was full and would take on no more passengers.

We lurched ahead with no stops. As we flew past corners, waiting passengers shouted and shook their fists at us. Meanwhile, some on the truck asked to get off and began their own chorus as we barreled down various streets and around corners. The more that passengers screamed, it seemed, the harder the father shoved his foot down on the gas. The scene was a chaotic Italian opera!

One passenger had an idea. Tear off the canvas cover and we might stop this madman. Others agreed, and one by one, each knot holding the canvas to the top of the truck's wooden sides was untied, and the rope was ripped away. Finally, whoof! The canvas sailed aloft before finally plopping down on a small car following us. The father apparently caught sight of the flying canvas in his rearview mirror and screeched to a halt. The son raced back to retrieve the canvas from the roof of the startled driver's car who had nearly smashed into the truck and was shouting one insult or another. Horns were honking. A police whistle blew furiously. A siren screamed in the distance. We were on the Via Barberini, one of the busiest streets in Rome.

Somebody found the ladder and several women descended. I and several young men jumped down to the street. Other women and the elderly descended via the ladder. The father and son were shouting at us, and some passengers were yelling back at them. The same man was still shouting *Porca Madonna!*

Che bel' confusione!

The strike lasted about a week. I almost bought a motor scooter, but decided against it because Joy wanted to save money and buy a car. She prevailed but it was glorious theater. I never forgot it.

* * *

Nor have I forgotten the coffee-bar strike. Coffee-bar workers had no union. No organization of any kind. No leadership and no bargaining power. But they did walk out. It was mass instinct.

The runner, or bar-boy, who raced *espresso* and other drinks to offices, commercial establishments, and apartments around town generally received a salary of between 5,000 and 8,000 lire ($8 to $12.80) per week. That included a half and sometimes a full sixth workday. Most of his earnings came from tips—from 50 lire (8 cents) to as much as 300 lire (48 cents) on a large order.

The runners demanded a wage increase of at least 1,000 lire ($1.60) per week in straight salary. It was a pittance, of course, but these young men were being paid meager salaries in the late 1950s.

When the strike began and the espresso stopped, the grumble from office workers all over Rome rose to a roar. The newspapers had a delightful time interviewing everyone from the strikers to bank presidents who missed having coffee delivered to their desks twice a day. Even police sergeants and captains were outraged—those cheap coffee-bar owners ought to be arrested. The outcry was tremendous and the salary increase was quickly won. But I faulted the customers. What cheapskates! They would tip a kid only 30 or 50 lire (8 cents) for delivering coffee.

"Porca Madonna," I told a friend. "You guys should be run out of town." He marveled at how Italian I was becoming. He didn't know the half of it. I had bought an espresso machine for the office and we didn't need to send out for coffee.

We were often involved in gas strikes. One of these, in the fall of 1959, lasted three months. The crews, which had a better strike fund than the bus and streetcar drivers, were a lot tougher—homestoves received a flame about as thin as a needle and a quarter-inch high. That was enough to boil water to heat a baby's bottle. We discovered that, for some reason, the skeleton crews at the gas company allowed a stronger flame between four and five each morning. I never determined the reason, but Joy and our maid, Elena, set early alarms and cooked at that hour.

As a matter of fact, during that time Joy cooked a pumpkin pie for Thanksgiving Day. Early the same day, she marched over to the local baker with three turkeys to be cooked in their coal-wood ovens. This was a special appointment at another special price. We needed all three because the largest Italian turkeys weighed only about seven pounds. Joy also brought three more pumpkin pies for baking (one for the baker) as well as a small can of cranberry sauce for the baker. Weeks before the strike, we had invited ten Italian friends to share a typical American Thanksgiving meal.

Now, Italian neighbors gathered at the bakery because they were curious about what went into an American Thanksgiving dinner. On arrival, Joy was surrounded by a group of Italian women. What exactly were the Americans celebrating? How long had this been going on? Was it really a national holiday? Did they invite Indian friends like those in the movies? What was in the turkey stuffing? What do cranberry sauce, squash, and American pumpkin pie taste like?

Our guests' reactions to our Thanksgiving dinner were mixed. Turkey meat was rated only so-so. Cranberry sauce was too tart. The squash didn't have a very distinctive taste. But the pumpkin pie swept them away. It may be a contradiction, I told Joy at the time, but the Italians were bananas about it. At the end of dinner, one of the ladies said, "Why doesn't Italy have one day to thank God for our blessings. We have a holiday for everything else!"

Amen, I said.

When Romans got a bellyful of bus, coffee, and gas strikes, many found their throats had run dry—no water. Well, not precisely. Coming out of faucets and showers, it was measured by the drop. That could mean a strike or, perhaps, a breakdown somewhere.

In the fall of 1963, a major pipe broke in our neighborhood. We were living outside the city in a tiny villa on the old Via Cassia. Some of our neighbors, who were local historians, said there had been no such break in a century. It had last occurred nearby at Nero's tomb.

With no water, our laundry began to pile up. There was water in town—we were six miles outside—but local officials promised us everything would be fixed domani *(tomorrow)*. As happens many times in Rome, domani never came.

Joy decided, with no water, to take a holiday from cooking. We would eat out, she said, until the broken pipe was found and fixed. That would be two days at most. So our family of five started eating lunch and dinner at a little *osteria* (country restaurant) nearby. We now had three boys; after Kevin, Terry was born in 1960 and Jeff a year later.

The boys got one whiff of that restaurant kitchen and suddenly developed appetites like Italian laborers. The bill, with five of us plus Elena, the maid, and sometimes visitors, was averaging $32 a day—considered a great deal of money in those days. This was almost nothing the owner and his wife claimed, saying we were receiving their special discount. I knew they had a private well and I thought of buying water from them instead of meals. However, their high meal prices dissuaded me from asking. I didn't want to be put in the position of refusing since Joy and the boys were crazy about the place.

Within a few days, the bill began rising. Jeffrey, then barely two years old, liked rum cake and had it for dessert at every meal. Terry and Elena had standing orders for *Zuppa Inglese* (English soup). This was actually hybrid pie and cake, soaked generously in rum, with whipped cream on top. I would manage to arrive for minestrone and the bill.

Before going to bed, we brushed our teeth in soda water, which a store owner sold to Joy at another discount. Morning and night, the soda flowed like a Roman fountain. We were able to wash our hands and faces because farmers sometimes came around and sold water by the bucket.

After five days without running water, we decided everyone needed a bath. We drove to the *Bagno Diurno* (daily bath), located under Rome's central railroad station. It was a day we long remembered.

The tubs were big enough to float motorboats. The water flowed like a river and so did the three boys. I frantically played lifeguard, diving after wayward bodies, as the boys bobbed up and down amid the soapy crests squealing with laughter. When we let the scalding water run, the clouds of steam became as thick as a Turkish bath. I couldn't see the boys so I held all three by their hair. They were furious. Nevertheless, we stayed more than two hours in the place. Total cost for the five of us was 1,500 lire ($2.40). That was the first price I liked in months.

The next day, the boys and I went to a nearby barbershop for haircuts. The total bill was $1.60. I was living! When we arrived home, Elena, who didn't accompany us to the public bath because it was beneath her dignity, announced she had found a well. After dark, Joy, Elena, and I piled every pail we had in the house into our car and drove to Elena's well.

The well was in the middle of a field and we had to use a flashlight to find it. Sure enough, there was water about twelve feet deep. One by one, I lowered the containers with a rope — pails, bottles, even two kettles with their spouts taped open. Elena kept saying the well was "public" but I knew better. Some farmer would find us and I would get a pitchfork up the rump. Nevertheless, with my gastronomic bills becoming astronomic, I wasn't about to argue with good fortune. I made four more trips to the well with Elena. At the end of it all, Elena heated the water and had a private bath!

Several days later, running water returned. Some neighbor families came home from their hotels in town. I paid off the restaurant owner and shut off the rum cake allowances.

We still had one more problem—all the laundry that had piled up. Joy and Elena eventually washed everything but we had no dryer and were in the midst of the rainy season. Joy always dried our laundry outside. It continued to pour and winter would begin shortly. When the weather was cold or rainy, most families dried their laundry anywhere inside the apartment or house where there was heat—atop room radiators, in front of the fireplace, and strung across rooms with electric heaters blazing. I scrounged among friends for stray heaters and kept a notebook to remember who owned what heater.

Amid the vicissitudes of daily Roman life, Joy and I longed for Sunday. It would be holy and happy—we hoped.

Chapter 7

Sunday in Rome

SUNDAY WAS THE jewel in the setting of Italian daily life. Since Italians did not live to work, they worked to live. Sunday was precious because most labored five and a half to six days a week.

Domenica wasn't Sunday without sunshine. If it rained, Italy had a national headache. Sunday was an outdoor day—to take the family out to lunch, a long walk in a park or somewhere else, to watch soccer, take a car trip, visit the relatives or play cards in the town square.

On Sunday, we were very Italian. This is how we spent a typical one. We went to early Mass at San Roberto Bellarmino in Piazza Ungheria. Unlike American churches, most worshippers stood. There were few pews. Italians explained that standing was an old habit—worshippers could more easily greet one another, exchange gossip, make appointments to talk business after Mass, or even make a date with a member of the opposite sex. Church didn't slow down Italian chatter. It merely muted it. Rapid-fire chitchat was especially prevalent in country churches if someone wanted to trade a pig for wine or chickens for olive oil.

Small children often flew large balloons in church—red, yellow, blue, green, and other colors soared on long strings to the ceiling. Parents bought these balloons from a peddler in the courtyard outside St. Robert Bellarmine. Worshippers told us the balloons helped to keep their children quiet. We always wondered why they didn't buy a few for themselves.

It soon became evident that Italians did not take the Sunday ritual too seriously—except for clothing. We once went to a church where the priest ordered Joy to leave because she wore a dress with short sleeves. Meanwhile, the jabbering continued as if it were intermission at the opera. But the priest was a shouter and could be heard throughout much of the church and above the din. Joy was devastated and we left. But we felt the glorious balloons made up for much of our embarrassment. They showed Italian humanity and made the church seem more human, like an old friend.

Each Sunday, we walked across Piazza Ungheria to a coffee bar. If the boys had been good in church—and somehow all passed the test no matter what they did—we bought them sweet rolls. Joy and I bolted down a couple of espressos with croissants.

We usually piled on the bus and rode downtown, often to Piazza di Spagna or Fontana di Trevi (Trevi Fountain, seen in many movies). I explained to the boys that the square took its name from the Spanish embassy to the Holy See which had been located there for centuries, and that a French ambassador built the famous Spanish Steps more than three centuries ago—out of his own pocket!

In the center of the square was a beautiful fountain, and traffic had to go around it. Italians called it "Bernini's (the great sculptor) Boat" since it was shaped like a boat. Some Italians told us that a great flood roared across Rome nearly four centuries before, and when the water withdrew, it left a boat where the present fountain stood. Bernini was said to have built his boat-shaped work to keep away future floods.

On hot Sundays, our kids would roll up their pants, take off their shoes, and walk in the fountain's water. They would splash one another and had a great time. The police never seemed to mind. They were often busy eyeing the many foreign girls who flooded the piazza. Young Italian men also were on the chase. The girls loved it! Our boys noticed this and, pointing to the girls, Terry said, "Papa, sono stranieri!" (Pop, they're foreigners!)

Our kids spoke Italian and English interchangeably and we never knew what language would pop out. They never considered themselves foreigners. I had a devil of a time explaining what flirting meant, though.

The *Professore* was a middle-aged gentleman who spent many days painting in the square. I introduced the family to him a number of times. I had gotten to know him by buying three of his works. The professor would arrive, start painting, and some foreigner would soon want to buy his work-in-progress. The professor spoke only Italian but, with grimaces and gestures, made it known to the foreigners that he couldn't bear to part with his creation. The tourist, of course, constantly pulled out more money until the professor could no longer resist. Of course, he was being very Italian. He said buyer and seller were both happier because of the bargaining session. I tried to impart this lesson to our boys.

Wherever we went, I tried to teach our kids. I pointed out the Memorial House of the poet, John Keats, located to the right of the Steps and open to visitors. Keats lived and wrote poetry there until he died in 1821. He was English, I told the boys, and we are Americans. I asked, "Are you going to leave behind good works when we go home to America?" They thought about that, but said nothing. Kevin finally responded. "Maybe I'll leave our coloring books. I'm not as good as the professor."

We often met Vittorio in the piazza. He was more than eighty years old and had been driving tourists around the city in his horse-drawn carriage since he was in his teens. All the cabbies parked their horses and buggies in the piazza.

Vittorio told us the same story more than once . . . In 1925, he said, there were more than 3,000 carriages carrying passengers around Rome. Now there were only 121. The reason was the *fanatici*! (the fanatics!) These were Italian car drivers who were forcing horses and buggies off the roads by revving their engines, honking, and spooking the animals. Also, the police forced the cabbies off certain streets, claiming the carriages slowed up traffic. As Vittorio put it, "The city is taking the oats out of life!"

Joy always insisted we walk along Via del Babuino, which flowed directly from the piazza. The street was famous for antique furniture and paintings. Store owners often used Sundays to ship orders and take in new furniture and other wares. I was surprised to learn that some of these were castaways which came from Rome's various flea markets. The owner would select a worthy item, fix or shine it up, and slap a new—and higher—price tag on it.

We made a purchase on Via del Babuino only once, a magnificent painting of Rome. The flea markets were more compatible with our style—and pocketbook.

We would sometimes walk from Via del Babuino to Via Veneto, a thirty-minute hike with small kids, where we would get sandwiches, cold drinks, and coffee. We usually went to Doney's adjoining the elegant Excelsior Hotel which had outdoor tables and colorful umbrellas.

There are no time laws in Italy regarding the sale of liquor. As early as 10:00 or 11:00 on Sunday mornings, when Joy and I sometimes had breakfast there, we saw couples having martinis. We knew, of course, they couldn't be Italians. No Italian would drink a martini on Sunday or any other morning.

Many Italians sat at Doney's just to watch the parade of foreigners. Some told us they didn't need to travel to London, Paris or Cologne because the English, French, and Germans came to them. I once heard an Italian man telling another a joke about foreigners. It went something like this with the storyteller playing both roles:

No. 1: Do you see that fellow? He's an Englishman.

No. 2: How do you know?

No. 1: You can always tell an Englishman because, when he walks down the street, he looks like he owns the world.

No. 2: You know, you're right. That's the way the English really are. But do you see that other fellow coming down the street? He's an American.

No. 1: But how do you know?

No. 2: Well, you can always tell an American because, when he walks down the street, he looks like he doesn't give a damn who owns the world!

One Sunday, we witnessed a fender bender on the Via Veneto and Joy chatted with one of the police officers on the scene. She bravely asked, "Why do Italians drive as crazily as they do?"

The reply was the officer's Sunday best: "Bravado! Abandon! Signora, the stage! The audience!"

Joy laughed. The officer offered an example: "Think of a girl on the back of a motor scooter. She has one arm around the waist of her boyfriend. The other holds her purse and umbrella. By some miracle, she balances herself. That is bravado!

"The same girl twists and turns on the seat as her boyfriend dodges through traffic. She can't hold down her skirt which is blowing above her knees. That is abandon! And when young men shout and cheer her on, that is the stage! Do you understand?"

Joy laughed so hard that she couldn't respond. The officer tipped his hat and smiled. She guessed he had told that story a hundred times. In Italy, even the police are actors!

We sometimes drove about 20 miles southwest of Rome to the hill town of Frascati for lunch. If an Italian family can possibly afford it, the entire clan—relatives and all—have lunch together on Sunday. These are perhaps the three choicest hours of the week. Italian Sunday lunches run somewhat longer than a good Broadway play. And good theater should not be rushed.

These family outings at Frascati and elsewhere always reminded me of an orchestra. Despite large helpings of spaghetti and chicken, interspersed with much chattering, laughter, and liters of wine (diluted with water for the children), the clan never seemed to miss a beat. Hands and forks waved madly. Fists pounded the long table. Napkins, tucked under collars, swayed with their movements. The chatter would rise to a crescendo until . . . *il conto* (the check). There was always respectful silence as Papa slowly added up the bill. He would often say, "Abbiamo bevuto troppo oggi!" (We drank too much today)! Everybody would laugh and Mamma would respond, "You drank too much!" And everyone would roar.

On Sunday afternoons, we usually went to Pincio Hill near Villa Borghese, the common name for one of the city's largest parks. Thousands of parents with their children, relatives and friends, courting couples, and sometimes a lonely elderly man or woman, would swarm across the park. Villa Borghese teemed with flower and balloon sellers, olive peddlers, open-air coffee bars and puppet shows, donkey rides, boat excursions in a lagoon, children's cars, and snoring grandfathers resting on the grass after a picnic lunch.

Pulcinella, a puppet of either gender, was everyone's hero. Rain or shine, the marionette appeared on its high wooden stage every Sunday afternoon. The puppet was dressed in white with a black mask. He/she originated in Sicily and Naples centuries ago when local folk used puppets to express grievances against foreign rulers. Pulcinella battled robbers, witches, and the like, and much of the time, the marionette beat the hell out of the devil with a stick. From about 11:00 a.m. to sunset, three men pulled the strings and gave voice to the puppets from behind a portable stage. The men passed a plate or basket among the crowds after performances. The normal offering for a family was 100 lire (16 cents).

We often went to Piazza Navona for late-afternoon ice cream. The boys invariably would let chocolate drip down their shirts and pants. Proprietors offered large paper napkins and I usually washed the trio in one of the fountains in the square. Piazza Navona was my favorite square in Rome because the place was so intimate, so homey, to say nothing of Bernini's great fountains in the center of the piazza.

Americans often preferred the square around *Fontana di Trevi* because of the movie, *Three Coins in the Fountain*. There was no doubt Trevi had charm because of the coin-tossing (a coin in the fountain assured one's return to Rome). But Navona is a family piazza, a square that moves and breathes like people. The many apartments and their laundry hanging over the piazza create a living family atmosphere with none of the gloss that often covers other squares in Rome, Paris, and elsewhere.

Sundays in Rome taught me a lesson, one of the most profound of my life. After several years there, watching our children grow, I concluded with the sages that we humans had so little time on earth. Rome itself was more than 3,000 years old. How infinitesmal was our fleeting presence at its shrines and monuments. How few Sundays we really had—for our children and to learn more of the world around us. Time was a great teacher and most of us had less than a century. Perhaps, the Italians had learned that lesson. Time was one of our great inheritances. Sunday was its most precious, eloquent moment.

Chapter 8

Maids

MOST ITALIAN MAIDS weren't much interested in reason, research, or even explanations. They were creatures of the moment. Their lives rose and fell on the latest emotion—from a boyfriend's still-smouldering kiss to an invitation from the butcher. Their lives were one big rollercoaster.

The drudgery of their work led to exaggerated hopes and dreams that somehow their lives would change. Many often lived and died dreaming the fantasies of movies and magazine articles about the lives of the rich and famous—from actresses to aristocrats.

Many Italians treated their maids as household gypsies, who would work until they took to the road again. Others gave them a home and affection until some man stole them away to cook and darn his socks. Most of our friends took their maids as they came, for better or worse, without any whys or wherefores. The relationship was merely a temporary alliance for both.

I left most judgments about maids to those who knew better. Their lives became so much a soap opera at times that, as my father used to say, silence was golden.

Signora Iole was our first maid in Rome. She was a quiet, dignified soul. I believed she was close to sanctity. Her husband, Toto, worked at odd jobs, and their son even more rarely. One daughter traveled with a theatrical group and the youngest was still in school. Iole's meager monthly earnings (30,000 lire or about $48) also helped support her husband's parents who drew a small monthly check equivalent to $40 in state social security. We paid Iole the standard wage for a live-out maid in 1957. Joy often tried to slip her extra money, but Iole usually refused. When Iole did accept, she would weep and explain her reason—usually her husband had been let go from another temporary job.

Iole often urged me to get Toto a permanent job. She did this with deference and grace, but was as determined as her character would permit. I heard of several possibilities but he would suddenly find a job for a few days and was unavailable for an interview. Toto didn't seem to want full-time work. The son constantly claimed bad luck. He was right. He managed to scrape up enough lire to play the national soccer pool every week but lost.

Iole was saved from her daily trials by a wonderful sense of humor. I remember finding her alone in the kitchen one day laughing heartily to herself. I asked her what was so funny. Iole said that Joy still had a few steps to climb in learning Italian. Joy had told Iole that she wanted to bake a chocolate cake, only she used the French word *gateau* for cake. In Italian, that sounds like *gatto* which means "cat," so Joy had told Iole she was going to bake a chocolate cat!

There were many similar laughs but one of the longest-running mixups involved the Italian words *pesce* for "fish" and *pesche* for "peaches." Joy often spoke of having peach soup and fish for dessert.

After a year, Iole finally left us. We wept when she departed. Her husband, Toto, had finally gotten a full-time job as a truck driver, and the son found employment in a chemical factory. A few years after Iole had gone, she returned late one afternoon to see Joy. They had always been good friends. She marveled at how much Italian Joy had learned and announced on leaving, "Signora Gioia, I was your greatest Italian teacher!"

From Iole the saint, we switched to Rosaria the sinner. Several friends, including a good padre, recommended we look for a new maid at a *collegio* (it wouldn't be correct to call it a college but a halfway trade school would do nicely) about 15 miles from Rome. The place, run by nuns, was a house for unwed mothers. We met Rosaria, who was nineteen, and everybody there—priests, nuns, and other administrators—said the same thing: Rosaria had been done wrong. She was still a child. She was the finest soul in school, superior in every category, a veritable lady anxious to make herself a lofty place in society.

I should have guessed that this character assessment was gushy, even for Italians. But everyone seemed so sincere. I believed them, and so did Joy.

I remember Rosaria saying goodbye to the nuns, talking of the great reformation in her life. She waved farewell to all her friends as we drove out the gate. Rosaria quickly explained she had already placed her child in a private home. When we had driven a few miles, she suddenly pulled out a pack of cigarettes, lit one, took a deep drag, and exhaled the smoke into the front seat. Rosaria, I concluded, was no rosary girl. She was a hot-blooded Sardinian.

Within two weeks of Rosaria's arrival, our phone started ringing with calls for her from Pietro . . . Antonio . . . Giuseppe . . . Giacomo. The names changed over the months but never the line—"I'm an old friend." I was working out of our apartment in those days with an office in a side room. Since most of the calls were about my news work, I answered the phone. I had to get up and go find Rosaria five or six times a day. She never batted an eye about all the calls, just picked up the phone and murmured, "Ciao" (the intimate, personal form of hello).

That summer we went for a week's vacation to Piediluco, a little lake town north of Rome. Rosaria was free from 9:00 until 11:00 every night, and did her swinging just off the town square where a local band played. She danced in tight, yellow pants. They were her trademark. Everybody in town marveled at them—or was it Rosaria's hips?

In less than a week, the owner of the *pensione* where we stayed gave us the breathless news—our Rosaria now had a *fidanzato*. She had become engaged.

"Listen," I told Joy, "that Sardinian swinger has been engaged since she came to live with us. And so have I, answering her phone calls. When you start losing, I say: disengage!"

Joy was torn between disengagement and our laundry. "I tell you she can wash more clothes faster than a laundromat. Besides, they don't have laundromats in Italy. She also has two eyes and can babysit. Two legs to get the food at the market. And enough brains to bring home the change. I can't let her go. Where can I find another maid now?"

When we returned home, I went back to being Rosaria's secretary. The national summer holiday of *Ferragosto* (a one-time pagan holiday falling on the Ascension of the Blessed Virgin) was coming. A telegram arrived for Rosaria. Her father was dying and she must return home to Sardinia at once. She cried a little. I told her father came first. She was packed and out the door in a flash and a half. That was Wednesday evening.

The following Friday was the holiday and, as Rosaria had carefully noted, it would be nice to be home with her family on the weekend. If all went well with Papa, she would leave Cagliari on a Monday flight and be back that evening.

Tuesday came and no Rosaria. In the afternoon, our phone rang. "Hello, this is Rosaria in Cagliari. It's just been terrible. Papa has been wavering for the whole weekend. Mamma cries and cries. It's fortunate that I came. Well, I can tell you that Papa is somewhat better now. The doctor says the crisis is over. So I'll be back tomorrow evening. Ciao . . ."

Suspicious, I called Joy, "Where is that telegram calling Rosaria home?" She recalled that Rosaria had thrown it in Kevin's wastebasket. I searched and found my answer. I summoned Joy.

"Do you know where this telegram originated? Not Cagliari in faraway Sardinia, but *Roma*—Rome of the Caesars!"

Joy saw the evidence. She sat down. I brought her the newspaper. She opened it to "Positions Wanted" and looked for the heading "Maids."

Two days later Rosaria returned. I showed her the telegram. She didn't bat an eye. "What about my good exit money?" she asked. (Severance pay was required by the state, even if an employee is fired.) I paid her that, her due wages, and she packed. She made a phone call and asked the other party, "Can you pick me up in fifteen minutes? I'm leaving . . . for good. Ciao!"

She needed a rest, Rosaria told us. Every girl needed a few days off. I was tempted to mention her "Sardinia" vacation, but decided against it. When a car horn honked, she picked up her valise and went outside. The young man drove a convertible. She tossed her bag in the back seat, got in, smiled at him, and lit a cigarette. They roared off.

I closed our apartment door, turned to Joy and called with a little wave, "Ciao!" If Joy's jolting look could have killed, I was a dead duck.

For weeks the phone rang for Rosaria. I remember answering one call in particular. "Rosaria isn't here. No, she's not out, she's gone—for good. What do you mean you demand to know where she's gone? You're her fiancé! Listen, amico mio, Rosario left here with a guy who she said was her fiancé. I suspect she counts her fiancés on two hands!"

A stunned silence. He lashed out with one word: "Women!"

Joy decided we should leave for our second week of vacation. She found a small *pensione* near Fregene, on the Mediterranean west of Rome. There we met Gina, a whiz-bang worker.

Gina cleaned at least fifteen rooms a day, swept out the entire place, emptied much of the garbage, helped in the kitchen, assisted at waiting tables, and, on her own time, did sewing and laundry as well as some baby-sitting to earn extra money. Gina was about 35, husky, humorous, and looking for another job. Joy said, "She's for me." We hired her.

Gina was a spectacular cook. She was also heavy duty around the house. With her good humor and easy way with people, she was as popular as Sunday afternoon chicken. I knew she wasn't perfect (she was constantly reading sensational pulp magazines) but she would do until a good Italian saint came along.

We later learned that Gina also was an unwed mother but she never attended a *collegio*, and thought references were a joke. I couldn't quarrel with her on either count.

Even Giulia, the porter, loved Gina, and Giulia could be like a high-court judge. The shoemaker fell for Gina and so did the man who owned the wine shop. Policarpo certainly had an eye for her.

Gina was with us for several months. I never ate so well in my life. So I had some trepidation when Nando, an Italian neighbor, asked if he could speak to me privately about our maid.

Nando was a calm, thoughtful gentleman. He began by cautiously explaining he worked nights downtown at a communications company near Piazza San Silvestro. "This is none of my business. Please excuse me if I am indiscreet. I hope you'll accept this in the right spirit . . ."

I ran out of patience, thanked Nando, but suggested he get to the point. He spoke circumspectly again. "I finish work about 2:30 a.m. A lot goes on out on the piazza at that hour. I'm only telling you this because . . ."

I cut him off. "Look, Nando," I said, "what are you trying to say?"

He blurted, "On her nights off, Gina is in business near my office."

Business? The meaning did not hit me for several seconds. Suddenly, I began to sputter, "You mean . . . our Gina?"

"Yes," hands said. "Walking . . . a street walker."

I gulped. Stumbling for an explanation, one word kept jumping up in my mind: *Fumetti*. Fumetti is the Italian word for cheap magazines that sensationalize romance. *Fumo* means smoke. *Fumetti* literally means little puffs of smoke. That referred to the circles filled with dialogue, as in comic strips, placed above the heads of those speaking.

Since coming to us, Gina was always up in smoke, dragging on those magazines' unrequited love. The pulps featured the jilted girl who got revenge, the orphan who married a modern knight, and other titillating smoke. Gina loved them.

One story affected her for a long time. It was the true story of Fausto Coppi. Coppi, the greatest cyclist in Italy during those years, became ill with a mysterious virus. He died within 48 hours of that medical diagnosis. All Italy mourned because Fausto had carried Italy's colors around the world. And he won enough medals to decorate an entire Olympic team. Coppi was a national hero, known to the smallest schoolboy as "Fausto — our Fausto."

The champion's wife, Bruna, wept and kissed her husband's hands on his death bed and at his public wake. Their daughter remained secluded. Shortly afterward, another woman arrived to view Coppi's body. Giulia Occhini kissed Fausto and hysterically cried their love would never die. The mistress revealed she had a child by Fausto, young Angelo. He remained at a villa his mother had shared with the cycling king.

This was the real fire of the *fumetti*. What smoke!

Gina relentlessly read every line in the pulps, the endless but divided love scenes between Coppi, his wife and mistress, and the fate of his two children. This was the pinnacle of passion: Did the wife or the mistress kiss Fausto in vain in death? Who did he truly love? Did Coppi renounce *La Dama Bianca* (The White Madame or The Other Woman) before he died? Had he called for a priest? The pulps finally revealed Fausto went to confession and received the last rites of the Catholic Church. He had given up Occhini in favor of his wife. Was that really true?

The debate raged for weeks. Gina told us, "We Italians are passionate! Only love matters!"

The pulps then disclosed that Coppi had left his medals and property to his mistress and their son. Gina was flying somewhere on a white cloud. "Was there ever an American romance like that? This could never happen in America!" she trumpeted. "We write operas about such things."

I got caught up in Gina's soulful emotion and wrote a news feature about Coppi's death. This was the last paragraph of the story:

"A white, winter snow is now falling quietly over the trails he blazed in his long career. Italians say snow rarely falls in Rome and never in Palermo, but it is now descending on a stunned schoolboy in the Eternal City and a sad-faced flower girl in the Sicilian capital. Over and beyond the Alps, where he rode to glory, the flakes float down slowly and softly. Time, the clock, now means nothing to Coppi. The fleeting seconds, the long grinds are over. His face, the face of Italy, has closed its taut lines beneath the white blanket falling today at the cemetery in his home town of Castellania. The legs are bones of dead glory. Coppi, man and mortal, has crossed the finish line."

For me that was a job. Gina breathed the stuff.

Gina left us quietly. I don't know if Nando's account of her was true. Perhaps he made a mistake. I would like to think so. We made up some kind of story. Joy and I still look back on her with affection. That was what she wanted—love.

Elena arrived. She was a tiny thing. About five feet, two inches, and perhaps 95 pounds. Elena was 26 years old. She had already been a maid for 15 years. The young woman began working as a maid for the family of an army colonel at the age of 11. Their home was near her hometown of Penna San Giovanni, a small farming community near Macerata. Both are difficult to find on a tourist map, but they aren't distant from Ancona on the Adriatic Sea in northern Italy.

Elena was the greatest house invention since the gas stove. She was a ball of fire. She had the oven lit by 6:00 a.m., hot coffee on the stove, sweet rolls and orange juice ready. The whole house was swept by 6:30 a.m. She would begin the laundry at that hour, singing above the bathtub where she dumped the dirty clothes. We had no washing machine because insufficient water was pumped to our apartment to run it. Elena did everything but fix the plumbing and deliver the mail. As Joy put it, "She's faster than Fausto Coppi."

Elena brought one particularly new quality to the household. She growled. In a household crisis, and we were not immune to them, her thin legs would stiffen and her lower lip would curl. Elena then gritted her teeth and, in a terrifying split second, she would begin to growl. It was not a hiss. Not a sob. Not an angry cough. But a very clear and distinct "Ggrrrrrr!" It meant, "Get out of my way!"

She sometimes growled on and off for two days. Not a single word from her. Just a glare and her elongated displeasure. Everything was speeded up—lunch, laundry, lights out. She banged everything—doors, windows, chairs, pots, pans, even the mail.

Episodes ended as suddenly as they began. In this instance, on defrosting the refrigerator, Elena mentioned to Joy we faced a very grave problem. "Signora, the ice is running out of the ice box." I would have accepted a flood in the kitchen rather than a growl from Elena.

She would say and do the craziest things. Once, when Joy and I were asleep and Elena was watching TV, she burst into our bedroom to announce, "You know Delia Scala, the actress? Well, she's dancing on television with NO clothes on!"

We bounded out of bed to catch the scene. There was Delia. Her costume was indeed brief, just some thin dots and dashes. Every inch of leg and almost everything else was manifestly displayed, but Delia did manage to cover the most important part of her message. I said so. "But Elena, she does have some clothes on."

Elena retorted, "Well, maybe for you, *Signor Gianni* (Mister Johnny), but she leaves nothing to my imagination!"

Elena's imagination was always vivid, but her facts weren't always so clear. I don't think, since the day we met her, she ever got any phone message completely correct. Elena and I had some real growling matches about it as a good number of the calls were urgent messages about my work.

This was typical: We were going out one evening to see friends. I wrote down their phone number and placed it next to our phone. I explained to Elena, if anyone called, she should do one of two things—either give them the number I had written on the pad or take their name and number and call me. She chose the latter, more complicated way. Elena phoned me at our friends' home, and the conversation went something like this:

"Hello, Signor Gianni. This is Elena. Well, he called. No, I don't know who. I didn't ask his name. He couldn't speak Italian very well. But I got his number. It's 870661 . . . What do you mean that's our phone number? That's the number he gave me . . . Why should I look at the number on our phone? I don't care what it says . . . That's his number. And hurry, he says it's important. What do you mean, do I have another number? That's it. Now, Signor Gianni, don't you dare use that language with me. What? Signor Gianni? Hello? Hello . . . ?"

Elena was with us for about six years. The boys grew up under her wing and she guarded them like a lioness. She was part of our Mafia—watchful, sometimes wary, devoted to family first, then friends, country, church, and conscience.

Elena never left us. When the sad day arrived and we packed to return to America, she carefully arranged and placed in our trunks about half the clothes she owned, including part of her dowry. She said, "These will be waiting for me in Washington."

Now, 30 years later, we still have the dress apron she wore on formal occasions. Most of her clothes were eventually given to the Salvation Army. I remember when we parted with them about a decade after our return—the old wool sweater that she wore in winter; a bright Sunday dress; a few small things like bed linen she purchased as part of her dowry, and a few household items. Elena was once engaged to a young man before discovering he was an epileptic. The memory was never erased from her mind.

We also gave to charity various presents she had once bought for the boys out of her small salary. It was particularly emotional to give up the old mandolin recordings she so lovingly packed one by one in the trunks, stuffing them in blankets so they wouldn't break. As the children grew older, however, they no longer listened to Italian music and some Italo-American societies wanted the records.

Elena never arrived in America. We tried to bring her, but immigration rules restricted her. We wrote one another for nearly twenty years, but somehow drifted apart. I once said, like many Italian families, I could take or leave maids. They came and went and that was it. Elena changed my mind. I still remember her growl, but today it seems more like the sound of some beautiful Italian mandolin. *Ciao, Elena, Ciao!*

Chapter 9

Leaping Lena

FATHER THOMAS LYNCH knew a lot about Catholic Church law but little about Leaping Lena and the laws governing her life on the streets of Rome. Lena was a grouchy, old girl who, for many years, was a troublemaker at the stately Old North American College on Via dell' Umilta (called The House on Humility Street). This was the home of American priests doing post-graduate study, as distinguished from the large New American College on the Janiculum Hill, overlooking the Vatican, where American seminarians lived.

Lena was a Vespa motor scooter, a longtime wreck with a motor on her worn hip, and subject to terrible temper tantrums.

I had known Father Tom, of Hartford, Connecticut, for about a year before he introduced me to Lena as a new friend of his. He was in the process of becoming her fourth owner—actually, half-owner. I didn't like the looks of Lena. She resembled a bit player in *The Bicycle Thief*, a street-smart Roman movie made just after World War II. Battered and rattling in front and back, her paint chipped, seat cockeyed, and an unsteadily mounted engine, she looked like a stolen mistake from some underground Roman flea market.

Father Tom, ordained a few years earlier, was then a postgraduate student in canon law. His knowledge of mechanics and slippery salesmen bordered on childlike innocence. I was to find this out after he had smilingly introduced me to the scooter.

Lena had difficulty in making up her mind about many things, particularly the days she would start and those she laid down tired. I was up on Janiculum Hill with the big Irish priest one day, and watched as he ran her down the hill toward St. Peter's Square. Lena sputtered to a stop long before she reached the giant piazza below, choking in a cloud of her own smoke.

Tom and I were pals, and met often. We would eat pizza together and exchange stories about the idiosyncracies of Rome and the Italians. Then, trying to start Lena, he would run, leaving behind a long line of broken cassock buttons. Little boys, who had been cheering him on during a second or third try, would follow his tortuous trail, tripping over themselves to pick up his black buttons. They tried to sell the good ones back to him for 50 lire (eight cents) each. The urchins would then settle down on curbstones, with pained amusement, to await Tom's next move.

The priest would try to start the scooter again and again. Men joined the boys in shouting encouragement from the sidewalks.

"Avanti, Padre . . . Avanti! Dai, Padre, dai!" (Forward, Father, forward! Go, Father, go!)

Sometimes, the bystanders could no longer control themselves. They tore off their coats, charged from the curbstones, and jumped up and down on the starter. The women shouted them on,

"Forte, Federico! Piu forte!" (Strong, Frederick! Stronger!)

The encouragement was often to no avail. Lena had already made up her mind to sleep, not to leap. I think back through the years now and can still hear other curbstone comments:

"Who is he? Must be a foreigner!"

"Maybe he's a German. Serves the Germans right!"

"An American. I knew it had to be an American. Only they are that crazy!"

"I thought the Americans had a lot of money. Why couldn't he buy a new one?"

"What crook sold it to him? It had to be an Italian!"

"But if he's so educated, how could he buy that old kettle?"

"Maybe the fool hasn't any gas in it. Somebody check the tank!"

"Maria, go up and turn the gas off under the spaghetti. We're going to be here a long time. Madonna, what a mess! Nino? Where's my little Nino? He could get hit with that junk."

"Mamma, will he be arrested?"

"Certainly not, he's a priest!"

"Look out, he's running down the hill with it again!"

Sometimes, Father Tom walked Lena home. Other times, he dragged her off to a mechanic. Still, on bright days, she leaped!

I recall one of the good times. The motor kicked over with a shot of flame. Lena was off and running. Father Tom desperately tried to grip the handle with his left hand. His right tried to haul up the skirt of his cassock as he chased the scooter down the street, attempting to mount her. He did! The Vespa swayed as it shot downhill with Tom plopped atop the rickety seat. The crowd of disbelievers went crazy:

"Bravo! Bravo!", they shouted, as the priest roared off with Lena coughing deliriously.

None of the scooter's hijinx dissuaded Father Tom. The good padre told me over an espresso he would become her fourth owner. True, only a half interest was available at the moment but, eventually, he would make Lena completely his own. This was despite the fact he, his fellow priests, and mobs of Romans knew Lena had a bad temper. It was said the scooter developed her devilish irascibility from her first owner, an Italian seminarian. It seems during summer vacations, he became a Roman taxi driver. There, he picked up the habit of fast starts. With Lena, he enjoyed leaping starts. Thus, her name.

The scooter always seemed in the process of being sold to a new owner. In Lena's case, two priests owned the vehicle but one needed quick cash. He asked $25 for his half-interest and Tom paid it.

Under Italian transfer-of-title law, it was necessary to show Father Tom had duly paid for half the vehicle. This was a side of Lena none of the priests cared much about—her papers. The scooter's ownership was perhaps an even more formidable problem than her starts. It is herewith related in grim but sometimes cheerful detail.

Father Tom sought advice about the title transfer at a Roman branch of the Italian Automobile Club. The gentleman who offered to assist suddenly had a knowing smile on his face as soon as the young American priest told him of the motor scooter. He said, "Ah, yes. It must be Lena. I know her. She's been here before."

The man, Tom quickly concluded, was an expert. He instructed the priest to go to the consulate of the American embassy and obtain a statement in triplicate asserting he was 1) a United States citizen, and 2) solvent.

The lady consulate official knew of Lena at once. She smiled saying she had known several of the previous owners. In virtually no time, the woman handed the priest a simple statement to the effect his passport demonstrated United States citizenship and his income was substantiated by his status as a clergyman. An innocuous statement if the United States ever issued one. She also offered some brief, informal advice: insure the vehicle. What she was really telling Tom was, if he had an accident and went to court, he would surely lose the case if the other party were Italian. With insurance, he had some protection.

Father Tom wasted no time and walked across the avenue to an Italian insurance firm. He filled out innumerable forms and was told to return in a day or so.

The priest then returned to the Auto Club with the official consulate statement. The same agent was on duty and expressed his pleasure at Tom's quick results. However, he explained, another statement was needed for the title transfer to be completed. The priest who was selling the one-half interest must draw up a bill of particulars, and sign it before a notary public.

Tom was crestfallen. The priest was on holiday in Florence and wouldn't return for a week. The Italian gentleman sighed. The priest gulped. After a week, the priest returned and signed a bill before a notary. Of course, Tom paid the charge.

The Auto Club agent beamed when he saw the notarized bill. He then looked at Tom a bit sheepishly and said, "Now for the next move."

"Next move?" Tom burst with surprise.

The agent wasn't perturbed. "You must, of course, submit a signed statement to the Ministry of the Interior. Since you are not an Italian citizen, we must show that you have insurance or the ability to pay possible damages should you injure an Italian citizen or anyone else with the Vespa. Don't worry. Just join the Auto Club and we'll take care of all that for you. There will be some fees, of course, but we can talk about that later."

Tom's head spun with swirling details, yet he remained calm. The agent felt sufficiently safe to venture forward. "There is also the Motor Vehicle Department."

That was too much for the priest to bear. He wailed, "What Motor Vehicle Department?"

Other agents and clerks as well as several customers turned inquiring glances toward the two. Tom's agent continued with pleasant but deadly efficiency.

"We'll have to register the number on Lena's motor in case of theft, future sale, etcetera. But don't worry. The head of the Motor Vehicle Department is a friend of mine. We'll take care of it for you. However, he has a death in the family right now and won't be in the office for four days. Why don't you return in a week?"

Tom sought me out for advice. I told him to dump Lena and take the bus. He insisted public transportation was no adventure. I retorted it called for the greatest heroics in Rome. Tom would not be dissuaded. He must have Lena.

A week passed and Father Tom returned to the Auto Club. His agent was smiling broadly. The gentleman said, "Father, I've cleared away our problems in the Motor Vehicle Department. Now, Father, don't be dismayed. I mean don't jump. But you don't happen to be an Italian property owner, do you? A little country house somewhere? A beach shack? Anything?"

Tom's shoulders slumped.

The agent continued without dismay. "I know, Father, that you're getting vehicle insurance. But that might not cover all damages—like death, for instance." The agent paused. He straightened up to let the enormity of the thought sink in. The man briefly leaned over the counter, staring, as if looking into the priest's conscience.

He quickly returned to his ramrod position, adding; "This presents Italy with a problem since . . . ahem . . . you could suddenly leave the country after running someone into . . . ahem . . . paradise with Lena. Believe me, Father, I know you would never do that—run somebody down and skip the country, I mean. But a vehicle owner is only a statistic to the government. A foreign vehicle owner, a bigger gamble. Italian law considers that."

There was an awkward pause. I remember it well because Tom would often recall these encounters, adding drama with each succeeding recollection. He never left out this pause. The priest recounted how the agent pulled away from him slowly, distancing himself, as if Tom had already plowed down some elderly Italian gentleman with a cane. After the full ramifications were allowed to splash like a wave of fear across Tom's head, the agent spoke again.

"In your case, Father, since we know one another so well, perhaps I can pull a few strings. Come back in a few days when we'll have your approved insurance. I've contacted the company where you applied. We'll send photocopies of the contract to several government ministries. Come back, and I will have spoken with my friends."

Father Tom walked away with more questions in his mind. Why "several" government ministries? Why not just one? When would all this end? He phoned me. I told him the Italians would eventually run out of their unrelenting red tape.

When the priest returned, the agent was smiling from ear to ear. He even shouted across the office as Tom opened the door. "They're here, Father! The ownership papers! You're the half-owner of Lena!"

Heads turned, of course. What was a priest doing purchasing a Lena? That went out with the Middle Ages. Oh, well, Rome was in the midst of *La Dolce Vita* (The Sweet Life).

But, Tom wondered, what about the photocopies and all the questions that had floated through his brain? The etceteras that never ended? The agent was shaking his hand, both hands. The priest thought the man was about to embrace him. He stepped back. The agent spoke in quick bursts.

"I got your insurance number from the company and sent it along to all the civil authorities. I fixed everything. Do you understand, Father? Everything!" The man was ecstatic. His fellow clerks smiled. So did the priest. Everyone knew that the hit would inevitably follow. Not immediately. Italians had too much grace for that. They weren't like the French. Wham, your wallet! No. Softly, delicately, discreetly, they picked your pocket with a gracious smile.

Yet, the pause was ominous. Tom didn't like it. The little helper behind the counter twisted his mustache, as if his shoes were too tight or his shorts were falling down inside his pants. His words exited slowly from his tight mouth. "Owning a vehicle in Italy is one thing, Father; legal use of it is another."

Tom gagged. He couldn't speak. Consolingly, the agent spoke for him, "Father, you have an American driver's license. That would be okay if you were a tourist, but you're a resident of Italy.

Italian law says you must have an official translation made of your license."

With the agent's instructions ringing in his ears as he flung open the office door and plunged out onto the sidewalk, Tom roared off to a special branch of the Auto Club near the central railway station for the license translation. He careened back to the agent aboard Leaping Lena, and even she was now panting for an end to the epic.

The agent greeted him cheerily. "Good work, Father. All is done—except for . . ."

"I know," the priest said. "One, final item."

"How did you know, Father?"

"There's always one more thing to do."

With a growing smile, the man pulled a small, square piece of paper from beneath the counter. The agent's face was a floral wreath of happiness when he handed an official-looking sticker to the priest and said. "This is your road-tax sticker, Father."

The man stood in triumph. He looked like a strutting Mussolini on the balcony above Piazza Venezia, only he was shorter and much thinner. But his chin stood up and out, pushing out to sea for the world to see. It was all over, with one, final exception—the bill. The agent didn't speak. Italians try not to talk of such things. With his right hand covering the total, he slipped the long list of charges across the counter. The flat message accommodated itself there without a whimper for a long while. Father Tom hadn't noticed it, that is, until the agent looked down and announced: "Ahem."

It wasn't a cough really. His throat clogged only slightly, just enough to be noticed. Father Tom saw the total and said:

"Forty-five thousand lire ($72). Is that the total?" (It would be about $400 today.)

"Well, ahem . . . ," the agent cleared his throat. Then, all the man's work at the ministries began to add up in the priest's mind. His contacts, friends, phone calls, the art of the bureaucracy. And, of course, the agent would have to pay his contacts off at some future time. It was an endless procession of fat hands.

The official bill of $72 was nearly three times Lena's cost. Tom paid in cash. He then pulled out a 10,000 lire note ($16), more than half of Lena's value, and handed it to the agent as a gesture of good will. The man, who accepted life as it came, showed no dismay. He pocketed the tip and said in a clear voice, "Happy motoring, Father!"

The priest shook hands with his benefactor—or was *he* the benefactor—and walked to the door. The other Italian agents and clerks called out, "Happy motoring!"

In taking stock of his finances that evening, the priest concluded canon law was much less complicated than Italian law.

But, oh, what a figure Lena cut through the streets of Rome. How many times our boys shouted *Avanti, Padre!* as Tom raced down the street trying to start her. How many countless Italians watched the circus performance.

Who owns her today? Father Tom went home to Connecticut and we lost track of him over the years. Perhaps a mechanic owns Lena and keeps her running. Could she stand in stately stiffness in a motor scooter museum? Perhaps a flea market antique? Wherever Lena is, I still see her wired for big coughs and flames shooting out from her motor. She is bounding over the cobblestones in clouds of smoke and crowds of children are shouting, *Avanti!*

Chapter 10

A Winter View

THE LAST LEAVES of fall and first snowflakes of winter cast a long, lonely shadow across the Italian countryside. The hordes of summer tourists in their bright regalia had long gone home. Dark smoke rose from chimneys and clung to the air like an old, frayed coat. Days were shorter and the sun often hid behind low lingering clouds. The storied *Bella Italia* (Beautiful Italy) was in semi-hibernation.

Joy and I decided this was the perfect time to take a two-week vacation. Hotel and other travel costs had plummeted. There were no crowds and no waiting at historic monuments or famous museums. Trains and buses had plenty of seats. Most of all, Italians had time to talk. We loved that.

Traveling north from Rome, our first stop was Assisi, the home of St. Francis. I wandered alone into an old, woodcarver's workshop just off the town's main thoroughfare. St. Francis stood there atop a carver's bench looking me. A bird was perched on his left shoulder. The small creature seemed about to sing and Francis ready to speak.

"He appears almost alive," I said softly to a carver in Italian.

The old man nodded, his eyes squinting behind small, thick glasses. He took another bite of his bread, tomato, and salami sandwich and washed it down with a gulp of red wine. Some of the wine ran down his chin, white with stubble. He must have been seventy. The woodcarver looked at the figure and said, "Signore, St. Francis *is* alive."

The old man lifted his head and his brown eyes searched mine. Two other elderly woodcarvers in the shop eyed me wordlessly. The man, apparently the shop owner, slowly swept his right hand around the large, cold room as if it were some private blessing. "He lives here."

What could I respond to such an evident truth?

A dozen statues, in various sizes, stood on a shelf against one wall. Others were mounted on other shelves and tables. Still more stood immobilized in various stages of completion. The old woodcarver spoke again, "We are the monks of wood, sir, and recreate God in St. Francis with ordinary, carpenter's tools."

The shop and the street outside were silent. I listened but heard nothing. The old man spoke again. "St. Francis travels from our small workshop around the world. His birds sing. His voice whispers again, 'Lord, make me an instrument of your peace . . . where there is hatred, let me sow love . . .'"

Once again, the shop fell silent. Only the wood shavings rustled, blown by a draft of air slipping through a crack in the entrance door. The noonday bells of the *Angelus* began to toll. I nodded, closed the door softly, and walked to the main piazza where Joy was waiting.

The monks were chanting inside the monastery of San Francesco. Their voices wafted across the square and into the hills, dropping into the valleys below. Time was rolled back seven centuries. On the hillsides, where the good minstrel of God had slept in rock niches, rays of sun broke through the gray clouds. Once in a while, our ears would pick up voices echoing in the hills where he once spoke. It was a haunting feeling.

A townsman explained to two Germans in the main square

monks were guiding tourists to some of St. Francis's caves. Their sandals also echoed as they shuffled along rocky ledges. The town was silent again except for a lone, chilled bird singing in the distance.

Assisi is easy to find on a map. For those looking for its spiritual message, it's just this side of paradise.

* * *

We boarded a bus headed toward Firenze (Florence). It was an interesting and pleasant ride. We passed through the hills of Umbria and its medieval towns and villages rose like sentinels in the sun. Rare indeed were the folk there who told time by a watch or clock. Their time was measured by the rise and fall of day and night—and the distance from Sunday to Sunday.

We alighted in Perugia, struck by the old-world splendor of the university town. An Italian guidebook told us from here up through Tuscany was one of the most civilized parts of human history. On that reflection, we found a pensione for the night.

The following morning, we visited the ducal palace. The mayor and city council held forth in offices near the tombs of long-dead aristocrats. We had the impression the living and the dead were shoulder to shoulder, side by side, marching in step for the greater glory of Perugia.

That was the story of all of Italy—from Sicily to Naples and Rome, and from Assisi to Perugia, Florence, Milan, and Venice. The living and the dead were side by side, sometimes even in competition with one another for space and public funds. And, as some Italians wryly observed, "Sometimes you can't tell the living from the dead."

Perugia measured wealth in terms of history, not modern amenities. There was no heat in the ducal palace. Thick walls kept the dampness and chill inside. Civil servants working there tapped their feet on the cold floors all day to circulate their blood and create body warmth. Years later, when we visited Perugia again, they were still tapping. We became pretty good at the old soft-shoe ourselves.

We took the bus to Florence where it was far colder in winter than most artists' conceptions would have one believe. We stayed at the Pensione Bandini, recommended by an English school-teacher who always pinched her lire. It was located at Piazza Santo Spirito, Number Nine, although the pensione wasn't visible. It was a six-flight walk up!

We could barely see as we climbed the winding staircase. I carried two suitcases weighing about 40 pounds each. Our footsteps echoed in the semidarkness. A 40-watt bulb hung on a cord from the top of the structure down to the third floor. It flickered as wisps of wind carried it back and forth.

We finally reached the sixth floor and Joy rang the bell. A women opened the door and smiled. That apparently was the reward for all the mountain goats who climbed to the peak.

Our meeting began a long but formal friendship with the two elderly ladies who ran the place. We never stayed anywhere else on visiting Florence. As Joy put it, "I couldn't bear with it—or without it!"

The beds were about as long and wide as a Florentine family chapel. Mine would have held Henry VIII and all his wives and mistresses. The bedsprings creaked like 16th century originals. The place was so cold, every breath created a puff of steam. As Joy observed with her hat and coat still on, "How does anyone heat a room the length of a basketball court with 20-foot-high ceilings of old-world atmosphere?"

The walls were several feet thick and retained all the chill and dampness. The only way to warm up was to run at least two laps around the room. I changed into heavy winter pants because it was colder in our room than in the piazza below. Joy put on ski pants. Michelangelo could take us or leave us.

Dinner was quiet and uneventful. There were about ten of us at the table. Few spoke except when passing the pasta and other food. We shivered through the meal and raced back to our room. Joy immediately announced, "I'm wearing my ski pants to bed." I laughed and put on heavy winter pajamas.

About 15 minutes later, I pulled heavy work pants over my woolies. At midnight, I still couldn't weather the cold and slipped on a jacket and a pair of sweat socks. Sometime during the night, Joy awoke and put on her wool socks. When dawn peeked through the ice on the windows, we were already awake. I made the first comment, "This is art?"

I hopped up and ran a few laps around the room to warm up. Our door reverberated with a heavy knock. I figured some neighbors were about to complain about my road work. It was a maid, smiling no less, with a pitcher of hot water. With this, I shaved—shirt, tie, sweater, and jacket still on. I told Joy, "I hope they spike the breakfast coffee."

We ate a breakfast of a croissant with butter, jam, and black coffee. On the way to see Michelangelo's *David* at the Galleria del' Academia, we rushed into the first coffee bar we saw and ordered an espresso—spiked with Italian brandy.

Florence is an artful paradox in winter. Where else could we slush along in the wet snow and look up at an archway where a della Robbia smiled like an orange sun? Or ask a policeman directions to the Palazzo Bargello and get a moment's lecture on the della Robbia family as well? He said their special room at the palazzo was a must. The officer had taken his wife there at least a dozen times. All the time he was talking, both of us were standing in a puddle of water.

We rose and fell with the tide of Florence for two days. We both had the impression of viewing more art than exists in the Museum of Modern Art and the rest of Manhattan.

Maybe it was the chill, but I never got into the swing of things in Florence although I admired Raphael, da Vinci, and the famous gold Baptistry Doors. I was always hungry, from morning until night.

For a daily total of 3,600 lire (about $5.75), which covered the two of us, Joy and I received our room plus breakfast and dinner. That was 1959, of course. I was famished by the time minestrone or thick barley soup was served for dinner. This was followed by veal or lamb, fruit in season, coffee, and a piece of cheese. Wine was extra. Most of the guests purchased a full bottle and they wrote their names on it. After each meal, the Italians marked the spot where the contents had descended. The same bottle was placed before a guest at each meal until consumed. Joy and I purchased a bottle every evening and poured all of it down in preparation for sleeping in our refrigerators.

We never tried the bath although we were told that, if we put coins in a hot-water heater, it would eventually give us enough hot water for a bath. I doubted the system and so did Joy. Both of us preferred the wine.

We understand the pensione still welcomes visitors but the price has jumped about 20 times. An elevator has been installed but the rooms in winter remain icy igloos. Still, we will never forget winter at the Pensione Bandini.

We slipped away from Florence's rain-swept streets and took the train to Venice. The face of the Lagoon City was shrouded in fog as we arrived. It was so thick we could barely see the people walking near us.

Venice reminded me of the women in the Casbah of Algiers, their semi-veiled faces slipping in and out of sight in the dark, crowded passageways like wisps of vapor. Venice was a city of winter veils, strange and somewhat mysterious, that many wouldn't recognize alongside its summer sister.

The famous gondolas were stored for the winter or covered to be used only on a few warm sunny days. Passenger ferries slushed cautiously through the lagoons, ringing their bells in the fog. Pigeons still swooped and skipped across St. Mark's Square, but many warmed themselves in the belfry of the cathedral and along the loggias of old palaces. The violins that serenaded Katherine Hepburn and Rossano Brazzi in their summertime romantic film about Venice were stilled and we looked in vain for one pair of bare legs along the beautiful Lido beach. St. Mark's Square was, at times, almost deserted.

We stayed at a modest hotel a few blocks off the square and, as in many encounters with the talkative Italians, some stories went with it. The owners said the place was important because the local prince of the Church, Angelo Giuseppe Cardinal Roncalli, was a character. He would sometimes slip out of his residence in the late afternoon, and often cut through a nearby beer hall to have a glass of wine at their bar and chat with whomever was around.

The owners said the cardinal didn't wear his red, just a simple black cassock. They added Roncalli was always talking with people. He wanted to know the souls under his care. The jolly, round churchman would exchange news and bright words of wisdom while washing down his tonsils. When his glass was finished, he paid his 100 lire (16 cents was the winter price for local Italians) despite the protestations of the bartender. Then Roncalli was off on a jaunty walk around the area to talk with others.

Like a second glass of wine, the hotel owners had another story about the Cardinal. They recalled a day several years earlier when the hot noon sun blazed across Venice. A group of laborers had been working for about five hours, repairing washed-away concrete from the sides of a canal. Unnoticed, Roncalli had been watching them from the lofty window of his study. As the workmen prepared to lay down their tools for lunch, a messenger arrived. He carried three large bottles of local *vino rosso* (red wine). He said, "A present from someone up there," pointing to the prelate's study. His mission accomplished, the messenger rushed off.

The hotel owners had made their point. One couldn't visit Venice without discussing its favorite son (the cardinal was actually born in Sotto Il Monte). Roncalli later became Pope John XXIII. After becoming pope, the prelate said to the delight of all Italians, "Before I am a priest, cardinal or pope, I am a man." John was called the jolly pope.

A few months after he was chosen pontiff in 1958, I met Pope John XXIII for the first time. We became friends through his private secretary, Monsignor Loris Capovilla, who was one of my closest pals in Rome. I had many chance encounters and several long talks with Pope John, once in his summer tower of San Giovanni inside the Vatican. We talked about the war in Algeria, where I had spent much time, the Ecumenical Council, and finally, America. Roncalli understood little about the United States. He was an Italian and European to the core and, remarkably, much of his interest centered on Eastern Europe where communism was still trying to crush religion.

One reason we visited Venice was to see some gondolas navigate the choppy winter waters. It was a great disappointment not to see the fleets in action. However, the time to speak with the gondoliers was perfect. Many of them worked only part-time at odd jobs while others were loafing until summer. All told the same story.

The once-gloried gondola may one day be gone from the Grand Canal. Once 10,000 strong, the gondolas were a fleet of less than 600 in the winter of 1959. The gondola also symbolized Venice itself because the Lagoon City was also washing away. It struggled to preserve itself from the continuing erosion of canal water, and had already lost artistic treasures to the sea. Centimeter by centimeter, the city was slipping into a watery grave.

The gondola was spawned on the lagoons of Venice nine centuries before in the year 1094. Two gondoliers related the story to us as one of them tossed stale bread to a flock of pigeons. Both were out of work due to winter weather.

Gondolas rode the crest of their popularity in the 16th and 17th centuries, soaring to a massive fleet of 10,000. Kings, princes, and diplomats then vied to see who could design and build the most luxurious model. Some gondolas were even set with jewels.

Italian folklore said the gondola came from a slice of the incandescent moon. It plummeted into the Venice sea to hide the romantic happiness of a poor, young, local couple from the eyes of the world. After the moon slice plunged into the sea, it later rose in the same shape—only black with silver tips at each end—to denote the joy of the young couple.

Although black was the color of mourning, the gondoliers said it was really a sign that eternity cannot be reached on this earth. The couple's greatest happiness was still ahead of them. So too for the happy gondolier.

Six small shipyards still built gondolas at that time in Venice. Construction was complicated. A typical gondola needed more than 200 different pieces of seven different types of wood. It was 35 feet long and weighed about a half-ton. The average cost in those days was about one million lire ($1,600).

Passenger ships and motor boats had slowly been washing the gondola out of the Grand Canal. Many hurrying tourists by-passed the gondola for faster-moving and less-costly large boats. The gondolier made most of his money from romantic couples who wanted to spin and spoon at night, and also wise visitors who wished to see the small, backwater canals of the city. Larger vessels couldn't navigate the city's superb little waterways. There, the gondolier was prince.

Gondoliers feared small, light, rubber rafts and other less-costly crafts might replace them. Perhaps. But Joy and I had no doubt the gondoliers would survive. What would replace that straw hat perched on his head? The birdlike whistle from his throat? The stroke of his oar that splashed gold in sunny waters? And his few words of English that spoke of romance and where to get candlelight pasta? To an Italian, the two were of equal importance.

Indeed, the gondoliers do survive today but their number is even smaller, their prices have skyrocketed, and few youngsters dream of joining their fleet.

Some Italians had long claimed that Venice might disappear before the gondolas did. The Lagoon City has sunk five feet during its 15-century history. It was then sinking into the sea at the rate of eight-and-one-half inches a century. But the rising sea of the past two decades has caused it to sink even more. In 1994, the waters of the Grand Canal splashed only a few feet below present street levels. Often, especially during winter, the canals now submerge the streets. Seawater even runs in to apartment windows. It rots not only the lower rooms of homes but also their foundations. The city had been spending about half a million dollars a year to shore up buildings, such as St. Mark's and other famous structures. Now, they're spending multimillion of dollars.

In two or three centuries, it may be necessary to jack up the huge thousand-year-old Basilica of St. Mark and other famous monuments. Parts of the city may not, however, be saved from invading waters. Workers keep rebuilding foundation after foundation and water wall after water wall. The entire world is now concerned about the fate of the lagoon city.

We loved Venice. It was, from a stylistic point of view, the most incredible city on earth. The dark, back canals coupled with its glorious open waterways offered both a magnificent panorama and mystique. To see Venice is truly to view one of the world's greatest combinations of God's and man's genius.

We left Venice by train in late evening. The sky was remarkably clear. A thin slice of moon shone. I watched it for several minutes before our train pulled out. The city had cast its spell. I no longer saw the moon up there—a gondola rode the crest of the heavens. It stroked across the sky and seemed to splash from star to star as if they were ports. The train jerked to a start and the reverie ended.

After stopping in Rome, we took another train to Naples. In the early morning light, we took a taxi from the Mergellina railroad station toward the center of the city. We struck up a friendship with Vincenzo, our driver, saying we wanted to see the *vera Napoli* (real Naples). He turned and asked, "Really?" "Yes, really," we emphasized. "Good," Vincenzo declared. "I'll show you something that you can see only in Naples."

We drove up Via Crispi and came to a two-story villa of white marble, surrounded by trees. A crowd of excited women stood before the villa. Vincenzo stopped and smiled. A man stood on the second-floor balcony. He seemed to be in his 70s. His face was bronzed with the sun and he looked very much like a *pezzo grosso* (big shot).

The man was dressed in a white bedsheet. He stood at the center of the balcony, with the bedroom shutters thrown open behind him. Smiling, he looked down on the women and waited for their loud chorus to subside. They were calling up to him in thick dialect.

Most were housewives between 30 and 60 years old. Many had worn dresses and unkempt hair. Most stood in slippers or wooden clogs.

The man began gesticulating grandiosely with his right hand. It was a combination military salute and priestly blessing. We thought he was crazy.

"Who is he?" Joy asked.

Vincenzo, with a smirk on his face, replied, "Our mayor, Signora. Achille Lauro. He's the modern Julius Caesar!"

Vincenzo spilled out the story. Nearly every day after sunrise, Mayor Lauro threw open the shutters of his bedroom. That is, after grabbing his bedsheet. He slept in the nude. He sometimes worked, ate, and swam in the nude.

After bursting onto the balcony, the mayor surveyed his city slowly awakening below him. Then, he bellowed far and wide in Neapolitan dialect, *Bongiorno a Napule!* (Good morning, Naples!)

The women below shouted back in dialect, *Bongiorno a tte, ca si 'o cohiu belle!* (Good morning to you because you are the most beautiful!)

Lauro, a fat-headed baldie, invariably was flattered. The mayor then tossed a shower of bills down on the waiting women who stampeded to catch them. Alms for the poor, Lauro once described the scene. Breakfast and sometimes lunch money for a hungry family. But Lauro's real message was: Vote for my Monarchist party!

Many Neapolitans claimed their Achille was a heel. The Lauro administration had dug the city deeper and deeper into debt. As some put it, "The treasury is lower than the cemetery."

Lauro filled central squares and other major parts of the city with beautiful flower gardens. He wanted to give Naples an elegant air. These grand gestures were seen as a cover-up for the various shennanigans Lauro and his cronies were pulling with public funds. Many Neapolitans said, "He's not giving us elegance. He's giving us empty air!"

Lauro also offered Neapolitans one shoe. A month before elections, the mayor would have a small army of flunkies pass out thousands of shoes to the poor—all for the left foot. Vincenzo told us Mamma and Papa would receive the right shoe only if they voted for Lauro and the Monarchists. The cabbie reflected, "Neapolitans are mutually tolerant."

We checked into a pensione off the Via Caracciolo. After breakfast, we wandered down to Via Forcella. Thousands of GIs who served in Naples during World War II remember the gentle grafters of yesteryear with affection. Via Forcella was known in those days as the "Casbah" of Naples. Its open wartime stalls and tents had been folded. However, smugglers' shutters still opened and closed to sell cigarettes and other American contraband as well as Japanese electronic equipment which was just making its debut on Naples's vast black market.

An Italian film company was making a movie there when we walked through. It featured Sophia Loren and Marcello Mastroianni and was called *Love Italian Style*. Sophia was born in a nearby ghetto.

GI Joe's paradise of pillage had changed to mostly common shops when we walked through. There was a big sale on black-market Japanese transistor radios. The only under-the-counter foreign cigarettes were Swiss. Still, they were in demand because the government taxed Italian cigarettes heavily and all had a flat taste. We saw some cheap cologne from France and makeup smuggled in from North Africa. The Muslims were very good at making lipsticks, mascara, and other feminine facial needs. In fact, the French learned much of what they know about cosmetics from the Arabs.

We watched a young Neapolitan dandy escorting a young German tourist along the street. He and the woman were speaking in English. A British naval officer, attached to the NATO base, was browsing with his wife—both very proper. A couple of Americans, like us, were looking for bargains, but there was no fire sale. No kids tugging at a pants or skirt saying, "I gotta great GI jacket for seven bucks, mister . . . Hey, lady, how about one for you?" Yes, I told myself nostalgically, GI Joe is over the sea and far away in the land of the big PX.

We wandered around the *basso* or poorer sections for several hours. Laundry hung from building to building over the narrow passageways. It often hid the sun. The voices of shouting women ricocheted off the walls and ceilings of their apartments. Every once in a while, a housewife would dump a bucket of dirty water on the street. Children ran from corner to corner in games of hide-and-seek.

I stopped to get a shoe shine from a *scugnizzo* (street urchin). The kid was seven years old and proud. He said his father owned a shoe-shine parlor. He pointed to the place across a passageway. It had two king-like thrones where customers sat. Both were covered in frayed, red velvet. The arms glittered with gold studs and were crafted of precious wood. After the shine, the youngster introduced us to his father, who told us proudly when the old kings of Naples sought to have the best shoe shiner of the city as part of their court, his forefathers lodged in the royal palace. We were impressed with this, but the man suddenly reversed himself. "Now business is bad. We're thinking of forming a union to get higher prices. Perhaps a Communist union!"

With that, the son began snapping at my shoes again with a rag. He said, "I just put wings on your shoes, sir." I gave him 200 lire (32 cents). It was double what he expected, and his face lit up. With two fingers of his right hand, he touched his forehead, lips, and heart. It was an Arabic gesture of greeting, friendship, and deference—and a reminder of God's blessings.

At that moment, I thought of what an elderly Neapolitan gentleman living in Rome had once said to me, "We Neapolitans are an old and crossbred civilization—Italians, Spanish, French, Greeks, Arabs, Turks, and others who touched our shores before and after the birth of Christ. Later came Jews and even Americans. We have the blood and culture of many other peoples. The blood of ages. But we have remained Neapolitan. We agreed with all of them by day and shit on them at night. We swallowed them all."

The same gentleman also said, "We have one and a half million people in Naples and three million souls. One soul is to cry and the other to laugh."

That evening, Franco Bucarelli, who was to become one of my best friends, and his girlfriend, Lucia, took us to church for a pizza. The pizzeria was located in the basement of the Church and Monastery of Santa Chiara (St. Clare) directly below the bell tower. Luigi Lombardi and his four sons ran the place. It had been passed from one Lombardi son to the next generation for some 400 years. The monastery itself was older than the pizzeria.

Bucarelli, a young lawyer and reporter, knew the father well and called him over to talk with us. Lombardi paid before dying, Pope Pius XII had named Clare the patron saint of television. He was slightly miffed at that. He thought she should have been blessed the patron saint of pizza. Nevertheless, he concluded, "She still knows that we're making her pizzas here."

Signor Lombardi told us pizza was born in Naples seven centuries earlier in an open brick oven, fed with wood and charcoal flames. He baked pizza the same way that evening, adding, "The secret of our pizza is in the water. It brings the bread to light and full quality."

The unpretentious entrance to Lombardi's place was just off the main church steps outside. Inside, the whitewashed walls had virtually no decorations; the room accommodated about thirty customers. The tablecloths were butcher paper. "Just the way my father ran the place," Lombardi explained.

A dozen customers were sprinkled around the room. Most were casually dressed. Voices rose and fell in sharp, loud bursts. A guitar player wandered in from the street and began to play and sing, "I think of Naples as it once was. . . ." Slowly, the chatter began to subside. The patrons listened almost in reverence to "Munastero 'e Santa Chiara" (The Monastery of St. Clare).

The postwar lament about an Italian prisoner of war who came home became a Naples classic. The POW recalled the days and nights he had dreamed of returning to Naples, but his girlfriend has found another. The entire city had become a sea of corruption. *Ma perche, perche?* (But why, why?) he asks. Once there were good girls here; now they walk the streets. Was the Monastery of St. Clare, where a few cloistered nuns remained, the only island of honor in the dirty waters around him? He remembered his old Naples with its head high. But now? Why, why? the dirge concluded.

Maestro Barberis, a soldier who returned from the war, wrote the music. Galdieri, the poet, crafted the words. The song, which became a virtual hymn in Naples, brought many men and women to their knees at the Monastery of St. Clare. Barberis, saddened by the postwar corruption that he saw about him, left Naples for Mexico City and never returned. The story goes he died there of a broken heart.

Neapolitans said the Monastery of St. Clare was the only song that ever made Pope Pius XII cry.

The guitarist, an elderly gentleman, played and sang a few more songs, passed a saucer around for tips, then left with a wave.

I noticed that the foundations of the church were visible along the walls. On one wall, some eight feet up a side, a candle stood on a small square of wood which protruded like a shelf. It flickered in front of a beautiful but faded painting, dimly revealing the face of St. Clare.

I suddenly realized the guitarist had not waved to Lombardi or the customers. He was saluting St. Clare. He waved because he had no hat. Those who did tipped their hats before leaving Lombardi's.

We were finishing our pizzas when one of Lombardi's sons told us a story. About 150 years earlier, some of the priests at the church began wondering about the propriety of having a pizza parlor in the house of their saint. Several of them suggested the Lombardis move. Many of the customers, members of the parish, objected.

A debate began. Finally, the wise old pastor said the rule of reason should prevail. The side with the most intelligent approach to the problem would decide the outcome. One of the parishioners won with this sage advice, "I will go to church to get food for my soul, and to Lombardi's to eat food for my body." The pizzeria remained.

We left Lombardi's about midnight. The bill for our large cheese pizza and four small glasses of red wine came to 600 lire (96 cents).

The Lombardi family has now moved to a new place nearby. It still serves delicious pizza but the prices have soared like dough under heat.

That was the first of our many journeys to Naples. I never left the city without tipping my hat—to St. Clare, the Lombardis, the street urchins, the magnificent bay, beguiling mandolin and guitar music, and a monumental heritage.

Chapter 11

Cables, Callas, Bergman, and the Cinema

ONE OF THE most nerve-wracking experiences of my news reporting in those days was working with Rome's radio signal and cable offices. We usually used RadioStampa which sent stories back to the United States via radio signal. However, I sometimes used Italcable, a cable company. *Commendatore* Mario De Medici, who ran RadioStampa, was the only person in the Rome office who spoke English. This was despite the fact his staff received and sent tens of thousands of words to the United States and other English-speaking countries each day— millions of words each month. Yet they didn't understand a word of what they were sending.

I typed most of my stories, later sent to New York, but often dictated them from home or some other part of Italy. I was then at the mercy of what I called the A-B-C system—Ancona, Bologna, Catania—of using the names of different Italian cities to spell out messages. As an example, let's begin this mournful tale by using the name of the opera diva, Maria Callas, in a story. This is the way I dictated it to the RadioStampa office:

MILANO . . . ANCONA . . . ROMA . . . IMMOLA . . . AN-

CONA for Maria. (PAUSE) CATANIA . . . ANCONA . . . LIVORNO . . . LIVORNO . . . ANCONA . . . SAVONA . . . for Callas.

The letters *H*, *J*, and *Y* don't exist in Italian, so no city in Italy begins with those letters. By mutual agreement with the Radio-Stampa staff, I used HOTEL, JUNTA, and YORK for *H*, *J*, or *Y*.

It took almost as much time in receiving or sending a message to New York as it would take to drive downtown and return home with the original message. However, parking problems dissuaded me from the trip.

Over the years, I had many mix-ups and battles with Radio-Stampa. Crucial words would sometimes be left out in dictation and there were other snafus between Rome and New York. One of the biggest headaches of all came one night about 1:00 a.m. That was 7:00 a.m. in New York (daylight saving time). Radio-Stampa phoned me at home. The message involved Maria Callas. It used phrases like "the Rome Opera House ablaze" and "a fiery riot." Still half-asleep, I couldn't understand the full meaning of the message. So I told the RadioStampa man I would drive down to his office to see the precise words myself.

The message was what was known in the trade as a "rocket," meaning another news organization had beaten you on a big story. It explained soprano Callas had walked off the Rome Opera House stage in the midst of her performance the previous evening, the opening night of the season. Further, Italian President Giovanni Gronchi was present and her walkout was considered an insult to him and Italy. Callas was Greek.

Callas had trooped off in the second act and locked herself in her dressing room, claiming to be ill. The packed house shouted insults at her from the orchestra seats to the gallery. It was "ablaze" with anger.

We had missed a very good story. I phoned the home of our night deskman but he was apparently asleep and didn't answer. I raced by car to a big Rome morning newspaper *Il Messaggero* where an edition was being dumped on delivery trucks. I grabbed a copy, giving a delivery man 500 lire (80 cents), and roared back to RadioStampa.

The *Il Messaggero* opera critic had written a masterful front-page news story with many details. He included some editorial comment, often slipped into Italian news copy, including the dramatic phrase that the temperamental soprano had hanged herself with her latest antics. The writer implied he and other opera lovers would lead a crusade against her future appearances in Rome. It was by then 9:00 a.m. in New York so I had to get off a story fast to the *New York Journal-American*. The lead was:

"World-famous soprano Maria Callas was hanged in effigy today by Italy's opera lovers after she walked out in the midst of the opening night of the Rome season . . ."

The story moved to New York quickly because I didn't have to dictate it letter by letter. I checked every word sent. In working with RadioStampa, I took nothing for granted.

I went back to our office and fell asleep at my desk. When day broke, I awoke and walked out to a coffee bar and read the rest of the morning newspapers. They were cutting Callas into Greek salad.

My phone was ringing when I returned to the office. Radio-Stampa was again ready to take me through the cities of Italy. Letter by letter, the message from our New York office said: CONGRATULATIONS STOP YOUR CALLAS HANGING STORY SPLASHED HERE STOP SEND MORNING STORY THANKS FARIS (Barry Faris was the editor in chief of INS).

His message was the old wire service refrain: What have you done for me lately—or for tomorrow?

The day staff began arriving for work. I had the feeling it was going to be a hectic day. Alberto rushed in with a new message from New York.

OPPOSITION NOW AHEAD WITH NEW ANGLE SAYING ANGRY CROWD GATHERED OUTSIDE CALLAS HOTEL STOP HOW PLEASE QUERY FARIS

"How please?" is the beautifully swift dagger of the wire-service business. It's eloquent in its cable-style brevity (saving the company money) and has the finesse of saying "please" while burying the knife deep into your back. There is also plenty of rope dangling from the innocent-appearing question mark: Why did you miss the story and what are you doing to catch up?

I phoned the hotel and battled to get the manager on the phone. He was plainly irritated but didn't want to be rude to an international news organization. This was no time for a waltz so I fired quick, blunt questions about Callas and the crowd outside. He answered in spurts, "Yes, Madame Callas (important personages are often referred to in Italy with the French "Madame") is indeed one of our guests. No, she doesn't wish to be disturbed. She is resting . . . Yes, there's an unruly lot outside the hotel. They're disturbing her and our other guests . . . I have called the police. They will get rid of these threatening people . . . One of these hecklers is particularly annoying. He's demanding that Madame Callas apologize to President Gronchi and the Italian people . . . Yes, some in the crowd agree with him . . . Madame Callas will not respond to these insults. She is a lady! You want my name? Sir, I am the management. That is who. The management!"

He hung up but I was already batting out a new story that would hopefully topple the opposition from power. The lead went like this:

"An unruly mob, shouting insults at opera star Maria Callas, threatened to storm a fashionable Rome hotel today unless the secluded soprano apologized to Italian President Giovanni Gronchi for walking off the stage at the opening performance of the new opera season.

"Police surrounded the hotel (they would be there by the time this was in print) after its management appealed for protection. Temperamental Maria refused to leave her suite, saying she didn't feel well and needed a rest. The angry crowd outside answered this with jeers, etcetera . . ."

I put that in appropriate cable language and fired it off to New York. The missile should hold down the opposition for a while, but I knew this was war and I needed reinforcements. I dispatched GianCarlo Govoni, our day deskman, and a cameraman to the hotel front. I told them to phone me immediately if anything unusual happened, otherwise every half hour no matter what. No sooner had the pair left than Alberto rumbled into my office with another urgent war communique from New York:

GREAT MOB STORY WHICH GETTING SMASH PLAY STOP IS THERE WAY WE CAN PUT LYNCHING ANGLE BACK INTO LEAD QUERY FARIS

"Murder!" I shouted to myself. "Do they want me to say the crowd wants to lynch her? What do they want, blood?"

I was sure the Associated Press and United Press were preparing another salvo against us. But what could I write? I wasn't going to send New York a lot of hot air. That was Callas's job. I sat tight hoping to hear from Govoni. Less than an hour later, Alberto roared through my door like a locomotive. New York had fired us another blast:

OPPOSITION REPORTS MOB STONING CALLAS HOTEL STOP HOW PLEASE QUERY FARIS

"Where the hell is Govoni?" I shouted to no one in particular. There was nowhere I could call him so I dispatched Alberto to the scene on his motor scooter. Govoni called me ten minutes later.

"Santa Maria del cielo!" (Holy Mary of Heaven) I cried. Where have you been? New York says the crowd is throwing rocks at the hotel."

"That disgraceful fellow!" Govoni shouted back. He was furious at another reporter who apparently had filed the story. It took a while to get Govoni to speak coherently. He finally explained:

"Workmen were cleaning the brick on the outside of the hotel. Two old bricks came loose and fell to the ground. On the way down, one of them shattered a hotel window. The crowd cheered. That's all that happened. But nobody threw any stones. I swear."

Okay, I told Govoni, but keep your eyes open. New York is screaming. Govoni promised to call me at the slightest ripple.

I then decided to gamble and phoned the hotel manager again: "Now listen, I am a personal friend of Madame Callas's husband, *Commendatore* GianBattista Meneghini (I paused, letting the full significance of my message sink in). This is most important or, I assure you, I wouldn't disturb The Management. I must speak with *Commendatore* Meneghini . . .

"You say that I cannot. Why? Ah, because he has gone to Madame Callas's bedroom to be with her a while. I see. Well, thank you very much, sir. I'll call later. No, there is no message. My name? It's not important. I'll phone again later. Thank you."

In seconds I had paper in my typewriter was clattering out a new lead to our story. "Milan millionaire-industrialist Gianbattista Meneghini rushed to the bedside of his ailing wife, soprano Maria Callas, after a window was smashed by a brick at their fashionable hotel today, while an angry mob of opera fans threatened the star with further violence unless she apologized to Italian President Giovanni Gronchi for walking out on him and the opera season opening last night. . . ."

I again put the lead into cableese and fired it off to New York. I was beginning to mumble to myself but shouted to Alberto to rush the copy over to RadioStampa. I prayed it wouldn't take Alberto longer to get to the transmission office than it would for the entire story to reach New York. So I warned him, "No stops on the way or you are fried fish!" Alberto saluted and took off faster than his usual gait, normally a crawl. He and the motor scooter disappeared down Via del Corso in a cloud of blue smoke. I knew he had gotten the message and I put my head on my desk. It was 11:00 p.m. I didn't awaken until about 7:00 a.m. when Alberto bounded in the office with a message from New York, OPPOSITION SAYS CALLAS MAY HAVE FLED HOTEL FEARING MOB VIOLENCE STOP HOW PLEASE QUERY FARIS

I was off and running again, "Hello, is this the hotel manager? Listen, this is a friend of Madame Callas . . ."

I can't remember the rest of the Callas story and, perhaps, it's just as well. I do recall she left town with her nose in the air and her husband toting her bags. Callas later dumped Meneghini and sailed out on the marital seas with Greek shipping tycoon Aristotle Onassis.

New York kept ringing its fire bells and had me chasing new sirens, many in the movie world. They included Anna Magnani, Sophia Loren, Gina Lollobrigida, Ingrid Bergman, Elizabeth Taylor, Anita Ekberg, and Linda Christian.

I look back on all of them now and wonder why our New York office became so excited about their antics. Personally, the only ones I ever met—and there were scores—with any genuine intellect were Bergman, Magnani, and Loren.

I went to Magnani's apartment one time and, at the close of a long photo session, she asked me, "Why do you want all these photos?"

I replied, "Your face."

"What do you mean?" she asked.

"I mean you have the face of Italy—earthiness, the wisdom of years, yet youthful passion."

She looked at me for several seconds and finally asked, "How long have you been in Italy?"

I replied, "A few years."

She concluded, "You sound like an Italian."

Loren had a rough background as a youngster, coming from a slum outside Naples. But she could taste the sweet smell of success at an early age and became very ambitious. She devoted herself to learning acting and speaking English. Loren was a very shrewd woman and her goals were laudable.

I interviewed her only once, in Naples. She was totally prepared and knew exactly what she wanted to say. Loran ignored many of my questions and answered with a prepared agenda. She was always thinking, always working, forever on guard.

Elizabeth Taylor was a heavy boozer during her Roman escapades with actor Richard Burton. Many reporters saw her drunk at restaurants and nightclubs while engaged in the filming of *Cleopatra*. I never had any interest in speaking with Taylor for any length because she was such a self-serving, selfish individual. Her only class was a cosmetic veneer.

One of the most dramatic stories I ever covered in Rome was the day that actress Ingrid Bergman left Roberto Rossellini and her family for Lars Schmidt, a Swedish businessman living in Paris. She had an affair and children with the Italian movie director, and was soon castigated by critics as an immoral woman. But I knew Bergman and liked her immensely because she was a gentle, gracious individual.

New York drove me crazy to get an interview with the actress before she left Rome to marry Schmidt in Paris. I phoned her and she told me she was leaving Rome the following day, a Sunday, and to meet her at the airport. I did.

We sat in the waiting room for a long time. Bergman wore dark glasses and a large scarf that covered her head and much of her face. Neither of us said anything significant. We talked of the sunny weather for the flight and some of her old movies. I told her I would always remember her performance in *Casablanca*. Finally, her boarding call was announced and we had only a few moments. I turned to the actress and said it all. "Ingrid, why did you do it? Leave Rossellini for Schmidt? That's what my editors want to know. Louella Parsons (a longtime Hollywood columnist) sent me a long cable asking the same question. They say everything comes down to that."

She looked at me and said, "Write that I said I am a woman. That's all. A human being. A woman."

I returned to the office, wrote a story in blurred depression about Bergman's years in Italy and her final quote. I closed the office door absentmindedly on the way out but forgot where I had parked my car. I was certain of one thing—I would remember Ingrid Bergman as a woman, not an actress.

I wrote thousands of stories while in Rome, from the tribulations of the Italian people to fistfights in parliament and the deaths of popes. In the back of my mind, however, I always asked myself whether the men at RadioStampa and Italcable had any real comprehension of the drama they sent day after day to New York.

Chapter 12

Via Veneto

VIA VENETO WAS called the giddiest, gawdiest, most glamorous mile in the world—and a lot of other things.

The so-called glamour girls of the film world giggled and wiggled here. Footsore tourists sprouted bunions, and footloose gangsters from stateside syndicates sported new Suzies. Grey-haired Italian gigolos waited for their American goldstrike. Business giants mixed themselves a whisky and soda while reading the *Wall Street Journal*. An ailing monk meandered home to die at his monastery nearby. Kings without thrones sipped orange juice at sidewalk cafes. And just plain guys and dolls, goggled-eyed and dreamy at the same time, came and went on a worldly pilgrimage to Rome's Broadway.

It was *La Dolce Vita* (The Sweet Life) where Magnani screeched the brakes on her fire-engine-red convertible and left the tank triple-parked in the street. Where, for years, Ava Gardner put out flame after flame with a slap across their faces. Egypt's ex-king Farouk squired a fat, bumptious tigress—a Neapolitan redhead who called herself an opera singer and sipped lemonade while watching the peasants of the world walk by—roundtrip, economy class from Hamburg, Helsinki, and Houston.

New Orleans jazz blared from a high-class basement saloon called "Bricktop's," where the legendary hoofer and singer hung her name and a lot of memories. For 17 years, she had been a hoofer and nightclub warbler in Paris and then for a decade in Rome.

Mary Pickford and Charley Chaplin had come and gone from the Via Veneto. So had Joe DiMaggio and actress Maureen O'Hara. Retired diplomats came to remember grander old days, and nuns came to die tomorrow or next week. The United States embassy stood in the midst of all this, swimming like an island in the middle of a colossal champagne glass.

I had gotten to know Mario Lanza, the singer and actor, around "the beach." That's what some of us called Via Veneto because of its thin-clad women and sidewalk umbrellas. I liked Mario. Sure, he was impetuous, at times even a kid. But he was open with nothing crafty or cunning about him. Not like so many others along the beach.

One day on Via Veneto Mario turned to me, and pointing to himself said, "Hollywood counted me out six years ago. I took the long count—three and a half years of no work. But I got up. Today, I'm belting out songs to the audiences. And now, the so-and-so's are calling me 'Champ.' Who am I? I'm still me—Mario Lanza."

He clenched his fist and continued. "The producers now say hello to me. They touch me, handle me—all because I put more money in their pockets. To them, my voice is just the ring of a cash register."

Lanza could be eloquent when he was angry. "Sure, I'd fought and ranted at 'em in the past, but with reason. Not because I wanted dollars. I wanted to be Mario Lanza, not the stooge of big-shoot movie executives. I wanted respect."

Mario owed Uncle Sam a bundle in back taxes, and had picked enough fights with movie moguls for a half dozen war flicks. He had come to Rome with his wife, Betty, and their four children. Lanza knocked off drinking and eating binges and made several good films. He also had a new long-term contract with a record company. We were having espresso together on the Via Veneto one evening and he said to me, "I feel like I'm on the right road now. Like I can go on forever."

A few weeks later, I came home one evening and my wife told me Mario had died in his Roman villa of a heart attack. Betty had called her. I sat down on a living room chair and recalled something he had said when we last talked on the beach: "I want people to understand me." I hoped some did.

* * *

Alberto Pinto retired from Via Veneto before we left Italy. He had been the master concierge at the fashionable Excelsior Hotel as long as anyone could remember. I always thought Pinto was as smart as Guglielmo Marconi or Enrico Fermi. He just took a different road. After his passing, an Italian friend told me "After the Pope, he may have been to American tourists the second most important man in Rome."

This deliberate, distinguished-looking gentleman could hold five conversations in different languages at the same time. I once saw him take 600,000 lire (nearly $1,000) from his "kitty" and loan them to a guest without asking for a receipt while ordering a bellboy to pick up the luggage of new arrivals who had checked in a moment earlier.

Pinto could get the private phone number of any person in Rome. He also knew when not to give it out. He could obtain two tickets to the opera at the Baths of Caracalla when it was absolutely sold out and not even an Italian senator could get a ducat. He could get you a fair price on any item for sale in Rome if you told him you were being taken. It would take only a moment's phone call. He was a master at getting tickets to semiprivate papal audiences an hour before they began. Pinto was seldom without wit but rarely had time for it. He was a model of dignified dynamism.

Pinto was a friend and counselor to the late Aga Khan, William Randolph Hearst, Sr. and many other international figures. He knew most sheiks of the Arab world, the jet-setters from New York to New Delhi, princes without castles, and flashy actresses who hadn't made a film in ten years. His phone never stopped ringing.

Nothing ever escaped his eye, but Pinto was the epitome of discretion. He could spot a guest who was a deadbeat in seconds and give the thumb to hookers posing as the wives of wealthy playboys. Yet Pinto rarely spoke beyond the necessary. He would sometimes allow the phonies to play their little games until he decided on a day of reckoning. He would suddenly present them with a bill and that was that. You paid immediately or you never stayed at the Excelsior again.

I used to go to Pinto for advice. He had one rule: Don't ask personal questions. When Pinto retired, Cosimo De Giorgio took his place. On moving behind Pinto's desk, De Giorgio said it all in four words, "I am his disciple."

* * *

Novella Parigini was a little time bomb about five feet tall with short hair, leprechaun shoes, and a rude smirk. Her favorite color was purple, like some of her prose and many of her paintings.

Novella was a ranking—some said rank—painter of European nudes. Also of the Cat Set—nude women in various poses, usually 21-year-old sex kittens—Novella was a publicity cat. To attract the media, she would explain in multicolored phrases, she would be pleased to hang up her purple panties forever and parade in Piazza del Popolo in nothing more than her smirk. She threatened this several times, creating headlines, but was always visited by the police and warned of the consequences. The Cat always demurred with the proper purr.

Novella's studio apartment on the Via Margutta was only a few blocks from our office. I often chatted with her on the street or the nearby *Re degli Amici* restaurant. However, I saw her mostly on the Via Vento in the company of some curvacious Cat who she usually treated like honey. Her throaty voice could often be heard several tables away, usually bemoaning the "cover-up" in the art world and culture in general. She often talked of "off-beat" beauty, painting that should be "sleek," especially around the eyes and mouth.

Novella was among the first of the Rome's "crazies" after the war, the far-out crowd who later proclaimed the 1960s as the decade of defiance. She was much before her time, but taught a lot of the Hip Generation how to market cultural and political tomfoolery and other put-ons to the media. I never thought she could paint worth a damn and just about said so in several chats with her. Novella didn't care. Her attitude was: Photograph my paintings, send them around the world, and spell my name right.

The Via Veneto swarmed with Novella types who were pounced on by the *paparazzi*. These freelance photographers roamed the Big Street and the nightclub circuit on foot and motor scooters. Aspiring actresses and the paparazzi were a perfect marriage. Both aimed to be splashed across the front pages, only sometimes it was necessary to stage some spicy scandal or state of undress.

Perhaps the best of these photographers while I covered Rome was Ivan the Russian. I called him "Ivan the Terrible" and bought our share of photos from him. Ivan liked me—I never knew why but perhaps we shared the same cynical view of Via Veneto. He would often offer me first crack at his best stuff. INS didn't pay more than the others, but I appreciated good work and said so. Despite his naughty game, Ivan was a gentleman. I never heard him swear or tell a lie. The red-haired hipster also spoke five languages. He would show me crazy photos, like bosomy Anita Ekberg doing a striptease in a Roman fountain at

3:00 a.m. with a church clock in the background to prove the hour. We might pay him 30,000 lire ($48) for a photo like that. That was a lot of money in Rome during the late 1950s.

The paparazzi also specialized in royal rumbles. Onetime Italian or Spanish dukes were often drunks and deadbeats. Their choice of women often turned out to be wild geese honking for attention. The paparazzi not only photographed the duke and the goose but were often lucky enough to catch him taking a swing at the camera. While this was a great shot for the European magazines, the big-money photos involved a famous actor or prince courting a sexy starlet instead of his wife. That was magazine-cover stuff with a big inside spread.

There was nothing, however, like that summer night when Via Veneto's high-class streetwalkers went on strike. The girls protested that the police were making too many public-nuisance arrests, and they wasted an extravagant number of working hours at downtown headquarters.

The girls formed their lines near the U.S. embassy where the cops were sure to leave them alone. The police gathered at the top of Via Veneto near the Porto Pinciana. They clashed midway between the two points with the girls shouting, kicking, and biting the law. Many of them were hauled off to jail, and it was a clean-cut victory for the police. That is, until early morning when the newspapers hit the streets. One photo showed a cop embracing one of the lovelies instead of making an arrest. Another officer appeared to be resting comfortably in the arms of a striking blonde. Still another sported a brunette where his badge should have been. The whole city roared with laughter, except the officers' wives and girlfriends.

The girls continued to play house on Via Veneto as long as we lived in Rome. This was always their standard reply to cops, "Me? I'm Princess Soraya. What's your alias?" (Soraya, the former queen of Iran, had come to live in Rome after the Shah ditched her.) I understand the girls still work the street.

There were always new, exotic escapades. One was the Bongo

Party. These took place among party folk of "the beach" who would sometimes throw an indoor house shindig. A male or female, invariably dressed in violet and black, would read verse while bongo drums beat softly in the background in cadence with the voice. As the voice rose and fell, so did the drums. The close of the reading and drums was always muted. This was the moment of voodoo. All the lights were extinguished. A candle or two remained.

Voodoo would enter the silent rooms, penetrate the souls, and speak in new tongues. These voices were described as sensations—about life, people, and places. The session would end with a drum roll and lights.

Bongo lovers said they were searching for something neo-experimentalistic. The fad eventually lost fashion, however, and sex returned along with a new social class from the States called beatniks. Romans dressed and ate well and beatniks never made a splash on the Street.

One of the characters along Via Veneto at the time was an aging black hoofer and chanteuse called Bricktop. Her real name was Ada Smith Duconge. She had come a long way from Alderson, West Virginia, where she was born some seventy years earlier.

Brickie, as her friends called her, had been a singer and dancer in Europe for decades. She had four interests in life—entertaining, her Catholic faith, Boys Towns of Italy, and an inseparable cognac accompanied by a small, black cigar. Bricktop opened the door for most black entertainers in Europe. Singer Nat "King" Cole once told me that. So did Sugar Ray Robinson, the onetime middleweight champ, who toured Europe as a hoofer after he hung up his gloves.

Despite her background of late-night nightclubs, Brickie saw life as a morality play. I asked her one time about her coming to Europe.

"I arrived in the late 1920s about the same time as Florence Mills, a dancer from Harlem. We were friends and drove Paris nuts with some hot hoofin', Harlem- and Chicago-style. The time I remember best was 1931. I was flush in Paris that year from hoofin' and singin' and went looking for a poor family. I was always a sucker for the down and out. I found a pair with eleven kids. The father was sick and the mother worked so they would have enough to eat. I bought a houseful of food and clothes. Their eyes were like Christmas-tree bulbs when I brought them the stuff by taxi. I couldn't understand all they said because my French wasn't so hot at the time. But, you know, I saw a lot in their faces.

"I saw my pal, Cole Porter, drinking champagne and eating hash at five o'clock one morning near the Paris nightspot where I worked. I looked at him and he smiled. He had had a good night. He said to me, 'You're a good gal, Brickie. I like you. We're friends.' That was happiness.

"I saw the face of Florence Mills, my hoofin' pal. She was probably the greatest American dancer who ever lived. At least Harlem thought so. When she died, they gave her the biggest funeral in the history of the place.

"I saw the faces of a lot of guys I knew—John Steinbeck, Hemingway, Scott Fitzgerald and others. They were saying, 'Hi, baby! Sing a song! Lift a leg and a glass!' That was happiness.

"I knew then that I was rich. And I was ready to answer a question that Fanny Ward's (an actress) husband once tossed at me, 'Can you handle success?'

"I looked at that French family and told myself, 'Yeah, I can handle success. I ain't got no swelled head. And never did have!'"

My wife and I saw Brickie fairly often. She invited us to dinner at her place several times a year. She would slip me a check for the Boys Towns of Italy and we would talk about Chicago. She had worked there and liked the town. I gave her a copy of my favorite book, *Gall and Honey* by Eddie Doherty, a Windy City (Chicago) newspaperman of yesteryear. She fell in love with the book and never returned it. I never expected her to do so. It was a present to a saint of the Big Street.

The Via Veneto wasn't Italy, but some Italians adopted it as their own. One was a young man who sat on a stool and stroked the notes of jazz piano. His name was Romano Mussolini, a son of *Il Duce*. Romano had one great love, jazz, and he played it hour after hour. When not playing, he listened to the records of America's jazz kings. He followed them note by note in American music magazines.

When I knew him, Romano lived in a modest Roman apartment with his mother, Rachele, and a younger sister, Anna Maria. Romano later wed the younger sister of actress Sophia Loren. In various chats we had, he never mentioned politics and declined to answer any questions about it. He didn't read a note of music, but what he didn't know about jazz wasn't worth remembering. Romano taught himself to play the piano.

"I first became interested in jazz" he once said to me, "when my older brother, Vittorio, then editor of a student newspaper, began receiving letters to the editor about this American music phenomenon. He purchased a few records and I was on my way in jazz.

"Neither of our parents ever stopped us from playing jazz. My mother thought it was strange music but my father never commented on it although he listened to jazz records when I played them. Later, when he became the national leader, my father published an article criticizing jazz. It wasn't that he didn't like jazz, but said Italy should play Italian music."

Romano was an unassuming individual who liked to be alone. He had his own jazz combo and they toured Italy and other parts of Europe. I sometimes saw him on the Via Veneto and we would usually stop and chat. Although I didn't know much about jazz, he thought every American did and always asked me about it. One evening Romano was quite upset. He had read a news article alleging blind jazz pianist George Shearing was ill. Although the two had never met, it was obvious Romano considered Shearing a friend. I thought it was because Romano lived in a world of semidarkness as a result of his father's life. He asked me about Shearing's illness, but I knew nothing of it. Romano walked off, deeply disturbed, and seemed oblivious to Rome's crazy traffic. I never saw him again but came to the conclusion that Shearing meant more to him than almost anyone in the world.

Via Veneto welcomed everybody. It had no particular language. You could hear a half dozen at almost any time of day or night. No one ran it. The Big Street had no stars or impressarios like Damon Runyon, Walter Winchell, Jack Dempsey, or the Schubert clan on Broadway. The only calling cards were getting your mug known and paying the check.

I never reflected much about Via Veneto and went there only because it existed. To me, it was a looking glass, no more, no less. A thoroughfare of daily life. Others who never went there criticized it as a blind alley with no purpose. For some, however, sitting at a cafe table on the Via Veneto was like listening to the music of a violinist leading them to the stars. The atmosphere sprinkled stardust on their ordinary lives.

In looking back on the street now, I become nostalgic. I long to hear the music of *Arrivederci Roma* and *Venticello di Roma* (Wind or Breeze of Rome). I watch in hope of seeing a little girl throw a coin in the Trevi Fountain and of hearing a sigh saying she will return. I'll never say good-bye to Rome.

Chapter 13

A Legend Must Die

THE TOWN OF Cariati in Italy's deep South lay on the shores of the Ionian Sea in the province of Calabria. The sea washed on the doorsteps of shabby one- and two-room houses as children watched from bare, open windows.

I had come to the South this early autumn of 1959 with Monsignor Andrew P. Landi, an American from Brooklyn. He directed the charitable work of the U.S. National Catholic Welfare Conference (now the National Catholic Relief Services) in Italy. The Italian Air Force loaned him a helicopter and pilot so the priest could visit as many communities as possible. Landi had an office in Rome, but spent almost as much time visiting the local Italian communities as he did in his headquarters. The monsignor had been traveling the length and breadth of Italy for twenty years and knew the country better than any American. He always maintained no one could understand Italy without knowing something of its South. In that spirit, I accompanied Landi to what Italians call their *Mezzogiorno* (literally Noonday but meaning the South). It was also called Italy's Africa.

Most of the people of Cariati were poverty-stricken fisherfolk.

A few farmed inland. Fishermen had a good day when they earned 500 lire (80 cents). A thousand lire ($1.60) was considered a gift of the gods.

I watched as a little boy chewed on a great chunk of hard bread with a slice of tomato between the crust. The bread suddenly slipped from his hands and fell into the sea. The child screamed. He splashed into the water and came up smiling with the soaked sandwich in his hands. He had saved his entire lunch.

One father of four children told us he hadn't seen his wife in two-and-a-half years. She was in London, working as a maid, and sent home the equivalent of 48 precious dollars a month.

The eldest child in the family, a daughter of 12, watched her younger brothers and sisters when the father went to sea. That was four or five days a week. She went to school when she could, but confessed it was not often. Later, at a town meeting in the piazza, a man in the crowd shook his fist and shouted, "I was better off as a prisoner of war."

I spoke with a woman in the Calabrian village of Isola Capo di Rizzuto. She said, "A shot of penicillin here costs four days' wages. So how can we afford it? I couldn't, so one of my young sons died." The woman paused, lifted an apron to wipe her eyes, and continued. "But one of the other women here will have a son on the bed where she sleeps with her husband. He'll take the place of mine in a fishing boat some day. There's no mystery about life or death here."

On seeing the name above the town, I couldn't help thinking of Phil Rizzuto who had played shortstop for the New York Yankees. How fortunate the Rizzutos, Joe DiMaggios, Eddie Arcaros, Rocky Marcianos, Frank Sinatras, Perry Comos, and Tony Bennetts (Di Benedetto) had been in America. How many potential star ballplayers, jockeys, boxers, or singers stood right before us here in this village—if they had enough to eat and the opportunity?

Poverty, sickness, and other daily suffering was the legacy and legend of the Italian South. That is why the DiMaggios and

Sinatras emigrated. Bread, tomatoes, a few other vegetables, and sometimes fish—that was the diet here, when they were available. Meat was eaten once a month, perhaps once every two months.

We flew to the town of Andria in the nearby province of Puglia. I watched the hiring of farm laborers in the main piazza. One landowner offered 400 lire (64 cents) for a full day's work in his fields. A young man, who told me earlier he had a wife and three children, accepted. He wasn't happy about the paltry wage, but hadn't worked for two days. He could find no job and was desperate. As the young man prepared to climb aboard a truck with other workers, he remarked to me "This is why we vote Communist."

We attended a public meeting in Puglia's coastal town of Molfetta. Local leaders said about 350 men from the town, mostly fathers, had emigrated to work in Venezuela. Some had forgotten their Italian families and started new lives there.

The city fathers asked that U.S. immigration quotas be increased so more local men could emigrate to Hoboken, New Jersey. That was where Frank Sinatra grew up. About 6,000 men and women had emigrated there over the years. They described Hoboken, never a pretty sight, as *paradiso*.

We flew to the towns of Crotone, Mileto, Castellana, and Catanzaro, a large administrative seat of some 80,000 people in central Calabria. I stood outside the Hotel Moderno in Catanzaro one afternoon, talking with a young man about 21. He was anxious to show me a billboard so we walked to a nearby piazza. The billboard was emblazoned with one name, Primo Carnera. The young man poured out his feelings.

"You remember, he fought Joe Louis in America two decades ago for the heavyweight boxing championship of the world. The same Primo Carnera. His parents had emigrated from Catanzaro to the States. Well, he was just here. It was billed as the world's heavyweight wrestling championship. Twenty years after Louis knocked Carnera out. My father laughed because Carnera is now older than he is. Sure, Carnera won the wrestling match. We knew that result before the contest began. But what we really thought was this—the Carneras had the right idea. Get out of Calabria. That would be the biggest championship that we could ever win!"

* * *

In 1950, the Italian government established the *Cassa del Mezzogiorno* (Southern Redevelopment Fund). In the decade of the 1950s, Rome had poured multimillions of dollars into the South—from Naples to the tip of the Italian boot in Calabria as well as the islands of Sicily and Sardinia—to create electricity, running water, decent housing, hospitals, schools, and jobs.

When the project began, the flatlands of the South were almost as malarial as the swamps of Africa's Upper Nile. Across some 70,000 square miles of the area, most of the roads were mule tracks. Virtually every year, mountain streams flooded arable land and carried topsoil into the sea. Other farmland had no irrigation whatever.

Hunger, starvation wages, no running water or electricity in many homes, illness, and illiteracy on a vast scale—these were the beds on which communism was born and bred in the South.

To fight communism, the Southern Redevelopment Fund began programs of land reform and reclamation. Feudal-like estates were divided among small farmers and shareholders. In its first eight years, the Italian government claimed the program gave the South 160 million man-days of labor.

It listed other results. About 9,000 miles of new or reconstructed roads were built; electricity tripled with the installation of hydroelectric plants; some 700 towns and villages had water pumped to them for the first time; thousands of public buildings, including hospitals and schools, arose.

The Communists, who regularly held protests and sometimes instigated riots against poverty, accepted the government assistance in the areas of the South they controlled. They attempted to block it in other regions.

In Communist-dominated areas, the Reds claimed the gains were due to their leadership. In others, poverty bred Communists and progress would strangle it. Landowners were capitalists; hired hands made good card-carrying members of the party. New schools, which they couldn't control, meant a capitalist education; illiterates followed leaders with the loudest promises.

Despite some economic and social gains, much of the South remained in the grip of poverty and communism when I left Italy in 1964. One reason was the government program had been loaded with graft. Much of the funding filled the pockets of building contractors, lawyers, middlemen, and politicians. The program was also mired in government red tape with millions of dollars in aid wasted. The people themselves differed as to how the money should be spent.

In the 1960s, communism continued to pose a threat because many southern Italians still didn't eat enough to meet what the United Nations considered a minimum daily diet for normal health. Unemployment and only part-time labor left thousands without sufficient money to live. Even many who worked earned only about $50 a month. Families were often large, from four to a dozen children. The United States government poured a vast amount of aid into Italy following World War II. This included not only food, medicine, and other aid, but millions of dollars to help the Christian Democratic Party fight communism. American Catholics, through Landi's work, also contributed considerable assistance. The aid was unable to keep pace not only with the need in the South but also the people's developing sense of economic and social justice.

Where did this new social pressure come from? Virtually every man in the clergy I met on the trip, answered in one word—television.

One explained, "There may be only one community TV set in an entire village but, for the first time in his life, the southern

Italian was able to take a close look at his brothers in the North. Week after week, month after month, he saw the northerner had work, food, a house, and even his own television set. That was the stuff of revolution.

"The southerner followed the TV commercials with great interest. Why cannot his family have a refrigerator? His wife a washing machine? Why not a family savings account in a bank?

"Life on the TV screen became an obsession. Southerners had been changed forever."

Monsignor Landi was transferred back to New York by National Catholic Relief Services in the 1970s. Now in his mid-eighties, he still works for the agency and retains his interest in the Italian poor.

Looking at the South from the perspective of the 1990s, it continues to be the greatest challenge to the future of Italy. The Communist party still actively captures blocks of votes. Many northern Italians, industrialized and thriving, fail to comprehend its needs; yet the South today is one of the most important economic and social issues in Europe. It's still poor and struggling to catch up with the rest of Italy and Europe.

Continuing political corruption exploded in the 1990s when hundreds of Italian politicians and businessmen were indicted on a sweeping scale, not only in the South but in all other parts of the country.

The historic *Risorgimento* (Rebirth) of Italy's political unification in 1861 will never truly unify the country until the South rises to live in dignity. Its legends of poverty must die.

* * *

During our years in Italy, I returned time and again to the South in search of answers to its problems. One of those journeys took me to Sicily in the early 1960s. I went to the birthplace and grave of its most famous son, Turiddu (an untranslatable nickname in Sicilian dialect). That's what Sicilians called Salvatore

Giuliano, the bandit, in their heavy dialect. Turiddu was born in the early 1920s in the poor, tiny town of Montelepre, a few hours by car from Palermo. He was long known to the world as Sicily's Robin Hood.

Giuliano stole from the rich and gave to the poor. For a decade, he and his gang raided and robbed landlords and others, then disappeared into the Sicilian hills. For years, police feared to follow.

Turiddu became a living legend. The poor protected him. All Sicilians shared *omerta* (literally "shade" but meaning the law of silence). Some considered Giuliano a Mafia chief, but I never accepted that. He was his own man with no ties to a broader network of crime.

The Italian government offered Giuliano a pardon if he would surrender and promise to obey the law in the future—or if he left Italy forever. Authorities promised his followers the same freedom if they betrayed him.

Giuliano didn't surrender nor did he abandon Sicily. Hundreds of federal police were sent to the island to track him down. He and his men killed at least a dozen of them and wounded more.

In the Sicilian spring of 1953, Turiddu was betrayed by his most trusted accomplice who shot him to death. When police arrived, they shot him again for good measure.

I went to the Giuliano home in Montelepre where his mother lived with a daughter. They lived modestly across the road from the local *carabinieri* headquarters. The mother spoke only Sicilian so the daughter translated into Italian. Turiddu's mother said over and over to me, "My son always fought on the side of the angels. He's now with them in heaven."

I walked to his tomb atop a hill, knelt, and prayed. It was a large, imposing brick vault. Some boys were playing there. They showed me the nearby tomb of the man who betrayed Giuliano. He died from a poisoned cup of coffee while in prison.

I was about to leave when one of the boys said something that gave me a clearer comprehension of the South than anything I had seen or heard there. In four words, this small villager amassed all the cries of the South against poverty, lifelong toil, and sickness. He pointed to Giuliano's tomb and said, "Turiddu is now free."

In the South, a man was free when he died.

Chapter 14

At the Bedside of the Pope

On October 3, 1958, the sun splashed on the orange-brown summer palace of Pope Pius XII at Castelgandolfo, about 17 miles south of Rome. Some 200 American pilgrims, mostly from New York, waited silently in the palace courtyard for the pope to address them. The blue water of nearby Lake Albano was calm. All appeared serene in the tiny, hilltop town of about 1,000 villagers.

Pius appeared on the balcony and spoke in English about guardian angels. He hiccuped. No one seemed to notice. I thought back to 1953–1954 when a siege of hiccups threatened his life. Rumors in Rome indicated that the Pontiff was unwell.

The Pope hiccuped again. I began to feel uneasy and strained to view his face, but couldn't see him well because I was about 25 yards away. Just before finishing his homily, Pius hiccuped for the third time. It was quite pronounced. He quickly completed his blessing and disappeared inside.

I saw Cardinal Francis Spellman of New York and approached him at the gate as he was leaving. Spellman had seen the Pope privately during an extended meeting that morning. The Cardinal saw me coming and knew what was on my mind. "Jack, don't ask me."

"But you heard the Pope," I said, "and I heard him. Some reporter is going to find this out, and no one knows what he may write. I just need the truth."

Cardinal Spellman and I knew one another well. Over the years, we shared many confidences. He knew I wouldn't quit until I had the story. Spellman finally said, "He's weak. Not particularly well. I don't know . . ."

It was a heavy, sad moment for the Cardinal. He and Pius had been close friends since the two had worked together in the Vatican as young priests.

"I'm sorry," I said. We shook hands and separated. I found a telephone in the town square and called in a story for Radio-Stampa to send to our office in New York. It was the first confirmation from a responsible Church official that Pius was unwell. The story included Pius's previous hiccups and illness. My three hundred words could be expanded into a thousand-word story when New York added more background.

We had a world beat on the papal illness. I was now reporting for Hearst Headline Service since INS had merged with United Press to become UPI. The Hearst newspapers splashed the story. I received cables of congratulations, but glory in the news business lasts only one news cycle, twelve hours. The entire foreign press corps in Rome descended on Castelgandolfo when our story was published. I smiled as officials of the papal household refused to confirm or deny my story. Eventually, a couple of reporters got through to Cardinal Spellman on the phone and he confirmed everything. Everyone then had the story. However, for two days, the Vatican refused comment. It finally issued a statement saying the Pontiff was suffering from a "mild indisposition."

Reporters from around the world poured into Rome and later Castelgandolfo. The famous papal "death watch" had begun. The Vatican suddenly made a dramatic announcement: Pius had suffered a coronary stroke. Doctors were in attendance. All papal appointments were canceled.

I was still at Castelgandolfo but managed to go home and sleep for a few hours each night while shaving, showering, and changing clothes. Each day, although there was virtually no news, reporters battled over the few public phones. I had paid a local family 50,000 lire ($80) for exclusive use of their phone. I also paid them for each call to RadioStampa or home. After several days of this jockeying, the Italian phone company placed emergency news phones around Piazza della Liberta (Liberty Square), which faced the closed central gate of the 16th century palace. The electric company added power for television lights. Lines were strung for radio broadcasts. Italcable and Radio-Stampa moved in lines and trucks with teletype machines to transmit stories to Rome where they were fed overseas.

We worked in a jigsaw puzzle of languages. I found myself translating for Americans, English, and other reporters and also managed to help some of the French and Spanish. At the same time, I was trying to file my own stories. At 10:00 a.m. on October 8, Rome newspapers hit the streets proclaiming the death of Pope Pius. We had no such word at Castelgandolfo. The confusion and excitement were electric. I recall sitting down at a sidewalk cafe, shaking my head in weariness, and thinking, "This could only happen in Italy."

Vatican Radio's sacred music, playing on my new transistor radio, was suddenly interrupted. A brief announcement said the Pope was still alive. No mention was made of the Rome headlines. I told those around me and everyone cheered.

I later learned the reason for the false rumor. A secondary Italian news agency had made a deal with a priest inside the Vatican. If the Pope died, he was to lower a shade in a particular Vatican office. Someone else pulled down the shade against the sun, and the plan misfired. With obituaries already prepared, however, Italian papers took to the streets.

Some international news agencies, quoting the Italian news

service, flashed the Pope's false death around the world. The report caused radio and television stations from Rome to Rio de Janeiro to interrupt programs and broadcast the incorrect news.

Shortly after the false alarm, the three physicians in attendance issued their second statement of the day: Pius had suffered a second stroke.

Reporters began writing their final stories, leaving blank the exact time of death. Since the Vatican was saying little, these stories were what some newsmen call "off the west wall." That means whatever one can dream up that seems safe. They wrote of weeping pilgrims at Castelgandolfo and at the Vatican, the prayers of people around the world, and the great void that was left by the Pope's passing. It was all there, including Pius's years as nuncio to Germany and Vatican secretary of state. Finally, his joy when American troops liberated Rome and the many papal encyclicals that followed.

In the early hours of October 9, 1958, at precisely 3:52 a.m., six days after his last public appearance, the Pontiff succumbed. That was 9:52 p.m., October 8, New York time. I remember the words of an old Italian woman when she heard the announcement at Castelgandolfo. "It was time." Pius had been pontiff for 19 years.

After announcing the Pope's death on Vatican Radio, Father Pellegrino came to the gates of the papal villa and into the square. Television lights bathed the eerie darkness. The little priest had been broadcasting almost without sleep for days and was on the point of exhaustion.

Slowly, meticulously, he answered reporters' questions. The priest described how, hours earlier, the Pope had lapsed into a coma from which he never recovered. Before slipping away, Pellegrino said, Pius asked to work. Pellegrino concluded, "Now his work is ended."

* * *

Cardinals of the Roman Curia, the church senate, came to the papal villa to see the fallen pope who had ruled them with an iron hand. Bishops, priests, and the Pacelli family arrived.

On the afternoon of October 10, Bob Considine, the Hearst newspapers' star reporter, and I were standing in the square outside the palace's central gate when we noticed a priest motioning to us from inside. Considine was puzzled. Monsignor Quirino Paganuzzi of the Vatican staff was insistent. We moved to meet him. Paganuzzi recognized us from an earlier meeting. He quietly asked, "Would you like to see the Holy Father?"

Considine and I looked at one another, momentarily speechless. We nodded. It was the understatement of our careers. The monsignor led us inside the gate and upstairs. As we walked, he confided that, apart from some cardinals, the papal household and the Pacelli family, we would be the first people to see the dead Pope.

We knelt together to the right of the brass bed in the Pontiff's bedroom. Pius was dressed in red velvet robes. Four priests stood at the corners of the bed. Three tall candles flamed on each side.

I had always considered his hands the most striking physical aspect of Pius. The long, delicate fingers of the sculptured hands were entwined in a black rosary. It seemed as if Michelangelo had come into the room, chiseled them there in white marble, and slipped back into the centuries. Even in death, there was style, elegance, grace, even movement in those hands.

I looked at the Pope's face. The lines were noticeably deep, etching the human struggle that had consumed the thin, frail body now hidden by vestments. The Pope's spectacles were gone. His eyes were closed but Eugenio Pacelli was already looking into eternity.

We remained kneeling at his bedside for about ten minutes. I noticed the cross above his head and recalled Pius's words, "My mission is peace. The only weapon I carry is the cross."

We rose from our trance. Monsignor Paganuzzi noticed that I had been staring at the Pope's hands. He motioned us toward

Pius. I nodded and elbowed Considine to move closer to the bed. The two of us bent over the prostrate body and kissed the hands of the Pope of Peace.

The papal Fisherman's ring was gone from the Pope's hand. I thought of how many times it had been raised *Urbi et Orbi* (to the city and the world) over the earth in blessing; the red birettas those hands had placed on the heads of some 40 new cardinals of the church, and the papal encyclicals they had carved from centuries of Roman Catholic learning.

The two of us tiptoed out of the silent room, down the staircase and into the lingering sunlight in the town square. We walked to a coffee bar at the far end of the square to be alone. Bob ordered a double Scotch on-the-rocks. I had an espresso with a shot of cognac tossed in. Bob spoke first. His words trembled. "After 25 years as a newspaperman, I thought I had been everywhere and seen everything. And now, I kiss the hands of a dead pope."

Bob raised his glass and said, "I'm sure the good Lord won't think it's blasphemous. Here's to Pius the Twelfth, Jack. To the Pope!"

I had covered many stories with Considine but that was the first time that I had seen him visibly shaken. He said softly, "In that ten minutes, my whole life passed in front of my eyes. Fifty years or so. History in the present tense. It humbles a guy."

We compared mental notes on the bedroom scene. Detail by detail, we pieced together a composite photograph. Then, we placed our typewriters on a sidewalk cafe table and began to write. Our dateline read: AT THE BEDSIDE OF THE POPE, CASTELGANDOLPHO . . .

Considine did an eyewitness piece about the dead Pope on the bed, the bedroom itself, and the atmosphere inside the papal summer palace. I wrote an "I remember" piece — two private audiences which my wife and I had earlier with Pius. The first fell on his eighty-second birthday, while the second occurred in June about four months before he died, after INS had closed.

I remembered being struck by the delicately chiseled hands of Pius during that first audience. How he opened his hands to draw people closer to him and closed them to indicate the audience was at an end. The Pope was about six feet tall and, I recalled, he walked like a basketball player, careful not to bump his head on low arches. He also had a lot of spring in his legs. In that first audience, we talked about the Harlem Globetrotters who once had a papal audience and performed in a Vatican courtyard for him. Pius beamed. He loved the Globetrotters.

The Pontiff understood English well, and picked up some of the slang from GIs who had audiences with him after the fall of Rome. Some of us were relieved they didn't teach him some of their foxhole phrases. A Vatican prelate told me, "GI talk really got to him. They would say: 'Howdy, Mister Pope, I'm a Jew from the Bronx . . .' or 'Hiya Pope, this is quite a joint. I'm a Protestant from Iowa and we got nothing like it back home.'"

After one such audience Pius told the prelate "The Americans are so expressive. They're teaching me a new English!"

The Pontiff spoke more than a half dozen languages, but he never quite mastered all the lingo of cartoonist Bill Mauldin and his GI Joe drawings.

After INS merged with United Press, the Pope received the INS staff and their wives in private audience for about a half hour. I believe we were the only newsmen in history to explain to a pope how we got fired. When the two news agencies merged, all INS employees received letters that our services were no longer needed.

His Holiness wanted to know every detail. How many men were without jobs; could any of us be hired by the newly formed agency; whether everyone would receive severance pay; and what prospects did we have for new jobs? Turning to me at the close of the audience, the pope said,

"Please tell the directors of the new agency that We are most anxious and hopeful that they will take every measure to find employment for all those now without work. You may quote me." Pius added, "Say also that I believe journalism to be a noble mission of truth, justice, and light. We need dedicated people to undertake these great tasks. We need all of you."

The Pope was acting like our parish pastor. He was down to earth and we liked that. For the moment, the scholar who wrote encyclicals on social justice had become like our father. I wondered what the Notre Dame football team would do if he ever gave them a pep talk before a game. No doubt the goal posts at that stadium would now rise in the Vatican gardens!

I did send the Pope's job message to New York. They must have been astounded, but nobody ever responded to it. All of us eventually found jobs but it took months for some. Bill Hearst cabled me an offer to remain in Rome as a correspondent for his newspapers, and I accepted.

* * *

Those were fond remembrances, but now the funeral procession for Pius was taking place. It was awesome. At the ancient Coliseum, thousands upon thousands of priests, monks, and nuns met the hearse which bore his body from Castelgandolfo. They marched with the body from beneath the high walls up the broad boulevard to Piazza Venezia where Benito Mussolini had so often called on the Italian people to march with him. I wrote these words:

"The Pope was borne past the balcony from which *Il Duce* harangued his cohorts and vast crowds of men, women and children. Today, there was not a single echo of the hoarse cries that once rattled from the throats of his militant blackshirts. There is only silence in this mammoth square and, when it is broken, it comes to life only in breaths of prayer . . ."

Even now, I cannot forget the shuffle of their sandals, the bare feet, legs and tonsured heads of the monks. The multicolored religious habits of various Catholic orders rustled in the autumn breeze, extending mile after mile. The throaty chant of priests soared above their white surplices into the clear sky. This was the Church Militant victorious in death. This was the answer to Stalin's insolent question: "How many divisions has the Pope?"

I tried to find the face of a certain nun in the crowd. Her name was Madre Pasqualina. Few knew who she was and fewer still had ever seen her. For more than 40 years, Pasqualina had been the Pope's chief housekeeper.

I once studied a photo taken of her with a telephoto lens when she was standing in the choir loft of St. Peter's Basilica during a papal ceremony. Every cameraman in Rome would have given away a hundred or more pictures for just one good photo of her. For years, they had tried to photograph her face up close—from the gates of the Vatican at dawn to hospitals that she would sometimes visit at night. Only a few managed to even see her and, even when they attempted to photograph her, the pictures were of poor quality.

Eugenio Pacelli first met Sister Pasqualina in 1912. He was then a young priest from the Vatican's Secretariat of State. She was a nun at the Einsiedlen Abbey in the Bernese Alps where he had gone for a rest. He was a frail man in mediocre health.

The nun spoke to the future pope in blunt terms. If he wanted to continue his career and do well, he must live on a lot of milk and cheese. Pacelli was never to forget the iron-willed taskmaster. He too had an iron will. When appointed papal nuncio to Munich in 1917, he asked and received permission to have Pasqualina take charge of his household. When Pacelli was later named secretary of state and a cardinal, she accompanied him to the Vatican.

Sister Pasqualina became Madre (Mother) when Cardinal Pacelli was chosen pope in 1939. She needed additional help to run the papal household, and sent for three younger German nuns to assist in the chores.

Madre Pasqualina watched over the Pope's health until his death. She supervised his meals, interrupted him when he worked too long and hard, kept visitors—even cardinals—from disturbing him when he was tired, and even broke off papal conversations with guests saying, "The Holy Father must go now. It's time for him to leave."

The papal household spoke German under Pius. He had spoken it for years when stationed there. Even Augustine Cardinal Bea, the papal confessor, was German. Pius's work schedule proceeded with strict German preciseness. It was a common saying in the Vatican that one could set his watch by the pontiff's activities.

I never did see Madre Pasqualina, although we received various tips she would be somewhere at a certain time. I would assign a photographer to go and wait, sometimes for hours, but we never obtained a photo of her. Eventually, a few weeks after Pius's passing, she took up residence at Rome's Salvator Mundi Hospital.

There were insinuations in some Italian magazines and tabloids Pasqualina and Pius had a platonic romance. Most of these rumors came from anticlericals who attacked the Church on virtually any count. Other comments reflected the cynicism some Italians always had toward the Church. But not even the Communists I knew believed that tawdry gossip.

Pasqualina was interesting for two reasons: the mystery she created about herself and the amount of power she wielded behind the papal throne.

My thoughts returned to the funeral. The long street procession finally ended and the body of Pius was placed on a sloping red-draped dais inside St. Peter's Basilica. The Pontiff's head and the golden mitre atop it pointed upward toward the papal altar. He wore a red chasuble, symbolic of the blood shed by church martyrs for their faith. The Pope also wore white gloves, red and gold slippers, and a long white cassock, symbolic of his office. White represented the purity of the papacy.

As I stood looking at the body, resting directly before the Altar of the Confessional, I reflected that he had stood on that precise spot each Wednesday of his long reign where he received millions of pilgrims from distant lands in general audience. These audiences were not interrupted for Italians even during the dark days of World War II.

Pius requested in his will no monument be erected in his name. Some were, however, even at the direct instruction of his successor, Pope John XXIII. Yet, rather than any material reminder, Pius will live on in his voluminous writings and the texts of his many addresses. They were far greater in scope than any pope in history. His monuments will be in the minds and hearts of men.

Pius's thinking extended far beyond matters of the Church. For example, long before the United States and the Soviet Union launched the era of manmade satellites or Americans walked on the moon, Pius was writing about the conquest of space. He privately studied and even wrote about the possibility of life on other planets and what bearing that might have on Christianity.

I have read articles in various journals depicting Pius as betraying Jews in favor of Hitler and the Nazis. Nothing I ever read or heard at the Vatican convinced me of that. A vivid story added a personal touch to that conviction.

While living in Rome, my wife and I made the acquaintance of a charming Jewish physician named Lelle and his wife, Anna Maria, a nurse, who lived with us in the apartment building on Via Adelaide Ristori 22. One day we were watching TV together. It was the broadcast of a solemn High Mass from St. Peter's and we were listening to the Sistine Choir. Lelle began to chant with them, loud and clear, "Gloria in Excelsis Deo . . . ," until the final "Amen."

I was astonished, not only at his knowledge of Gregorian chant but his joy in singing it. However, I said nothing. As the Mass progressed, the physician would join the choir from time to time. I could no longer contain myself. "But not even most Catholics know that."

"Some Italian Jews, yes," Lelle replied. He then told this story: In early 1943, after German troop reinforcements began moving into Italy, Jews in Rome learned the Nazis were planning their arrests. Actually, the Vatican learned of the impending action and privately warned Jewish leaders who passed the word in their community. Pius secretly sent an emissary to Count Ciano, Mussolini's son-in-law, at his post in the foreign ministry.

Ciano reported neither he nor Mussolini could do anything about the purge. Italy couldn't control the Germany army or secret police. The truth was even Ciano was about to be shot by Il Duce on the unsubstantiated rumor he had abused the dictator's trust.

Lelle said Jews soon learned that Pius had ordered word to be passed from the Vatican: the doors of all monasteries, nunneries, and other Catholic religious houses would be opened to Jews. In the doctor's own family, children were sent to different religious houses. Only his father knew the whereabouts of all. Lelle put on the robes of a novice monk and sang Gregorian chant for the rest of the war. The chief rabbi of Rome later became a priest as a result of his long and close contact with Catholic nuns and priests.

On the day of his coronation, Pius said, ". . . In the course of centuries, the office of the supreme pontiff has had but one purpose: To serve the truth, that is to say, the complete and pure truth, not obscured by clouds nor enervated by weakness and never separated from the love of Christ."

I told myself after Pius's death, if he could return to defend his papacy, he would have happily noted the Jewish physician's beautiful Gregorian chant.

The author in St. Peter's Square, 1959.

Christmas of 1957 at the INS office on the Via Del Corso.

The author with Papa Giovanni—Pope John XXIII—in his Vatican study . . .

. . . and in audience with Pius XII in 1958.

Joy, Jeff, Terry, and Kevin pose for a family portrait in 1962.

Chapter 15

Under the Mountain

THE SMOKE FROM the Sistine Chapel chimney appeared to be dark, indicating a pope had not been elected. In the past, following ballots of the sacred college of cardinals, the disappointed throng dispersed quickly when black smoke billowed from the chimney. They knew well only white smoke indicated a new pope had been chosen. And this smoke, while not black, was dark.

This time, however, the thousands massed in St. Peter's Square didn't leave, despite the fact it was 6:00 p.m. and the dinner hour was approaching. As the crowd waited quietly, time seemed to stand still on that calm, placid evening of October 28, 1958.

I stood on the outskirts of the crowd and watched a few bystanders trickle down Via della Conciliazione. Perhaps, I thought, I should get a taxi and return to the Foreign Press Club. But the throng held me there. I couldn't understand its unwillingness to leave.

Suddenly, lights began to sprinkle along the corridor leading from the Apostolic Palace to the central loggia of St. Peter's Basilica. I still didn't understand the movement because wisps of dark smoke were still visible in the sky. Suddenly palace windows near the Sistine Chapel swung open and arms were waving white handkerchiefs. White! That was the signal we had all been waiting for. We had a new pope!

People began to cheer. A woman cried. The crowd waved back to those in the upper windows. The cheers had now become a roar. Finally, the glass doors of the Basilica's central loggia opened. Nicola Cardinal Canali, old and nearly blind, stepped to a waiting microphone. The crowd was hushed until it heard one name—"Angelo . . ."

The throng went wild. An Italian name. The new pontiff was Italian. After all the speculation that a non-Italian might be chosen, a more Italian name could not have been announced. Angelo Giuseppe Roncalli of Venice! As many observers were quick to add: A compromise Pope. An interim Pope. They concluded he had been chosen only after many ballots since the favorites had failed, and Roncalli's advanced age indicated a short reign.

Early the following morning, I left Rome with Bob Considine by train for Milan. We would drive to the little town of Sotto Il Monte where the new Pope John XXIII had been born. It was located in the hill country of the northern province of Bergamo, about an hour's drive from Milan's industrial-financial center.

Sotto Il Monte (Under the Mountain) was a picturesque farm community with perhaps 1,000 souls in the local parish district. All were poor. The area was strong in wheat, corn, wine, and laborers' backs. Little had changed since young Angelo had left his family farmhouse nearly 70 years before to attend a seminary.

Driving into town, we noted a single gasoline pump, one butcher shop, a vegetable market, pharmacy, a tobacco shop, and some nearby family dwellings. The parish church was some distance away.

I had spoken with Monsignor Loris Capovilla, the Pope's private secretary, before leaving Rome that morning. He knew me and called ahead to the Roncallis asking them to receive us. We drove up to the family home in mid-afternoon. The Pope's three brothers, all wearing coats because of the autumn chill, worked at various chores in the farmyard. Zaverio was 77 years old, Alfredo 71, and Giuseppe 66. All wore old, work shirts, frayed work pants, and heavy work shoes.

We introduced ourselves. I did the translating and joked with Alfredo about his battered, black hat. He said he had worn it for about 10 years. It was still good against the wind and snow, Alfredo said with a wink, and especially the hot summer sun.

Roosters and chickens roamed the farmyard where Angelo had learned to walk and play. Zaverio was piling freshly cut firewood at the side of the mud-brown stucco house. He had cut and carried it there himself. It was obvious all of the men, despite their ages, were in exceptional shape.

They invited us into the house and immediately led us to the room where their brother, Angelo, had been born. The curtains in the bedroom were dark from fireplace smoke, but the room itself was spotlessly clean. A farm helper, Giovanni Micheletti, and his wife, Sofia, now slept there. Zaverio suddenly said of Angelo, "He was always studying. He never could get enough books or time to read them. He didn't play as much as we did because he had no time. But he used to laugh and joke a lot, more than any of us."

Zaverio paused, searching his memory as he tried to be helpful to us, and recalled, "Our parents always wanted me to walk to school with Angelo. That was because the moment he left the house—and it was a very long walk—he had his nose in his books. They were afraid he would fall into a hole!"

The Pope's niece, Enrica, a woman of about 40, ran the household. She was a hard-working, God-fearing woman with a strong, clear voice. Enrica explained everyone ate on the two long wooden tables in the kitchen. She said they needed the space because the Roncallis had 15 nieces and nephews, and some always seemed to be visiting.

I asked Enrica if the family would go to Rome for the coronation of the Pope. She replied, "Of course, we would like to go, but we don't have clothes for such an occasion. Why, the men hardly leave the farm except to go to church. I also think we would get lost in that big city. We have never been there, you know. In fact, some of us have never ridden a train. And, with this large a family, who could afford such a ride?" The words sparked a delighted laugh from everyone.

I asked if the new Pope had contacted his family. Enrica said he had telephoned them from his new apartment in the Vatican. I looked around for the phone and, again, everyone laughed. The Roncallis had no phone.

Enrica explained, "He called a family friend. The fellow pedaled out here and I went back into town on our bicycle. It's a kind of community phone. Some people had already gathered around to hear what Angelo would say now that he was Pope. More people kept coming as I called back the telephone operator. They kept yelling and made me nervous."

The Roncalli brothers hung on every word. It was as if Enrica was telling the story for the first time. She continued, "First, I got his secretary, Monsignor Loris Capovilla. Then, Angelo came on the line. He asked first about everybody's health and I said all were fine. He said he was sorry not to return to Sotto Il Monte for his vacation last summer. He always came here on vacation, even when he was the papal nuncio in Paris. I told him it was all right. He could come back any time.

"Then, Angelo told me that he wanted us to come to the coronation at the Vatican. He said Monsignor Capovilla would take care of all the arrangements. He asked me to tell everyone to pray for him. He said it twice to make sure I understood. The line wasn't so clear.

"Finally, before hanging up, Angelo said, 'My blessing to you, all the family, and the people of Sotto Il Monte.' Just before Angelo hung up, he said, 'Kisses to the children!'"

Enrica's face was flushed with the emotion of retelling the story. It was getting dark and time to go. The brothers said they had more chores. As we rose to leave, Zaverio invited us down to the cellar. There, in the darkness, was a large cask where the family stored its homemade wine. He invited us to have a glass and we carried it upstairs. It was a full-bodied red.

"Ask him for a bottle," Considine nudged me. "Go ahead."

I carefully explained that Bob had come all the way from New York and that he would like to take a bottle back to his friends in the United States. We would gladly pay for it. Zaverio disappeared in the cellar and soon returned with two bottles of red, one for Bob and the other for me. "Good health!" he said with a smile. I tried to pay him but he shook his head.

We waved good-bye as darkness set in. Some of the nieces and nephews playing in the farmyard returned our waves. They had been talking about Uncle Angelo. There wasn't the slightest awe of him or his new high office, only a question mark about whether he would ever return to Sotto Il Monte again.

Pope John never returned to his family farm. Wherever he went, the Pope once told me, Sotto Il Monte went with him. That was the secret of his greatness. Papa Giovanni (John) carried within his mind and heart the simplicity, humility, and love characteristic of his hometown. He never ceased to be one of them. I write this in the humble thanksgiving of having known him well.

Considine carried the bottle of wine back to New York on board his plane. He asked a stewardess to put it in a safe place where the cork could not be loosened. Before leaving, Bob told me, "I'm going to bring it over to Toots Shor's joint. Then, invite some of the sporting fraternity. Not one of them picked Roncalli!"

Despite running into one another often after that, I deliberately never asked Bob about the wine. It might have spoiled the way I imagined the scene . . . Bob is standing at Toots's bar, sipping a double Scotch on-the-rocks. Various guests began to show—Joe DiMaggio, Yogi Berra, the old sportswriter Red Smith, Rocky Marciano, Eddie Arcaro, Phil Rizzuto, and maybe fighters "Sugar" Ray Robinson, Barney Ross, and a few other guys. Maybe a few bookies and the ghost of Bill Corum, another old sportswriter. One by one, they arrive at the bar, most of them Italians who would appreciate the moment. Bob counts noses. Finally, Toots shouts, "Play ball!"

The bartenders then set up wine glasses and pour the Roncalli red as if it were liquid gold. Bob clears his throat. There is a reverent silence. Bob says a few words about visiting the Roncalli farm, and that the brothers had given him the bottle. Finally, Considine offers a toast, "Gentlemen, to a very fine wine maker. To his strong, home-brew red. To the man you guys thought never had a prayer. To Angie Roncalli, the Pope!"

There is stunned surprise. Then, a cheer. They raise their glasses and call out in unison, "To Angie, the longshot Pope!"

I would like to think it went exactly like that.

* * *

The three Roncalli brothers and a sister watched transfixed beneath the cold, leaden sky of November 4, 1958, while their Angelo was crowned Pontiff of the Roman Catholic Church. The massed multitude in St. Peter's Square bellowed his name into the gray-cloaked heavens as the triple-tiered tiara was placed on the new pope's head at 1:00 p.m. Rome time.

A pink-faced little band of fifteen nieces and nephews stood on the loggia of honor above the waving sea of humanity in the rain-washed square below. They were in awe of the scene, surrounded by bemedaled noble princes and their ladies as well as red-robed cardinals and their priestly attendants. *Viva il Papa!* thundered the hundreds of thousands as if the sky were unleashing another torrent of rain that had lashed the city and Basilica during the night. *Viva il Papa!* echoed the little nieces and nephews.

"Long live Father Angelo, too," a small niece sung in golden notes. The Pope was still only a country priest to these humble farm folk. The Holy Father turned his crowned head, covered with the jeweled tiara, and smiled at them. Zaverio whispered to the family, "See, he's seen us!"

The other brothers, Alfredo and Giuseppe, their somber faces brightening, turned to their sister, Assunta. The brothers were dressed in rented long black coats with tails. Assunta was heavily veiled in black. A worn gold cross was pinned to her dress.

Monsignor Capovilla had provided the seats but villagers had given the Roncalli family part of their meager savings to rent suits and pay for the railroad tickets to Rome. The family slept free in a religious house. The Vatican had offered to pay the costs but the Roncallis declined.

Alfredo still carried his battered black hat. He held it like a relic in his strong, rough hands. The tall black hats of the Vatican diplomatic corps dwarfed him in the crowd.

There were striking differences between the stately figure of the late Pius and his homespun successor. Pius was tall and thin. John was short and round. Pius spoke elegant, eloquent Italian. John addressed people with traces of Bergamo dialect on his tongue. Pius loved solitude. John didn't even went to eat alone.

In his first address to the cardinals after being elected pontiff, John was quoted as saying, "Pardon me if I appear embarrassed. I must get used to this new state of things. I was a cardinal a short while ago. Now I am the pope. Pardon me . . ."

Roncalli used the proper noun *I*, not the usual papal *We*. For his entire reign of more than four years, John XXIII rarely used *We*. This was despite the fact he had been a Vatican diplomat and lived its protocol for many years—nine in Bulgaria, eight between Turkey and Greece, and seven in Paris.

I recall a general audience shortly after John's election. He walked into the midst of the crowd, something Pius would never have done. A papal chamberlain hurriedly stepped up and said to him that he must return to his place. John was heard to reply, "Well, that's fine. But I am the pope, am I not?"

John continued to mix and talk with the pilgrims.

The new Holy Father spoke fluent French and, of course, his

native Italian. He also knew a fair amount of Bulgarian, Greek and Turkish, some Russian, a smattering of Spanish and German, and greetings in other languages.

On becoming pope, John decided to learn enough English to carry on a simple conversation. His teacher was Monsignor Thomas Ryan, who had been at the Vatican about 25 years but was still very much an Irishman—six feet, three inches and 230 pounds, with a brogue that couldn't be cut with six steak knives.

I found out about the lessons and wrote a story about them, quoting Ryan as saying, "We're just talkin' to git the sound o' things. But he'll be givin' a few words, for sure, before ye know the difference." I also wrote, "Tis likely the good Pope'll be talkin to the world with a bit o' the Irish brogue."

Newspaper clippings of the article began to arrive on the monsignor's Vatican desk from the United States. Ryan was furious. One particular headline sent him into orbit: WHAT—A POPE WITH A BROGUE?

A very angry Ryan phoned me. He threatened to take off his collar and punch me in the nose. I told Ryan I had quoted him correctly. The Irishman hung up without so much as a "Top o' the mornin."

Most Vatican prelates laughed about the story. The few who kidded Ryan about it learned it was no joke. Whenever I bumped into the monsignor from then on, he gritted his teeth and called me "Sir."

Pope John's first public flight into English took place at a general audience. After addressing the crowd in Italian and French, he pulled a small card from an inside pocket, smiled and said in self-mocking English, "Here we go!" John then said a few simple words of welcome.

The Pope used the same "Here we go" phrase in English when President Eisenhower visited him at the Vatican. Ike immediately burst into laughter. The picture of the laughing Ike and the smiling pontiff was splashed around the globe.

As the Pope and Eisenhower ended their meeting, John turned

to Ike and said of his English, "Next time, I hope to do better!" The president again roared with laughter and John smiled.

The Pope once made an interesting observation about my own style of Italian when he referred to me as a *scugnizzo*. The word *scugnizzo* is Neapolitan dialect for a street urchin. It literally means a spinning top, one who twists and turns to escape the arms of cops.

The reason for the Pope's unique blessing was because I had learned my Italian in the streets, not in a classroom. I spoke it like a typical soccer fan would in a close game. I also had a reputation for being street smart when dealing with Vatican officials. My favorite line was, "I know the answer is no, but how do we do it?"

A few years after my run-in with Ryan, he was appointed bishop in his native Ireland. Just before he was to leave for home, I met him by accident in St. Peter's Square. He walked over to me, said nothing, but shook my hand. I guess he was saying that I would live after all. The incident left me with a sentimental lump in my throat. I loved Ireland and meant no offense to Ryan. My own mother spoke with a brogue. Ryan's teaching the Pope English had just seemed to me a very funny story.

No time or incident so summed up Pope John to me as a day I visited Castelgandolfo. The Holy Father was there on vacation. The man next to me in the crowd wore a red carnation, which sometimes indicated he was a Communist. I asked him if he were a party member, and the man replied that he was. Why then, I inquired, did you come to see the Pope? The man replied, "Because he's the pope of the people!"

An American priest put it to me another way, "You can take the boy out of the country, but never the country out of the boy."

John himself once said publicly, "Before I am a priest, cardinal or pope, I am a man. I want people to like me because of what I am—Roncalli, the man. Because of this, I can understand the sadness in the hearts of men, and their joy. I want to meet every man who comes to see me. Who knows, he might want to go to confession to me?"

Papa Giovanni was a man of all seasons—of fields, hills, and the breath of country air. I recall, in particular, John's face. Pius had delicate, chiseled hands, but John had a furrowed brow and face. The lines of a hoe burrowed down both sides of his mouth. The rugged chin had been flattened and slightly rounded like a garden spade. His ears were as uneven as potato peelings. His hands were heavy and thick and his feet big and slow. But the mouth opened softly, and his eyes twinkled. It was obvious John harvested laughter. But it was his good heart and soul that elevated him above the mountain at Sotto Il Monte.

Chapter 16

Franco

FRANCO DELIVERED HIS credentials with Neapolitan oratorical flourish. "The name is Franco Bucarelli. Citizen of Naples. Lawyer, newspaper reporter, radio sportscaster, part-time movie actor, poet, sometime songwriter, bachelor, and 22 years old.

"I began my career at 12—unofficially. I join the Fifth Army of Mark Clark. The general, he knows Franco Bucarelli. I learn GI English and a few other languages from the American soldiers—also how to get along far from home. I go with them up north. I become an unofficial interpreter because pretty soon my English is very good.

"My parents call me back home. I get my father a job with the Fifth Army in Naples. My mother, she's a teacher, and she puts me back in school. But I'm way ahead of the class because I already saw most of Italy and the GIs taught me a lot.

"I go to Naples University. The professors there are pretty smart, too. They give me my law degree. I broadcast soccer and other sports on the radio. I work in some movies about Naples with Vittorio de Sica. Then, I become a good police and all-around reporter for a Naples newspaper, *Il Mattino*. When I have time, I get some poetry published and a few of my songs become music records. I go out with girls and to church when the Lord and the Madonna call me. I'm Jewish but it doesn't hurt to have friends in high places. For references in Naples, I got the chief of police, Lucky Luciano, the cardinal and Franco Bucarelli. That is, I'm my own lawyer!"

After a deep breath I asked, "You mean the American Lucky Luciano? The gangster?"

"Yeah," Franco replied. "He's my very good friend. He says I'm a good, smart kid. I agree with everything but the kid. Maybe he's a mob man like some people say and, I think, if he needs a good lawyer some day, I'm ready. I'm also a reporter. And, maybe some day Lucky has a big story for me.

"Lucky goes his way, and I go mine. When we meet, we shake hands. I got no time for troubles; he has no time for wise guys. That's one time I got no time—no wise guys, just friends. I like everybody to be Franco Bucarelli's friend."

I got to the point. "How much money do you want to start as our stringer (part-time reporter) in Naples?"

"Nothing," Franco said. "Now I go to Naples. I find some stories that will interest Americans. When I send you a good story, you pay me. When I call in a very good story, you pay me more. And when you don't like what I send, you don't pay me. But I need some expense money once in a while. Not much. Shoe leather."

We shook hands. Franco worked for me at INS, with Hearst Headline Service, and became our office manager in Rome when I became bureau chief of ABC News there in 1961. I never regretted the partnership. Seven years later, when I left Italy, we parted with the same handshake.

We covered many stories together. Perhaps, it might be best to start with Jacqueline Kennedy, when she visited Italy in the early 1960s as First Lady of the United States. I was then a correspondent for ABC News. Mrs. Kennedy, with her sister, Princess Radziwill, had rented a large villa at Ravello, a magnificent little town atop Amalfi Drive that looked out on the Mediterranean coastline, as well as the beautiful Bay of Naples and Sorrento. It is one of the loveliest spots in the world.

A United States Secret Service agent, who appeared to be in charge of the operation, laid down the law—no interviews. We sent Mrs. Kennedy a dozen roses anyway and spent two days scouting the place. It looked hopeless. There appeared to be no way to get inside for an interview with Jacqueline.

The head of the Secret Service detail apparently was receiving reports about our snooping around. He met us once in town and warned he would have us tossed in the clink if we persisted.

One day, Franco and I visited some local winemakers and toured their plant. They told us Mrs. Kennedy was sipping their wine with dinner. They had a connection in the Kennedy kitchen—a cousin of a cousin. So the next day, we promised to get publicity for their wine in the States if Franco could go along when their truck made the next delivery. After gaining entree to the kitchen, Franco played Romeo with the chief cook and reported back, "Look, I wouldn't give that cook as a girlfriend to my dead grandfather, but I got a date with her. We're going for a walk in town. She says she needs to do some shopping anyway. I carry the packages. I'll take it from there but, believe me, she is no bargain and this is no picnic. I think that if my father saw me with her, he'd ask if I found her in a cemetery. That's the worst in Naples, a grave robber."

Franco paused, as if he suddenly decided to drop the idea, and then said, "When she looks at me, I get the chills. Like pneumonia is coming to take me out of this world. I see my sins before me. A rabbi and a priest are coming to get rid of my sins. 'Confess!' they're saying. 'Confess.' "

I tried to calm him down but he continued, "And my fiancé, Lucia. Madonna! Do you know what it means to be engaged to a girl with Sicilian blood? Of course you don't. First, she takes out your eyes with a kitchen knife. That's an act of mercy. Then she cuts off your . . . I can't even tell you the rest."

"Okay!" I surrendered. "You're not going?"

"I'm all set!" he said without blinking an eye.

We faced a major problem: how to sneak a camera, sound gear, plus a cameraman, soundman, and me into the villa.

Franco went shopping while I pumped some Italian workmen who were making repairs at the villa. I needed a mental layout of the place. Franco and I met late that afternoon to compare notes.

He reported, "The chief cook runs the kitchen. Whatever she says goes. Tomorrow evening, Mrs. Kennedy is having a reception for the mayor and other town officials. I think we can take the equipment and everyone up there in the wine delivery truck. We climb the back stairs into the kitchen. But I gotta go, Jack, not you. That's because, if somebody questions me, I'll say we're the local TV crew. We go everywhere the mayor does."

I agreed and would wait outside in the wine truck in case he needed me. Franco would do the interview with Mrs. Kennedy. He smiled. That magnificent, wonderful, watermelon grin. He was still smiling when he asked, "And if the head of the SS grabs me, what do I say to him?"

I replied, "You're the lawyer, Franco."

Franco assaulted the back stairs. As he later recounted the events to me, the cook met him, the cameraman, and soundman at the kitchen door. The reception had already begun. A buffet dinner was being readied for placement on a large table in the dining room. A hallway led from the kitchen to the dining room. A large, heavy drapery separated the dining room from the hallway.

Franco peeked out from behind the drapes trying to figure out his next move. The cameraman and soundman prepared their equipment. Franco decided he would slide under the table with a microphone when Mrs. Kennedy led the mayor and other guests to the buffet.

The soundman was to open the drapery and turn on his two frezzolites, holding one in each hand, shining them in the direction of the First Lady. The cameraman was to run both sound and film. Franco would get up from the floor, walk up to Mrs. Kennedy, holding the microphone at the end of the cameraman's longest cable. It was complicated stage managing, but it worked.

Franco tunneled under the buffet table and came up at Mrs. Kennedy's side. The SS chief was nowhere in sight so Franco said, "Hello, Mrs. Kennedy, I'm Franco Bucarelli of ABC News. Welcome to Italy! The American television audience would like to know, how do you like Italy?"

Mrs. Kennedy was speechless. Meanwhile, Franco waved away some of the guests who started to block the camera's view. Mrs. Kennedy was still so surprised that she couldn't respond. Franco began answering for her, "It's very nice, you say. What do you like most? You say the sea. And the people are so warm and friendly. Ah, Signora, that's Italy!"

Mrs. Kennedy had begun to smile. Never before, perhaps, had she seen anything like it. She was laughing. It was a Neopolitan operetta.

The film was still rolling and so was Franco. He asked about daughter Caroline, son John, her Italian shopping, and what Mrs. Kennedy would tell her husband about the visit when she returned to the White House. Franco supplied his own answer, "That he, too, should visit Italy. Brava, signora!

"One last question, Signora. When do you hope to return to Italy? As soon as you can, maybe next year. Wonderful! Thank you, Mrs. Kennedy. This is Franco Bucarelli, ABC, Ravello, Italy."

Jacqueline took it all with continued surprise and amusement, and shook hands with the intrepid newsman. But there was trouble ahead. Out of the corner of his eye Franco had seen the advancing SS chief and began a diplomatic retreat into the kitchen. But the chief and another agent were right behind the ABC trio. Franco tried to beat the chief to the punch, "Mister Agent, glad to meet you. Franco Bucarelli is the name. ABC News."

But the chief cut him off cold. "Ooooouut!" he gritted between his teeth. "Oooooouut!"

As the trio hustled their gear down the back stairs where the wine truck waited, the agent demanded, "How did you get in here?"

Franco was brilliant. All he answered to the rapid-fire questions was, "Yeah."

When the chief demanded the film, Franco said "Yeah" but didn't move to hand it over. He also answered "Yeah" to the threat of being arrested and put in jail.

"I'll be back in Rome in a few days," the SS chief said, "and I'm going to write a letter to the ABC bureau there. What's the address? Never mind. I'll get it myself. Now get out!"

"Yeah," said Franco, bolting for the truck.

We sent the film to New York. It created howls of disbelieving laughter. Obviously, it never made the evening news. The film was even shown to Jim Hagerty, former White House news secretary, then the vice president of ABC network news. I was later told Hagerty doubled up in laughter. His only comment was, "No one would believe it, even if they saw it."

I don't think Mrs. Kennedy believed it either.

*　*　*

Franco and I traveled to Bologna in one of the most unforgettable experiences of my life. I am reminded of it every day since by a gold medal and photo of the occasion hanging from my study wall in Arizona. The medal was the highest honor which the city and its longtime Communist mayor could bestow on anyone. The picture was autographed by the city's Roman Catholic prelate, Giacomo Cardinal Lercaro, one of the strongest anti-Communists in Italy. Lercaro thanked me for my role in producing "The Remarkable Comrades," a documentary which ABC did in the Bologna area on the Communist party. Giuseppe Dozza, the Red Mayor, gave me the medal for the same reason. This was one for Ripley's *Believe It or Not.* Franco deserved most of the credit.

Franco went to see Dozza in his office. The mayor hadn't been defeated in a popular vote since the war, 16 years before. Dozza carried Bologna by a margin so safe the Christian Democrats said he might last longer than the Communist party in the Soviet Union. Some local people said that perhaps not even a pope could beat him. Of course, Lercaro did. Therein lies our drama.

Franco and Dozza played cat and mouse over the mayor's desk in the old ducal palace for more than an hour. The mouse won. Dozza finally agreed it would be a good idea to show an American television audience how the Communist party worked for the people in Italy. Specifically, how it made their bread, bottled their milk, canned their olive oil and even provided a suitable box for their funeral—all at popular peoples' prices.

We filmed the Communists in all these businesses. Also, how the party found them lawyers, jobs, or introduced them to new friends at a Red Cell meeting. Perhaps, one day, the aspirant would even receive a party card.

Cardinal Lercaro agreed to show how he and other Catholics fought the Reds. We filmed his Catholic workers' cooperatives, flying chapels, and, of course, the good prelate himself on the stump blasting the party.

Dozza would give a speech to factory workers in the morning, and we would film Lercaro addressing one of his workers' cooperatives in the afternoon. Dozza played soccer with children at one of the Reds' summer camps, while the cardinal held a raffle to raise money for orphans under his care.

We managed to keep each group from knowing what we were filming of the other side. But Judgment Day had to come. Both the cardinal and mayor expressed keen desires to view the finished product. After the documentary was shown to rave reviews in the United States, Franco and I haltingly got on a train for the reckoning in Bologna. We had an appointment with Dozza in the morning and Lercaro in the afternoon. We crossed our fingers and our toes.

When we arrived at the mayor's office, we were told he was

waiting for us in the council chamber. Dozza and the entire city council were present. We gulped.

We showed the film. Since it was in English, Franco gave a running commentary in Italian. Dozza watched scenes showing his workers singing *Bandiera Rossa*, (The Red Flag), his speeches to thousands of clapping workers, and the party at work in a host of different businesses. This was militant communism with a face of goodness. I watched Dozza as Lercaro came on the screen. The cardinal lashed out at the Communists. He, too, had his clapping workers and children. I watched Dozza's reaction with some trepidation. He had a wry grin on his face. At last, the lights went on.

Dozza rose and beamed. He embraced us. Tears welled up in his eyes. He shook our hands. Finally, he addressed all in the room, "It was the truth. That's the way things really are. We oppose Lercaro and he fights us. But you know what that film said? Let me tell you. It said that Lercaro could never be elected mayor!"

The council cheered.

Without a council vote and beaming from ear to ear, the mayor announced that he was bestowing the city's gold medal of honor on Franco and me. They would be mailed to us when he had them minted. Indeed, they were. Joy opened the package and said the large medal was 18-karat gold. I never told my parents. They would never have allowed me to accept a medal from the Communists. Franco, ever the lawyer, said, "We got the medals from the city of Bologna."

If Dozza loved it, I told myself nervously, Lercaro would excommunicate us from the church. Lercaro also had a surprise audience for us. He had invited many of his orphans to view the film at his residence. Franco gave another running commentary in English.

Lercaro and the children seemed mute for the first twenty minutes of the documentary since most of it dealt with the Communists. Finally, there was a long stretch featuring His Eminence and his followers. The orphans stomped, yelled, and cheered. Lercaro moved among workers, smiling, laughing. Then, among children, chatting and playfully mussing their hair. Cheering Catholics appeared in other scenes. Finally, the documentary was over. The orphans cheered again.

The cardinal addressed us as the youngsters listened, "An extraordinary film! Now the world sees what I am fighting—the opposition that I face and the battle that we must wage."

How unusual, I thought, that each side paid indirect tribute to the opposition. Each respected the other's fighting qualities. Lercaro continued, "But do you know what the documentary says beyond any doubt? The mayor cannot win! We will defeat him!"

The cardinal shook hands warmly and autographed his photo for each of us as a remembrance. We leaped out the front door of his residence and bounded happily down the street.

"Franco," I said, "you were magnificent."

Bucarelli replied, "I think I could have made a good mayor . . . maybe even a cardinal!"

We laughed as our train hooted happily all the way to Rome.

* * *

When Pope Paul VI decided to visit the Holy Land in 1964, Franco began pacing the floor in the office. I had never seen him so agitated. Finally, he came to me and said, "I know what to say to priests and cardinals. And I know what to say to Communists, Italian politicians and Americans. But to Arabs and Jews, I confess, I don't know what to say."

Since he probably would make the trip to the Mideast in some capacity, Franco tormented himself about the Arabs and Israelis for a week. Finally, I said to him, "Franco, I've solved half your problem. You're going only to Israel. Figure out what to say to the Jews."

He grinned. "Shalom! I'm already thinking."

I flew to Jordan to cover the Arab side of the Pope's visit and

Franco enplaned for Tel Aviv. He was to coordinate our film shipments to New York. To Franco, of course, that meant he had to line up his own private Mafia.

I had told him to spend as much money as he felt necessary in making sure that NBC and CBS didn't ship their film more quickly than ours to New York. Those weren't the days of fast camera tape and satellites.

Franco said little about his hopes and plans. That made me uneasy. Before we left Rome, I cautioned him, "Don't give away the White House, just Brooklyn—and Boston if you must."

I caught the plane for Amman, still wondering what Franco had up his sleeve. Despite his silence at times, it was never empty.

The papal visit to Jordan was utter chaos. Arab crowds broke through police lines and barricades to touch Paul. The Via Dolorosa was so mobbed that the Pontiff was forced to seek safety in a small building while police and Jordanian army troops moved people back. Broadcast newsmen had to battle our way in and out of these throngs. Otherwise, we wouldn't be able to get our stories on the air. At the end of the papal pilgrimage, because of endless hours of work and physical beating, I collapsed in bed for a day.

In a view of the Pope's visit, by special agreement, reporters were allowed to go from the Jordanian sector of Jerusalem through the Mandelbaum Gate into Israel. Newsmen wouldn't do it previously because their names would be placed on the Arab blacklist, preventing them from obtaining visas to Arab nations.

I crossed over under this agreement to meet Franco and my ABC colleagues. I hadn't seen or heard from Franco during the papal coverage, and wasn't sure whether he was in Jerusalem or Tel Aviv. I started to look for him at the King David Hotel in Jerusalem. I asked the concierge if he knew where any ABC men were staying. He replied, "I know only one ABC newsman—Franco."

I asked, "You mean Franco Bucarelli?"

"Yes," the concierge said. With that, he pulled a small, colorful object from beneath the counter. It was a toy Swiss Guard. I was transfixed. What was this all about? The concierge smiled and said, "Franco has returned to Tel Aviv. Could you be Mister Jack?"

"Yes," I replied.

"Franco has left a car and driver for you. We've been expecting you. I'll show you his car."

I was still very tired and didn't say much to the driver during the ride. However, as we approached the lights of the city, the two of us began to chat.

Yes, the driver knew Franco well. He grinned and added, "A sleepless man. He worked all hours. I was his driver."

The man said it with pride. I talked to myself, "*Mamma mia*, what kind of tip did Franco give him?"

We arrived at the Dan Hotel. I gave the driver a big tip, assuming Franco had treated him grandiosely. The man had turned on the lights inside the car to count the money. Suddenly, I saw another Swiss Guard. He was hanging from the right sunshade. The driver noticed my interest, smiled, and said, "Franco gave it to me."

Everyone at the Dan seemed to know Franco, but none knew where he was. However, Franco had left me a note, saying he was bidding farewell to friends. We were booked out on a flight the following morning. I went to bed.

A familiar voice rang out as I walked across the lobby about 7:00 a.m. Franco was shaking hands all around and promising to return to Israel with his wife, Lucia, and their son when he was born. It would be a boy, Franco assured them. He knew it would. Another Franco.

He greeted me, firing away in Italian a mile a minute. We never spoke English together. Both of us had eaten breakfast and we hailed a taxi for the airport. By the spirit of the many *Shaloms* from the hotel staff, Franco had tipped them handsomely.

On the road to the airport, Franco said the ABC brass in New York were delighted with his film shipments. We had never been beaten and some of our most important film arrived hours before the other networks. He said all the credit belong to his Israeli Mafia. I stared at him to explain, but he ignored the look of inquiry. This made me more suspicious than ever. I knew then that Franco had become a prince of the poor.

On the tarmac walking to the plane, I heard a burst of shouts. Two Israeli policemen were running in our direction. I turned and asked Franco, "Are we in trouble?"

Boarding passengers stopped and waited to see what would happen. I was relieved because the two officers were smiling. One shouted, "Franco! Franco!"

The pair embraced him. Franco introduced the gentlemen to me. The pair worked in Israeli airport customs. They had cleared much of our film to New York. One said with a grin, "For Franco's film, we even held a plane once for 10 minutes."

The trio talked of Franco's return to Israel one day. They saluted each other's families and relatives. Franco promised to come back and we continued toward the plane. As we walked, one of the customs men called out, *Arrivederci, Franco!* Franco shouted back, *Shalom!*

We found our seats on the plane and I looked out the window. One of the customs officers pulled something out of the side pocket of his suit. He began to wave the object. It was another Swiss Guard.

Yes, Franco said with a sheepish grin, he had carried a half-dozen boxes of the red-, yellow- and blue-striped dolls to Israel. Seventy-two in all. These were his tips. He explained, "I told the Israelis that these young fellows, who guarded the Pope at the Vatican, could not make the trip to the Holy Land. So the Israelis were taking their places. But they had come in spirit. In these tiny dolls. These Swiss Guards would help protect Israel."

What could I say to that?

* * *

As Franco had predicted, Lucia gave birth to a son. He never considered their wedding, a year before, as important. They had been engaged for years and marriage was only a matter of having enough money to launch their ship. Joy and I went to their Naples wedding. It was a wild, crazy blast no one would believe if I wrote it down. Rather than strain credulity, I pass—except to say that Neapolitan women could outdance a brigade of Russian cossacks.

The child was named Angelo after Angelo Giuseppe Roncalli. It seemed messages arrived from all the globe's important points: the Vatican, United States, Israel, Sicily, Naples, and Bologna—from both Mayor Dozza and Cardinal Lercaro.

Angelo was baptized in the Vatican (Lucia was a Catholic). I was the godfather and Joy, godmother. Lucia was so proud. Franco wept. Relatives came by the dozens and we celebrated elegantly with champagne at Casino Valadier, the fashionable restaurant atop Pincio Hill overlooking Rome.

Everyone kissed each other. I never kissed so many men in my life. Franco, holding the child, sat next to me. He whispered softly to his son again, "Tu sei una stellina." (You are a star.)

"Yes," I said to him, "a star is born."

It always seemed to me Rome was never lovelier than when a child was born. The blood of the ancient city was renewed. A baby is a fresh breath in the famous *venticello*, the breeze of the city. It is also a star that lights the way into the future.

Chapter 17

We Kiss Your Hands

IN THE SPRING and fall, whenever possible, we would return to Naples. We would visit friends and acquaintances there, including the parents of Franco and Lucia Bucarelli, Padre Mario Borelli, Lucky Luciano, and *San Gennaro*. Also, I would do stories on Americans at the large NATO base and features about the city.

San Gennaro was a particularly fascinating friend of ours, and we used to pray to him every first Sunday of May and on September 19. On those two days each year, the congealed blood of the patron saint of Naples liquified before the eyes of his "relatives," friends, and even unbelievers. Joy thought it was good to have a friend with such power.

Tradition says that *San Gennaro* (St. Januarius) was born in Naples around the year A.D. 270 and eventually became a Catholic bishop. In A.D. 305, however, the Roman emperor, Diocletian, chopped off his head in a wave of religious persecution. Gennaro's head and body were thrown to the lions, tradition recounts, but a woman bravely stepped from the crowd and carried off the remains of the saint to the nearby town of Pozzuoli. She is said to have extracted his blood and placed it in two vials. The persecution ended in A.D. 449 and one vial of blood was carried to the cathedral in Naples where the local folk came to venerate it.

More than 600 years ago, on the September 19 anniversary of Gennaro's martyrdom, the first "miracle" occurred. Neapolitans say the saint's blood began to liquify as they prayed before it. Ever since that day, as well as the first Sunday of May—the anniversary of Gennaro's return to Naples from Pozzuoli—the blood has liquified, except for the year in which Benito Mussolini declared war in World War II.

Physicians and scientists have, at various times, been allowed to extract some of the liquified blood from the vial. All reported it was human blood but were unable to explain the "miracle" scientifically.

On each anniversary of San Gennaro, a little after dawn, women arrive one by one at the cathedral. They walk to a side chapel where the gates are securely locked. A bust of the saint, an air of severity about it, looks through the bars of the gates at the faithful. Several rows of rickety, wooden chairs are lined up in front of the small chapel. These are gradually occupied by the women who wear black shawls and carry prayer books. The candles near the saint are lit by an altar boy. A priest opens the gates and places the vial of congealed blood on a pedestal before the faithful. Meantime, the cathedral fills with other people, including foreign tourists.

Centuries ago, the ancestors of these woman formed their own religious "order," independent of church and priest. They gave their organization their own blessing and called themselves "The Relatives of San Gennaro." The unorthodox group became a local tradition and, like any Neapolitan tradition, no one dared try to abolish it.

Badges of honor, passed down from mother to daughter, ordained the seating arrangements. The longer a continuous family line had been established with the saint, the closer each "relative" would be to the vial of blood. The women, in no need of a priest, led all the prayers themselves. Joy and I had never heard such invocations:

"Alright, Genna', make the miracle!"

The thick Neapolitan dialect rose in pitch with each supplication. Perspiration broke out on the foreheads of most of the women. The tones rose higher and angrier:

"Can't you hear, Genna', make the miracle!"

"Start, Genna, don't let us make a bad showing!"

"Don't you love us anymore?"

"What are you waiting for?"

"Come on, you yellow face, make the miracle!"

Some visitors, especially foreigners, were somewhat aghast at the rising crescendo and angry faces of the women. As any Neapolitan would tell them, however, the ladies spoke the genuine tongue of local relatives.

During one visit, we waited nearly three hours for the blood to liquify. The chanting became more intense as the blood processed itself. Toward the end, the women broke into frenzied shouting and, finally, their voices roared. When all the blood had liquified, the tumult subsided into reverent prayer. The "relatives" said a thanksgiving aspiration to their patron saint, and then rushed out of the cathedral. No one was allowed to precede them. On the street, they proclaimed to all who could hear, *Miracolo! Miracolo!* (Miracle! Miracle!)

The glad tidings were shouted from apartment window to window and piazza to piazza. *San Gennaro! Il miracolo!*

The protector of all Neapolitans thus assured the faithful he would continue to be with them on their daily journey. The perfume of his promise carried across the city like a fresh breeze from the bay. Neapolitans sighed, "Amen."

An evening *festa* followed with music, dancing, food and, of course, local wine. Naples, often described as the Sin City of Italy, trumpeted salvation. Dock workers—"spinning tops," a local description of street urchins spinning out of the arms of the law—and 130,000 Neapolitans named Gennaro cheered.

The "miracle" and feast are still celebrated today, not only in Naples but in New York and other parts of the United States that have large numbers of Neapolitan descendents. Joy and I attended the block celebration in Manhattan's Little Italy in 1990. It was a mild imitation of the Naples festivities, but the food was good and the music and street dancing exuberant.

* * *

Mario Borelli was a priest whose faith took him from the altar to the darkest, dirtiest alleys of Naples. He became a *scugnizzo*, a rough ragamuffin of the streets. Shuned by shopkeepers, hunted by police, Padre Borelli became an animal in the gutters of Naples — by choice.

Franco introduced me to Borelli in the early 1960s. The priest told me his soul was torn apart by what he had to do, starting a decade earlier, to become a street urchin. He had stolen with them, worked the black market, and slept in the back alleys. In bad days, he went hungry with them. Borelli's dream was to bring "my street urchins" to the light and grace of God.

In 1963, the last time I saw him, he was standing in a junkyard, his junkyard. He was saying the most important thing in life for a boy was to believe in something or someone. Around him were scraps of iron, brass, broken furniture, and demolished cars. He compared them to the boys he was trying to salvage from Naples's mean streets — *his* boys.

"I was angry," he said. "I was bitter. I knew I couldn't remain a priest unless I did something worthy of a priest. It's like what I said to Morris West, the Australian author, when he came here. I said I couldn't stand at the altar of God and hold the body of Christ in my hands while the bodies of his children slept in the alleys of Naples."

With the permission of his cardinal, Padre Borelli walked out the door of his church one day in a dirty shirt and pants, an old cap, and workmen's shoes. Plus a couple of cigarettes. He was 28

years old, five feet, six inches tall, and sandy haired. He was joining the street urchins.

A scugnizzo carried the soul of a man in the body of a boy.
He was shredded of innocence, locked out of a home and even
society itself. He was empty of any paternal love, hungered for
pasta and water and a sweater to cover his raggedy shirt. He was
a thief and a liar who lived in terror of the police. He slept much
of the day and robbed at night. His home was the black market
and his love the price of a prostitute.

Thousands of these urchins moved into the streets of Naples
during and after World War II. They were still there after the
Korean war. Some were still in the streets when we left Italy in
1964. For most, they had no other place to go. Some are still on
Naples's streets today.

Padre Borelli became a lookout while they robbed shops and
offices. When they harangued "fences" for more money in return for their stolen goods, Borelli argued too. He ate their bread
and smoked their black-market cigarettes. When these ran out,
he squatted down to pick up butts and got in line at a nuns'
kitchen for soup. No one in the back alleys knew Borelli was a
priest. He later explained, "It was the only way I knew to get into
their hearts."

I asked him about his priestly vocation and vows. He replied,
"I always tried to withdraw myself from the direct act of sin. For
example, I never personally stole. My life was, so to speak, on
the razor's edge. I lived by my wits."

One night in a back alley, Borelli faced his scugnizzi as he really was, a priest. They looked at his cassock and collar in disbelief. The priest's words were simple, "Come with me. I have some
bread, shelter, and love you because I am also a street urchin."

Borelli told me he felt like Damien on the island of Mo-
lokai. He recalled Damien's dramatic words to those misbe-
gotten souls after he had been stricken with their disease, "We
lepers . . ."

About a dozen boys got up and followed him. Borelli led

them to an abandoned church. It was a slow, halting march for the street urchins because they habitually trusted no one.

When the group arrived at the church, the priest made a promise: all were free to come and go from the "House of Urchins" as they pleased. There would be no rules and no sermons. Just some mattresses, old bed covers, worn clothes, spaghetti, macaroni, bread, tomatoes, and water. Borelli made one more point, "I love all of you and will try to protect you."

That was the 1950 beginning. Until 1964, more than two-thousand boys—five years old and up—came to him for a hand-out and a bed. Some stayed a week, others hung around for months and years. When I last saw him, the priest had two houses for his urchins, one in an old church and another in an abandoned granary. He also fashioned a small chapel and a school. Through the years, several priests and others assisted Borelli as volunteers.

The priest had not changed much through the years. Borelli was in his early forties when I left him. He was still a fighter, a rugged little man with a tongue sharpened in the streets. He and his urchins were still living hand-to-mouth. The boys were collecting junk in the later years and Borelli ran his own junkyard. It was small but regular income. As the priest put it to me, "As you Americans say, I ask no quarter."

To me, Borelli was a symbol of Naples. He was a personification of passion. I can hear his voice now, calling one of his boys. I can see one of them spinning out of the arms of a policeman. He is running and running and running. Only this time, someone waits for him.

*   *   *

Joy and I met Lucky Luciano, who lived in Naples, by chance one evening in Palermo, Sicily. I had known him for about three years. We met during various interviews and several other encounters in Naples. Luciano had been the reputed longtime king of the New York underworld and was undoubtedly one of the worst criminals in U.S. history. He was a crime figure of staggering proportions—in murder, robbery, drugs, prostitution, union and underworld beatings, and a host of other criminal activities. When he was finally extradited to Italy as an undesirable alien, Luciano insisted he was as American as Jack Armstrong, the onetime, figurative all-American boy. That astonished a lot of people but never Luciano. He wore the American flag on his sleeve wherever he went in Italy.

Luciano asked us if we would like to have dinner with him later that evening at a restaurant overlooking the city. We agreed. Luciano didn't show up. A few months later, I met him by accident outside a restaurant in Naples and mentioned the dinner engagement. Luciano never offered an explanation. He merely asked me to convey his apologies to my wife.

Unpredictability appeared to be his living pattern—never doing the same thing two days in a row, constantly changing restaurants, nightclubs, and other hangouts, rarely keeping an appointment on time and sometimes not at all.

I concluded he feared a contract hit, but if that were the case, Luciano hid it well. He was always jovial with me, usually inquired about my wife and kids, and constantly asked if I had any big news from the States. We were sitting at the California Bar having espresso one day and Luciano suddenly blurted, "They call me an Italian gangster. That doesn't make sense. I left Sicily when I was four years old. If they want to call me a gangster, they have to call me an American gangster."

The sudden, brief speech surprised me. But that was Luciano, master of the unexpected. I asked him why he mentioned the subject, and he simply shrugged. He returned to the discussion of my family and asked if we were willing to educate our boys in Italy. I replied that grade school would be fine but not high school. They would then become too Italianized.

Luciano's own life centered around a woman by the name of Igea Lissoni. They shared a modern but not luxurious apartment on the fifth floor of a building on Naples's Via Tasso. Igea was an attractive middle-aged woman who spoke little and only quietly when she did. The story on the street was the two met at a Naples nightclub in 1948, and Igea became Lucky's companion shortly afterward.

She became seriously ill after I met her, and was in poor health for about a year. Luciano never revealed what was wrong with her, but once mentioned she had had an operation. He was said to have told the Italian surgeon, "She's not going to make it. She's lost her hope."

Luciano was right. Igea died shortly afterward. Lucky was never quite the same after her passing. Igea was 37 at her death; Luciano was then 66.

In later times, Luciano went out of his way to hail me whenever he saw me in Naples, but he spoke less and less. He was hungry to hear news of the States. I noticed his well-barbered gray hair was becoming white. He was a lonely man and, several times when I saw him walking around Naples, he seemed lost. Yet he clung to his impeccable dress, a blue-serge suit with a silver or dark silk tie.

One night, Luciano invited Franco and me to a nightclub. He ordered a bottle of champagne, took a sip, and left with only a brief good-bye. I presume he paid while walking out. I turned to Franco and said, "Luciano's a very complex guy."

Luciano always maintained he was an American, not an Italian. He spoke "American" whenever possible although he was fluent in Italian, Neapolitan, and Sicilian.

The last time I saw Lucky was in early 1962. I was on my way with Franco to cover a story in the southern town of Molfetta. He was sitting, reading the *Rome Daily American* at the California Bar and Grill. We decided not to interrupt him and sat by ourselves. Luciano soon spotted us and invited us to his table. I fired a quick question at him, "When are you going to write your book?"

Luciano chuckled. He habitually never showed surprise. He

mentioned a movie—a producer was coming from Spain to meet him and talk about doing his life story. Lucky turned to me and said, "You know more about me than this guy. Why don't you write it?"

I replied, "Lucky, you'll never write your story. But I'm ready if and when you are."

He laughed, hunched his shoulders, and his eyes seemed to say, "Yeah, in a thousand years."

As Franco and I were leaving, a raggedy Italian man of about 50 walked up to Luciano and whispered in his ear. I caught a few words, "Wife . . . children . . . food."

It was a touch. Lucky was known to be one of the softest touches in town. I watched him pull out a large note. It was 5,000 lire ($8). Lucky slipped it to the man. I shall never forget what the man said, *Baciamo le mani, Don Salvatore!* (Charles). *Baciamo le mani!* (We kiss your hands.)

Don is a term of maximum respect. It's used primarily from Naples south into Calabria and the islands of Sardinia and Sicily. The honorary title goes back centuries to the times of barbarian and later conquerors. It comes from the Latin *Dominus*, meaning Lord. A servant would thus address his master. The poor addressed nobility and landowners in this manner. The term also came to mean an elder or wise person in terms of age or profession. Priests were referred to as *Don* in most southern towns.

Baciamo le mani is also expression of supreme respect. In earlier centuries, serfs showed deference to their lord by kissing his hands. The kissing died, but the custom remained in the form of language and was usually uttered with a slight bow of the head.

The plural *We* was usually used. Southern Italians often spoke in the plural—from my family to yours.

In 1962, during the Algerian war, I was standing in the lobby of the Aletti Hotel in Algiers. Winston Burdett, a CBS news correspondent who also lived in Rome, crossed the room and said, "Lucky Luciano is dead."

Burdett explained he had received the news while speaking

with his Rome office. Luciano was standing at the airport in Naples waiting for a movie producer from Spain. Suddenly, he keeled over and was dead shortly afterward. Lucky, true to his code of silence, never uttered a word during his final moments. An examining physician later said Luciano had died of a heart attack.

I didn't respond to Burdett. There was nothing to say. I thought of the time that Luciano hunched his shoulders at the thought of collaborating on a book and said with his eyes, "Yeah, in a thousand years."

* * *

Pupetta Maresca was big, buxom, and with child when she pulled a pistol out of her purse and pumped three slugs into one of the brothers who allegedly killed her man. *Pupetta* means Baby Doll and her name was splashed in bold headlines from Sicily to the Alps. They called her the Pistol-Packin' Mama and Pistol-Packin' Pupetta. It was the most sensational murder trial during our years in Italy and I covered it for months.

Pupetta's sole defense rested in these simple words, "There was no other way to preserve my honor. I loved my husband."

This was the oldest and best defense in southern Italy—a crime of honor committed in passion. The honor of the family.

The truth was much less chivalrous. Police reported that Pupetta's husband was the leader of the notorious Neapolitan *Camorra*, a band of thieves and muscle men patterned after the Mafia. He and his mob allegedly were involved in price fixing and protection payoffs in the Neapolitan vegetable and other markets. They were also big in other rackets. The man accused of killing Pupetta's husband was part of a gang of brothers said to be trying to take over his turf. Murder was the price of their trade.

Another crime of honor rocked Sicily about the same time. Vincenzina confessed to Enzo, her fiancé, that she had an earlier affair with a certain Ernesto. Ernesto left her, however, to marry another. Enzo and the girl's parents were outraged at the 21-year-old's tearful revelation. Vincenzina was told she must uphold the code of family honor. She followed her first love, caught up with him at a bus stop, and plunged a butcher knife into his chest and stomach. The wounds were fatal.

Vincenzina was sentenced to three years in jail. The judge explained the light sentence, "A woman must be the guardian of her own honor."

The crime of honor also infiltrated the north. In Milan, pretty Maria and her mother defended the family name. Swept away in a torrent of love, Maria had an extended affair with a young man who promised to marry her. The suitor got cold feet, however, and the mother told Maria what to do. Maria whipped out a pistol and murdered the young man in cold blood. Northern courts were less accommodating about crimes of honor. Maria was sentenced to 14 years for murder and her mother got nine as an accomplice. Civil rights groups appealed the verdict to the Italian Supreme Court in a passionate outcry of injustice: Why did Vencenzina receive only three years from a judge in Sicily and Maria nearly five times that sentence in Milan for a similar crime?

Northern and southern legalists argued for months about their different scales of justice. The debate set the stage for Pupetta Maresca's trial in Naples. Northern newspapers shipped down a railroad car of reporters to cover the proceedings. They were to determine which system of justice was more in keeping with the times and the crime.

Pupetta was ready for her dramatic hour. She played her role like Elenora Duse, perhaps the greatest Italian actress in history.

Pupetta and her family slipped this story to newsmen. The afternoon before the shooting, the young expectant wife drove out of Naples to the small church of Our Lady of Pompeii. There, seen by only a gardener, she knelt before the Madonna and asked her guidance. Tears of her husband's loss washed down Pupetta's cheeks. But did they wash away the stain of dishonor left by her husband's killing? Baby Doll heard the Madonna. The Virgin cried for vengeance. Baby Doll would return to Naples and uphold her husband's good name.

When the trial opened before a packed courtroom, the prosecutor quickly pointed out the significance of Pupetta's visit to the Madonna. He said it was the clearest possible proof that Baby Doll had committed premeditated murder. It could therefore not be argued, he insisted, that the defendant acted in a moment of uncontrollable passion.

Pandemonium broke loose in the courtroom. The crowd hooted the prosecutor. Women called out to Baby Doll: "The Madonna is with you, child! Long live the Madonna!"

Pupetta's lawyers—she had a battery—wisely never introduced the Madonna scene.

Throughout the trial, there was never an empty seat in the courtroom. The national debate about light and tough sentences for major crimes of honor continued in heat and headlines. Most of Italy had chosen one side or the other.

It became obvious the defense cared much more about public opinion than their judge's views. I thought that was a big mistake. But who was I to challenge Neapolitans on their home turf? You could get shot for less than that.

Baby Doll's lawyers spent virtually the entire trial electrifying the courtroom with emotion, from wails of sorrow about this pregnant widow to the passion that had overwhelmed her heart and mind. Pupetta's greatest defense was her unborn child.

I remember well the day the judge rendered his verdict. Pupetta Maresca rose from her chair and, beneath the veil of sadness that covered her face during the trial, she wore a smirk. A confident smirk.

Carabinieri stood at attention throughout the courtroom. The waiting crowd spilled out onto the street. The two families— Pupetta's and that of her victim—stared coldly at the judge. Except for occasional heavy breathing, the room was still. The judge then issued his verdict, "Guilty!"

Violent screams and curses whipsawed the air. Women fainted. Men shook their fists at the judge. One woman, looking at the stone-faced Pupetta, shouted, "You are a martyr!"

Another woman barked at the judge, "You wretch!"

Still another woman wailed hysterically, "The Madonna proclaims your innocence from the heavens!"

Giving the judge the cuckold sign, a man called out, "God forbid, you bastard!"

Amid the uproar, Pupetta's triumphant smirk now gone, the judge sentenced Baby Doll to 12 years in prison. However, because of the child, she was to be placed in a women's correctional facility, Pupetta's face was crimson with a mixture of consternation and rage.

In the continuing pandemonium of the courtroom, the whole South seemed to rise before my eyes. Some of the voices and heartbreak of the past welled up in my mind . . .

The voice of the youngster at the grave of Salvatore Giuliano, "Turridu is now free."

The mayor of Molfetta, "If only we could emigrate to Hoboken, New Jersey."

The fisherman holding the hands of his little children in the village of Cariati. His wife had been working as a housemaid in London so the family could eat and be clothed. The man said, "I have not seen my wife in two and one-half years."

And those terrible but reverent words of the poor man, "We kiss your hands, Don Salvatore. We kiss your hands."

As Pupetta stood there mute, I was drowning in emotion. All the agony I had witnessed in the South overwhelmed me. The poverty. The hopelessness. The pervasive sorrow in the black dress of the people.

A feeling of deep longing overcame me. I wanted to see the United States. I was a foreigner here. I wanted to go home.

Chapter 18

A Grain of Sand

EVERY AUGUST, LIKE most Italians, our family went on vacation for a month. Each year, Signor Antonio Garbrielli, the mover, would come to our apartment for the children's beds, linens, the medicine chest, kitchen utensils, and the boys' shovels and pails. Every August first, the boys kissed Signor Garbrielli on the cheek and told him his van wouldn't be large enough. Each year, except our first, we rented a house on the beach near Anzio from Signora Vetriani. And all of us got a tan as dark as ripe Sicilian grapes.

We shopped at the same fruit market in Anzio every summer. It was just off the main piazza, run by the father with the bad eye and his four sons. We bought our meat from the same butcher, who had two good eyes and a big thumb. His place was to the right of the church in the square. We always shopped at the delicatessen across the piazza from the pharmacy. The boys and I went to the same barber every vacation—the fat little man with the small place on the left as one walked along the port. And each year, Joy bought at last one new dress at Tato's boutique while the boys and I sat there unable to understand why their discussions were so excited. Nothing seemed to change at Anzio. That was the way we liked it.

Our daily schedule ran like clockwork. In the morning, we swam in the Mediterranean and played in the hot sand on the beach. After lunch, everyone had a siesta (Italians adopted the Spanish word). Then all of us piled in the car and went for a drive to see the nearby towns and beaches.

The scars of the Anzio beachhead, the blood and bones of the many young Americans who had fallen there, had disappeared. But we often drove to the American military cemetery at nearby Nettuno, knelt at the graves and prayed. Thousands of crosses stood in neat rows. Many Italians brought flowers to the graves of these youngsters they had never known. One afternoon, I heard an Italian gardener say to a visitor, "This is the only territory that the Americans ever kept."

At least once each summer, we stopped at Nettuno's Church of Santa Maria Goretti. We viewed her preserved body beneath the altar. Few American visitors seemed to know her story or why the Roman Catholic Church had canonized little Maria a saint. She was not yet in her teens when the girl was beaten to death defending her virginity. The man convicted of the crime was sentenced to prison but later was freed to become a monk. He still lived in a nearby monastery in the early 1960s. The man publicly asked her parents' forgiveness and prayed to Maria every day to pardon him.

On return to Anzio, we had pizza or ice cream in the main square. This was merely an appetizer before dinner. We headed home and the boys and I usually went in search of new seashells along the beach. After finishing dinner about 9:00 p.m., the boys went to bed and Joy and I would sit on the open porch to catch the evening breeze. We scanned the sea, watching the bobbing lights of small fishing boats.

Every once in a while, Joy and I would drive to an Anzio cliff and look out to sea from the ruins of the summer villa of Emperor Nero. We would compare notes on ancient Roman history, and Joy always knew the most. But I knew much more Latin.

One day stretched into the next in a seamless pattern. None of us would have changed a thing.

On many Saturday evenings, there would be an orchestra concert in Anzio's central piazza. People would come from miles around, bringing small armies of children. The youngsters always made more noise than the orchestra, but it was great fun for all.

When we ate out, it was always at Zia Genevra, a tiny, vine-covered trattoria near a church. The man and wife who owned the place became our best friends in Anzio. Their one waiter, Angelo, carried to our table year after year the most magnificent fish dishes we had ever eaten. That was also the testimony of the many friends and acquaintances we invited there for dinner. The *zuppa di pesce* (fish soup) was so good that Joy and I would sometimes sneak away from Rome during the winter and drive the hour and fifteen minutes to Anzio to enjoy it. The soup consisted of more than a half dozen types of seafood, cooked in a special thick juice that had a wild tang. The bill, including dessert and coffee, was never more than two dollars per person. Ye gods, I had finally found paradise!

We had heard from an Italian friend about an intriguing island called Ponza. He said it was paradise. The man described it rising out of the Mediterranean approximately three hours by ferryboat from Anzio. Joy and I went there several days a year, once for a week, over a five-year span. The island was as memorable to us as Anzio, a spectacular rock at the end of all our rainbows.

The first time I saw Ponza, I thought the island was a scene from *Paradise Lost*. It was crescent-shaped, blessed with a natural harbor and several magnificent beaches. Above its port, the land was terraced just as in the times of the ancient Romans. As the ferry entered the harbor, these terraces and white-washed cottages seemed to rise from sleep in a gesture of greeting. In the port itself, scores of small fishing boats danced lightly on the water. Fishermen sat on them tending their nets.

Joy and I got off the ferry that summer day in 1959 looking for a place to sleep for the night. We were surrounded by shouting children. None sold anything. None tugged at our arms. They were shouting, "Americano. Americano."

"They've got our number," I said to Joy.

"And how!" she hollered back.

Then, we got an indication why. Emblazoned across their T-shirts here: NEW YORK YANKEES . . . NEW YORK GIANTS . . . BROOKLYN DODGERS.

That was before the Giants and Dodgers moved to California pastures. I feel sure today some shirts say NEW YORK METS.

I took a youngster by the arm and asked in Italian, "Where did you get the shirts?"

"America," he responded.

"From whom?" I asked.

"Relatives," he answered. "Everybody on Ponza has a relative in America."

"Everybody?" I inquired.

"Everybody!" the youngster repeated.

It was *Ferragosto*, August 14, the biggest summer holiday. The one hotel was filled. Rooms in private homes had been booked for weeks by mainlanders. We slept on makeshift cots in a school room that night. Several local housewives had appropriated the school and established their own hotel. Undoubtedly, the local fix was in.

Some 5,000 persons resided on the island. And about 10,000 Ponsese, as they called themselves, lived in the United States. Mayor Gennaro Valiante explained this to me:

"For every man, woman and child here, we have two in America. Nearly 5,000 of those, equal to our entire population here, live in New York City. Most of those live on three streets in the Bronx—149th, 150th and 151st."

That explained the baseball T-shirts. The mayor continued, "There's not one family on the island that doesn't have a relative in America. They send us clothes, money, and other things. Nine out of ten homes standing here today were built with American dollars."

I went to see the local priest since more questions arose each day. Monsignor Luigi Maria Dies had been pastor of the island's patron church of San Silverio for 20 years. He received me in his kitchen, offered cookies, and American instant coffee. He looked out on most of Ponza from a kitchen window and said, "Every boy on the island, without exception, wants to go to America. They study 'American' in school. We don't say 'English' because nobody's going to England. *America* is a holy word here.

"These souls are entrusted to me but I seem to raise them only for export. Few return except a few souls to retire. This is a poor place. But it bothers me to give away our only valuable possession, our sons and daughters."

The gray-haired pastor had been holding a book in his hands. He handed it to me. I was surprised to see it was an Italian translation of *No Man Is an Island*, by the American monk, Thomas Merton. I understood the priest's message.

A ferry carried tourists to Ponza three times a week during the summer season. Visitors also came on three-time-a-week supply ships from the nearest mainland city of Formia and also from Naples. During the rest of the year, supply ships arrived from Formia and Naples only once a week. Sometimes, because of rough winter seas, they weren't able to make the trip for two weeks or longer. Ponza was, therefore, cut off from the mainland except by telephone, Italian radio, or helicopters during a medical emergency.

The island was dependent on the mainland for pure drinking water and so the delay of a tanker by blustery weather was a serious concern. Meat and vegetables, even necessary milk and fruit for babies, sometimes became scarce or even nonexistent at times because of high seas. Although many island folk had summer gardens and canned their own fruits and vegetables, the gardens were so small due to the rocky soil, and canned food didn't last through the winter.

When food was scarce and money scarcer, fishermen would

defy the dangerous seas and take to their largest boats in an attempt to haul in fish. Women would gather in the church to pray for the safety of their men and light votive candles at home. They closed their shutters so as not to look at the stormy waves.

I sat on a rock one summer morning talking with Sam Scotti. Sam was known around the island as an *Americano* since he had worked in New York. Scotti was a balding little gray-haired fellow in his late sixties with an elfin grin.

"The summer is nice for kids here," he reflected, "They can play, swim, and fish. But the winters wash away whatever dreams they have. They are cold and cruel without much food. So youngsters begin to look beyond the island, over the horizon to America."

Sam paused to collect his reflections and continued, "I was a kid in 1912. All I had, when I took the boat from Naples to New York, were the clothes on my back and some hard salami and cheese. A friend of the family was going to meet me in New York. When I got there, I found work on a construction gang. I was lucky because I could start paying back the boat fare. In all, I spent 35 years in New York construction. I helped build Manhattan. Buildings in every part of town. I kept mixing mortar, hauling more than my weight, and making money. You didn't have to speak English on the job in those days. And the Italians stuck together. We all learned enough English to get by."

Sam pointed across the harbor and smiled. "Some of us returned. See that small beach area with the houses in back? That's La Forna. People here call it 'The American Colony' because all 60 husbands, sometimes their wives, worked in America. They're now retired and drawing U.S. Social Security. Local folk say we're rich. A family is fine here on $70 to $80 a month. If a guy can swing $100 a month, he can consider himself a king."

I asked, "What brought them back? Why did you return, Sam?"

Scotti tossed a small stick in the water, watched it for a while, and finally replied, "Many never left Ponza. They were always homesick for mother and father, brothers and sisters. They missed the sea, the fresh air, the old Italian ways of doing things. Others returned because it's cheaper living here."

"You, Sam?" I inquired again.

"I don't know," he said. "I really don't. If I had to give an answer, I'd say that I was like most. I never really left the place. New York was always fast, in a hurry, and I could never catch up with myself. I was a calm, quiet guy. I liked to think, to walk, to fish. It wasn't easy to work construction in New York."

"Do you miss New York?" I asked.

"I'd go back tomorrow," Sam answered. "It's exciting, alive."

"Why don't you return?" I questioned.

"I can't," Sam said. "There's no place for me. I got no place there. I'm nobody. One in millions. Here, I'm somebody."

Sam introduced me to others who had lived and worked in America: Biagiio Migliaccio, 25 years on Morris Avenue in the Bronx; Tomasso Tricoli, 45 years a longshoreman in Brooklyn; Aniello Esposito, 48 years a construction worker in Manhattan, and Salvatore Feola, who finally saved enough money to buy a small fishing boat in Brooklyn.

Danny D'Arco, born on the island and then living in New York, became the unofficial American ambassador to Ponza. Danny returned with his wife every two years and brought firsthand accounts of hundreds of Ponza people in the New York area. He owned a restaurant on Court Street in Brooklyn, and many Ponsese regularly gathered there. So Danny was full of news.

Ponza was a gift of nature. Magnificent beaches dotted its shoreline. As a lifelong swimmer, I was in heaven. The sea's blue-green water was so clear I could see to depths of 10 and sometimes 25 feet with the naked eye. The shoreline was excellent for skin diving and all-around underwater swimming. At least a dozen natural grottoes sliced under the walls of rocks and cliffs. One seemed almost as beautiful as the famous Blue Grotto of Capri.

No water ran in most Ponsese homes in those days. No cars bumped over the roads, only two island buses and some motor scooters. Several doctors were in residence but there was no hospital. During bad winter weather, a seaplane or helicopter from the mainland would arrive in a medical emergency. Patients would be rowed out to the seaplane in boats, and this was often hazardous.

School consisted of five grades. After that, boys often went to sea fishing with their fathers and older brothers. Girls assumed household duties. Some children were sent to higher-grade mainland schools but most families didn't have the money to pay for this. Teenage girls became maids in Naples, Rome, or other cities.

Fishermen, whose families constituted 80 percent of the population, earned an average of about $50 a month. Some made as little as $30 a month. Fish, caught at sea, was the basic food. Rents ranged from $10 to $25 a month for houses with two to five rooms.

The people of Ponza were outspokenly anti-Fascist. Mussolini treated the island as a penal colony. During *Il Duce's* dictatorship, political malcontents, including socialist leader Pietro Nenni, were shipped into exile at Ponza.

I once wrote a newspaper article about Ponza that included this statement: "Unlike the fabled Isle of Capri, no great story has ever been written about Ponza, no memorable music composed, no poetry . . ."

After sending a clipping to the mayor, he wrote to me a few weeks later. It was a kind letter of thanks but gently closed with, "There was a poet who stopped at Ponza. A Greek. We have a translation of some verse that he composed here. I should like to show it to you. His name was Homer . . ."

Ponza has a legend which is recounted by the smallest schoolboy. Centuries ago, Italian soldiers were stationed on the nearby island of Zannone. They were to signal coastal towns if any suspicious ships approached Italy. This was done by lighting bonfires which relayed various messages.

Winter blew in and the waves climbed high. The garrison exhausted its stores of food. One day, in their famine, some soldiers saw an old man rowing a boat at sea and they hailed him. The old man called back, telling them not to be afraid but to get into their small rowboats and follow him. He would lead them to food and shelter on the nearby island of Ponza.

The soldiers were afraid. But seeing the old man in the boat, and realizing that their hunger had become unbearable, several climbed into boats and began to row toward him. Others followed. They rowed and rowed, despite waves threatening to swamp them, and finally arrived safely at Ponza. The old man disappeared as they neared shore.

Some of the soldiers immediately went to church to pray for the old man and give thanks for their safe journey. On entering the church, the soldiers were stunned. There before them was the face of the old man in the sea. It was a statue of the island's patron saint, San Silverio, pope and martyr of the sixth century.

The feast of San Silverio falls on June 20. Every year, the Ponsese form a procession and march around the island. Then, through the evening and into the night, they celebrate the feast day. It is a day of thanksgiving, expressing their gratitude to the saint for protecting local fishermen. Most boys born in June are named Silverio. So are a good number born at other times. So if a Silverio crosses your path, you're probably correct in assuming he has some connection with Ponza.

I always felt sad on leaving Ponza. I would climb a hill to fetch Sam Scotti at his cottage. We would have a glass of wine and later take his favorite walk along a beach. I would wax poetic about the beauty of the place. He would promise to write me during the winter. Sam was always surprised by the fact that my work had taken me to more than 60 countries, yet I never felt any place was more humanly warm and beautiful than Ponza.

I recall one of our last meetings. I tried to get Sam to chat more about the island. We were walking along a beach. He suddenly stopped, reached down and came up with something in his right hand. Opening the palm, Sam said: "This is Ponza."

"I don't see anything, Sam," I countered.

"Look again," he insisted.

I looked but saw nothing. Finally, Sam said softly, "See it— the grain of sand."

It took some time for me to understand Sam's meaning—that the tiny grain of sand indicated the miniscule importance of Ponza in the world.

I remember the day I left Ponza for the last time. The ferry pulled slowly out of the harbor. I watched from a railing as so many of the island's sons and daughters had done in the past. Boys were diving from the rocks to the left of the church, splashing in the sea. The white-washed cottages climbed up the terraced landscape as the sun descended. Fishing boats, hung with lights, chugged after the falling sun. Soon it would be dark and the men would lower their nets.

What poetry, I asked myself, must Homer have written when he landed here more than 2,000 years ago? What an incredible odyssey—for both of us. I would not forget Ponza. All I had to do was reach down on a beach anywhere and pick up a grain of sand.

Before we left Italy, more tourists had discovered the island. Surprisingly, many were French and most of those came from Paris. I always found that somewhat ironic. The whole world wanted to visit Paris and Parisians went to unknown Ponza.

Today, the chic of Paris flood Ponza with their bikinis, long fingernails, cigarette holders, scented perfumes, and men's unbuttoned silk shirts. They come to escape the French capital yet bring it with them. The Ponsese women detest the flaunting nakedness of the French women on their beaches and the Ponsese men dislike the Frenchmen's airs of superiority. It's an uneasy atmosphere at times.

Ponza prices reflect years of European higher salaries and inflation. They have skyrocketed at least 15 times more than what they were in 1964. Other rich Europeans have discovered the island, and dock their yachts at the port. They're now buying local property for summer getaways. All this has been a great economic blessing for some families, but Ponza itself, we're told by Italian friends, will never be the same again. Old visitors like us, who sought its solitude and easy, earthy way of life, say it's now truly a lost paradise.

Chapter 19

Spaghetti on-the-Rocks

THERE WERE EIGHT political parties in Italy. Thus, eight days in the political week. This stretched the patience and imagination of all foreigners. I once called it spaghetti on-the-rocks— a contradiction in terms.

Millions of Italians ignored politics. They viewed politicians as universally dishonest. Others played the game in hopes of gaining a job, obtaining a favor or, the few, changing the direction of the nation. Italy's politicians were mostly lifetime professionals and, it seemed, talked forever. Italy has had more than 50 governments since World War II—more than the number of popes or even great tenors.

The Christian Democrats have been in power, until the most recent elections, since the United States and Vatican helped put them there at the close of World War II. A so-called National party, headed by a businessman, was elected in 1994. The Christian Democrats were divided into left and right. These two camps have always been further split by conflicting power grabs, money and other scandals, and clashing personalities.

Two distinct Socialist parties grubbed for votes during our

spaghetti days. One was run by Giuseppe Saragat, who was to become President of the republic, and were called the Democrat Socialists. The other, which simply called itself the Socialists, was divided into two warring factions. One group were fellow travelers with the Communists. The other took an independent road. Both were held together for decades by the worn reins of an extremely astute gentleman blessed with the balance of a juggler, Pietro Nenni.

The Communist party boasted it was the most unified but, paradoxically, it was ideologically split into four "collectives" for many years. The Young Lions eventually seized power from the Old Guards. One group followed the Moscow line as opposed to those who favored Peiping or Peking (now Beijing). The party was highly capitalistic since its collectives fiercely competed with many capitalistic businesses in open Italian markets. For example, the funeral business.

If that simple start seems confusing, add the Liberal party. It was not liberal at all. The Liberals spoke for big business and other major financial interests. Giovanni Malagodi ran the party for many years. He spoke impeccable English with an Oxford accent and was a profound student of Anglo-Saxon history.

The Republicans saw themselves as the defenders of the Italian constitution and often opposed the Catholic Church. They fought the increasing power of government, but still insisted on some of the political pasta. They blew up a lot of balloons which rhetorically sailed out to sea.

The Monarchists talked nostalgically about bringing back the king and other royalty. Everybody in the country knew it was a pipe dream, including themselves. King Umberto lived in exile. Much of the nobility had deserted the monarchy for political payola or sold themselves to the international jet set where they were ornaments at meaningless receptions and flashy parties.

The neo-Fascists, who called themselves the Italian Social Movement, weren't acceptable in most social circles. They had long ago abandoned Mussolini's cry: "Better to live one day as a lion than a thousand days as a lamb." The Fascists sometimes fought in the streets with the Communists and Monarchists, especially in Rome and Naples, but these were typical Italian fights—a lot of shouting and posturing but few haymakers.

Despite more than 2,000 years of civilization, Italy had been reunified into a republic for only a little more than century when we lived there—133 years in 1994. It was a youngster compared with old democracies, such as the United States and England.

Italians believed that government was necessary only to maintain a balance between public good and evil. Political balance was paramount. That was one reason why some voted for the Communists. The Reds were viewed as an instrument to keep the Christian Democrats honest. The Socialists represented the precarious but precious middle ground. The other parties diluted the strength of the larger groups. This was, to the Italian mind, beautiful politics—a public standoff.

Many Italians felt the same way about the Catholic Church. It shouldn't be allowed to become so powerful—as during the time of the papal states and a land-owning papal aristocracy— that it could again subject them to its moral and material dictates. Perhaps more than any people on earth, the Italians were aware that the Church was a divine institution, but in human hands. They didn't fear divinity, though mindful of their own failings, but rather the hands which administered Vatican economics and justice.

As with any generalities, these views are subject to controversy. In our time, however, they essentially reflected Italian life.

Virtually every American who came to Italy and inquired about the country asked this question: Why do Italian Catholics vote Communist? This seemingly simple inquiry was very complex. Placed in the profound background of Italian history and the labyrinthian corridors of the Italian mind, there were no easy answers. There were about a dozen responses but perhaps five would suffice. Even these weren't satisfactory for someone who had lived in Italy for a long time. Nevertheless, they offered a general overview:

1) The promises and highly effective opposition and organization of the Communist party. The Reds ran the most competent labor unions in the country. These were, apart from doctrine, the only truly effective national labor party in Italy. The economic gains and rights that the Communists won for laborers were sweeping. Italy's factory owners and landowners, with some notable exceptions, lagged in economic and social justice. Wage increases were rarely offered willingly or on the basis of fairness. Workers were forced to strike for wage and other benefits. The Communist party itself maintained highly efficient services to laborers—from lawyers to family benefits. These were never effectively matched by the Christian Democrats.

2) Financial and other scandal constantly dogged the Christian Democrats. Internal friction, often involving personal power grabs and personally conflicts, drained energy and cohesion from the party. The Christian Democrats never quite presented themselves to the public as a united party with a clear division of leadership and specific principles. For years the party was its own worst enemy. The United States continued to pour millions of dollars into the Christian Democrats to keep them in power despite the fact that a good number of these lawmakers were not only crooks but brazenly corrupt. All of this exploded publicly between 1990 and 1994 when politicians and businessmen were accused (some have already been found guilty and imprisoned) of longtime complicity in financial kickbacks and similar scandals. Not even Giulio Andreotti, a prime minister and longtime CD leader, was spared. I was somewhat surprised because of Andreotti's long and close association with Vatican officials.

3) The popes have offered many encyclicals on social justice and other public issues, but Italy's Catholic hierarchy had engaged in relatively little organized and effective social action to help the country's masses. The bishops disagreed sharply as to whether social action and justice should come down from an

elite leadership or up from the bottom through the great mass of workers. This disagreement crippled their work and greatly aided the Communists. The Church left the impression among millions of Italians it was incapable of action or merely paying lip service to the great teachings of Leo XIII, Pius XI, Pius XII, and John XXIII. The Church was also burdened, as a onetime feudalistic power, by its past injustices.

4) Through the centuries, the Italians had developed a sense of rebellion against whoever was in power. It was the most developed of all revolts—all the nonviolent means to slow and wear down an oppressor. This had sprung from a history of domination, division, and deep, bitter memories of oppression among all classes, not just the poor. Those memories had become virtually an inbred quality of the people. Few foreigners comprehended how basic this was to the Italian personality.

5) The independence of the Italian character. Contrary to popular belief, including some of their own recent writers, Italians are a conservative people. In the Italian makeup, the state exists only by virtue of the family and the family only because of individuals. Individual freedom, therefore, is the single, most important element of human existence. Consequently, there is no particular attraction to government, civil laws, or tax collectors. There is no genuine government, no legitimate law or tax if it interferes with the rights and sometimes even the interests of the family. I used to call it government by individual, not by an expanding state.

I once met Giorgio La Pira when he was mayor of Florence. La Pira represented another important but not often-considered element of Italian society—the mystical idealist. It must be remembered that Italy had produced the stuff of many great artists and saints. La Pira preached universal brotherhood. Some Italians considered him a political crackpot, yet La Pira exemplified many of the virtues and faults of the Italian political character.

I stood in a crowd one day in Rome, waiting to hear La Pira speak. Idly chatting with a man next to me, I asked about the Florentine leader. The man replied, "He's a political mystic and, therefore, a contradiction. I listen to him because some of his politics is good for my stomach and a bit of his mysticism is good for my soul. He feeds both the physical and spiritual appetites. Not too many Italian politicians do that."

La Pira arrived and I took some notes as he spoke. "I am La Pira, one of you. I have two slices of bread, both blessed, and I give you one of them. I am La Pira and I have two coats and I hand one to you, my brother. I am La Pira and I, too, am poor but we must not despair. Hail Mary, full of grace, the Lord is with thee, blessed art thou. . . ."

La Pira told the crowd his character wasn't created to give rousing speeches at political rallies. He preferred to go to Lake Tiberias, where Christ preached, and contemplate the words of the Divine Master. (I began to feel compelled by this man and, years later on visiting Lake Tiberias, I thought of La Pira and the saintly ideas that flowed from his beliefs.) The mayor told the crowd life was a service. One's calling, no matter what time or circumstance, was to contribute to the common good.

La Pira was called a radical and sometimes even a Communist. He was neither. The mayor was a reformist, especially assailing the high rate of unemployment. Italy had two million unemployed, most of the time that we lived there, among about fifty million people.

La Pira was born in Sicily, an island of hot-blooded people. He grew up in poverty. Social justice became his cause. His message of Christian enlightenment fell, for the most part, on a wilderness of public indifference.

It was commonly believed that the onetime mayor had taken the vows of the priestly life. He did live with monks at times, though it was disobedience that won La Pira the Florentine mayor's post. The Christian Democrats had been unable to dent the city's Communist regime and were desperate to oust them. They chose La Pira as a candidate who would challenge the Reds on their own turf—poverty and social abuse. La Pira launched his campaign by distributing bread from church steps. No one accused him of insincerity or of being a crackpot. After Communist party chief Palmiro Togliatti met La Pira for the first time, he knew the Communists faced a tough foe, saying, "What a terrifying little man!"

As mayor of Florence, La Pira insisted on not only finding but creating work for the jobless. He thus ran the city treasury into considerable debt. Despite public protest, he argued no society has the right to deny any individual his God-given right to earn a living. Finally, assailed by both left and right in the city council, La Pira quit his post rather than compromise his conscience. The Christian Democrats and Communists didn't quarrel with his aims. They merely wanted power for themselves and would sacrifice some poor to placate those who wished to balance the city budget. La Pira's conscience forbade such compromise.

On leaving office, La Pira castigated all political parties. He accused his own Christian Democrats, in particular, of failing the trust of millions of voters. One Christian Democrat retorted, "La Pira has taken three vows—poverty, chastity, and disobedience!"

Sitting on a couch in his office and fingering his rosary beads, La Pira looked at me and calmly castigated his fellow Christian Democrats. For 15 years, he said, the party had failed to reform itself. It was a party of privilege and greed. It had sold itself into the slavery of materialism. Fixing his thick eyeglasses and fastening his ever-loose tie, he cut down in sharp words the most powerful men in his party. To the end, La Pira feared no man. I believe he later passed away without fear.

La Pira was right about the Christian Democrats.

Another Sicilian, Silvio Milazzo, burst on the political scene like an explosive firecracker. He bolted from the Christian Democrats and formed his own party on the island. His battlecry was: *Viva La Sicilia e Santa Rosalia!* (Long Live Sicily and Saint Rosalie!) Rosalie was the island's patron saint. I took Joy with me to hear Milazzo speak in Palermo during one of Sicily's regional elections.

St. Rosalie may have saved Milazzo. Palermo's Ernesto Cardinal Ruffini threatened to excommunicate the politician and anyone who voted for him from the Church. The Jesuit-educated Milazzo then quoted St. Rosalie in every speech and closed each address invoking her blessing. The crowds loved it. I never considered Milazzo a mystic like La Pira but some Italians did. They felt only a mystic could run the Mafia out of Sicily. No one, not even the Communists, challenged a saint. Milazzo had one-upped Ruffini but His Eminence had little praise for the candidate.

The Church and its priests weren't courted but, at the same time, they weren't completely ignored in any Italian election. What priests preached, and didn't preach, from the pulpit has long been imponderable in Italian elections. That later came into a clear but new focus during a trip Joy and I took one evening to the little town of Monte Rotundo, about 12 miles south of Rome.

It was about five o'clock in the afternoon as we drove up the hilly road to town. We noted the full crops on the slopes and in the fields below. A few artisans' shops stood near the old church on the main street. A benediction service was beginning as a group of elderly men and women entered the church in their uniformly dark, homespun clothes. We followed them into church.

Some of the young choir boys were vying for who could hit the highest note. It seemed, as soon as the director pushed down one head, another popped up with an even shriller voice. Later, in the midst of the sermon, one of the town dogs wandered in through a side door, loped up the middle aisle, and suddenly hopped over the Communion rail. One of the altar boys grabbed the mutt by the neck and pulled him out into the street.

The priest didn't bat an eye during any of this. He was a native son who had returned just for the day from Rome. He was celebrating the 25th anniversary of his ordination to the priesthood among his townfolk. We could understand why. There was a lack of pretension and nostalgia about the place and its people. The church, at least two centuries old, was chilly and dark. There were few lights so the altar and votive candles assumed an aura of long ago.

We knew the priest, Monsignor Alberto Giovannetti, who worked in the Vatican Secretariat of State. He was later named the Vatican observer to the United Nations. Giovannetti had invited us to the celebration and we proceeded to a nearby restaurant to meet and mix with the townfolk and priests from the nearby Abruzzi Mountains. All were country people, plain spoken, good natured.

Three priests, all in their forties, sat across from us. They talked about their vocations and lives. Italy then had about 44,000 secular priests, distinct from various religious orders. Most were spread out in small towns, like those of the Abruzzi, working among farm families. For every million Italians, there were fewer than 1,000 priests. One of every five clerics was above the age of 70. These men continued because they had little savings and couldn't retire. Others had no one to replace them if they did retire.

The priests said most of the men over 60 were tired from many years of service. The work was hard, lonely, and offered few amenities. Most walked the rounds of their parishes. They had no money for a car or even a motor scooter. Even if they did, a good number were too old to drive. Most had no health insurance, no old-age pensions. As one priest expressed it, "We're at the mercy of time."

The salaries of about half of Italy's secular priests were paid by the state. That resulted from agreements made between Church and state when the Italian government confiscated Church land and other property during the reunification of Italy, a century earlier. The state payment to each priest amounted to approximately $524 a year or about $10 a week. Few were able to live on this amount of money so they needed stipends for saying Masses, weddings, and funeral services for members of their congregations. This would often be less than $100 a month, but it was needed for the upkeep of the church and perhaps a part-time salary for a housekeeper. The normal offering to have a daily Mass said was 100 lire (16 cents).

Sunday and holy day collections in small towns and villages were meager because the farmers were themselves poor. Some priests grew vegetables to help feed themselves. The oldest priests often depended on the goodwill of parishoners or relatives for sufficient food. Others prayed to divine providence for help.

Of the 30,000 seminarians studying for the priesthood, four-fifths would leave for one reason or another. Only 6,000 would take the places of the elderly. One of the priests concluded, "These are merely the cold facts. They don't explain the pain and suffering."

During one year in the 1960s, the entire archdiocese of Bologna produced only one newly ordained secular priest. Only two priests were ordained to work in the diocese of Bergamo where Pope John was born and lived as a young curate. In Rome, seat of the Catholic Church, only one native-born priest was ordained to the secular ranks.

Priests and nuns in Italy and the Vatican itself couldn't operate as they did in those days without professional and financial assistance from their more fortunate brothers and sisters in the United States and elsewhere. This has continued to the present day.

Instead of the powerful arm of the Christian Democrats that the Communists made them out to be, Italy's clerics were actually a bedraggled lot. They had been beaten down by economic, social, and political forces that often made their priesthood a bitter chalice.

The sad memory of that nostalgic evening at Monte Rotundo has returned again and again over the years. The wreckage and destruction of the human spirit were etched in the faces of those weary men. They were dying but the Italian cardinals in the

Roman Curia thought it more important to preserve their dominance in the College of Cardinals from foreigners. No wonder so many Italians listened to the music of "Red Flag" and heard the call of the Socialists: Forward!

Through the years, Corrado Pizzinelli, an Italian journalist, was one of my closest friends. He was one of the most intelligent men I had ever met, and a prolific writer. Corrado had traveled the world, and written a good number of books, including one of the best early works on communism inside China. I often asked Corrado to analyze his homeland. He would answer this way: "Italy is incomprehensible. It is, like China, a great riddle. *Siamo pazzi!* (We're crazy people!). No one knows what we will do next."

We were discussing Italian politics one day, and Corrado damned everybody on the scene. He said, "This is a very mixed-up country. It snows in the north and there's sun in the south. People in the Alps don't speak the same language as those in the central region, and the Tuscans don't speak the same tongue as the Sicilians.

"Rome is our capital but Milan is our most important city. We have seas on either side of us, but mountains running down the middle, dividing the country into separate parts. We cannot stand the French, our neighbors, but like the Americans who live 4,000 miles away.

"We love wine but don't get drunk. We are always criticizing the government and just about everything else but, if we say a word against our neighbor, he'll take us to court. Few people want to be soldiers, but everybody loves a military parade.

"We often chase women, but invoke the Madonna at the first sign of trouble. We're always fighting among ourselves, but get along well with foreigners. Nothing makes sense."

He concluded, "Politics is the worst of all. Most of us hate politics but we still have fist fights in parliament over the issues. The Reds say that to be a good Communist, you should be a good Catholic. The Catholics say you can't be a good Communist under any circumstances, but they vote for the Reds by the hundreds of thousands. We're a society of nuts!"

I suddenly blurted, "Spaghetti on-the-rocks."

He asked, "What do you mean?"

I replied, "That's a perfect description of Italy. A contradiction. An absurdity. Nonsense. As the Italians say: It's beautiful confusion!"

Chapter 20

John Wallace's British Blazer

DURING THE YEARS we called Rome our home, other news assignments called me away about half the time. I covered the Arab world from Tunisia to Iraq and Iran. Most of that time was spent in Lebanon and Algeria. I roamed Africa when its hot spots blew up. And, since they were relatively close to Italy, I also covered Greece, Turkey, Yugoslavia, and, occasionally, Switzerland. On a few occasions, I substituted in Paris when someone was on vacation. In other words, the Rome correspondent was a fireman.

In these wanderings, no memory is clearer or more compelling than that of the Algerian war. I remember Algeria well because it was so drastically different from my other assignments during those years. This was a Muslim-European struggle. It was fought savagely and with incredible terror against the civilian population on both sides. One trip to Algeria stands out in my mind. It began in the first days of January, 1962.

I arrived alone from Paris at Maison Blanche Airport about an hour before curfew in Algiers. Our Paris office said I would be met by our cameraman, Claude Giorgetti, a Frenchman with an

Italian surname, who I had never seen. Giorgetti was new with us but those in the bureau said I couldn't miss him. They described him as "a Marseille dandy." They were right.

Giorgetti wore a tight-fitting, dark, pinstripe suit with a crimson handkerchief in his breast pocket. He sported a silk, silver-colored tie, and pranced about in narrow, black leather shoes with pointed tips. His black hair was slicked down, and he had a pencil-thin mustache. He looked like a pimp or piano player from a 1930 casbah movie. After we shook hands and he began driving to the old Aletti Hotel in downtown Algiers, Giorgetti warned, "Things have changed. *Oui!* Changed much—for the worse!"

After checking in and looking over my room, I went to the hotel bar, a large, magnificent room with the look of longtime wear and tear. A voice boomed as I walked in.

"GAWD! Good Gawd, Casserly, are *you* back again?"

John Wallace, correspondent of the *London Telegraph* who had been covering North Africa for three decades, bellowed from the bar. I liked Wallace. He knew more about North Africa than most of the other correspondents put together. He knew that and let us know it. I was constantly amazed at his depth of knowledge, and good humor.

"Well," Wallace announced to one and all, "I must play wet nurse again. We've got a damn war on here and they send me a choir boy from Rome—and a Yank at that. All right, assume your place in line, have a drink and I'll attend to you in a moment."

In public, Wallace was always furious with me. He had little affection for radio and television correspondents as serious conveyors of news, and less respect for what he considered American meddling in North Africa. The rotund, gray-haired Englishman believed us to be brash and naive with no real comprehension of the intricacies of colonial matters. Worst of all, Wallace regarded the Americans as Johnnies-come-lately to the area.

"You Americans are going to screw everything up as usual, and then start throwing money around," he would say.

After about 20 minutes of whispering with two men who finally left the bar, Wallace turned to me and said, "Awful mess. It's getting worse. Let's have another drink." The red-faced veteran quickly ticked off what he considered the essential facts: de Gaulle would definitely make peace with the Arabs (the Algerian National Liberation Front or FLN), but General Raoul Salan might lead his colonial underground OAS (the French acronym for the Secret Army Organization) terrorists in a desperate final drive to thwart an armistice.

"Right now," Wallace said, "it looks like there's going to be a bloody massacre. Keep your mouth shut, especially here in the hotel. The intrigue is fierce. I think the OAS might even blow up the bar. And we can't have that, can we!"

Several days afterward, late on a Sunday morning, Wallace asked me to accompany him on a secret trip. I knew Wallace had something big in mind when he said not to discuss our conversation with anyone, and not bring a camera or tape recorder. But I didn't envisage anything this important. Only when we got in the car with a driver, a European who obviously was a member or sympathizer of the OAS, did he reveal our destination, "We're going to interview Jesus."

I gasped. The driver noticed my alarm and smiled. Jesus was the colonists' top civilian killer. He murdered Arab "collaborators" and "troublemakers" with zeal and efficiency.

We had met the driver near the Aletti. He drove us around the city, constantly checking to see if we were being followed, until the car finally roared into high speed and swerved into the notorious European quarter of Bab-el-Oued.

The district was mostly populated by fanatical followers of the OAS in Algiers—Europeans from France, Spain, Italy, Corsicans, and a smattering of Germans (some ex-Nazis). A good number had been born in Algeria, considered themselves French to the core, and were dedicated to violently preventing Algeria from being "sold out" to the native Arabs.

Bab-el-Oued was a keg of dynamite. All types of high explosives, machine guns, small arms, and other weapons had been smuggled into the crowded quarter. Much of them came from soldiers in the French Army who secretly were members or sympathizers of the dreaded OAS.

We stopped on a side street not far from a cafe. The driver told us to enter, order a drink at the bar, and Jesus would eventually join us. We ordered the usual OAS drink, anisette mixed with water. It looked when stirred like watery skim milk but had a white-lightning kick. Two young women appeared to run the place. One was rather pretty.

Wallace was the first to be aware that someone was coming up behind us. He turned slowly on his stool, smiled, stuck out his hand for a handshake, and as if greeting someone after church, said, "Good morning, Jesus." Jesus shook hands but did not respond. He merely nodded in my direction. He was sizing us up.

The dark-featured young man with a mustache was about five feet, seven inches tall. He wore a black suit with an open-collar white shirt. His eyes flickered momentarily when Wallace described me as an American journalist. Americans were generally considered enemies because U.S. foreign policy favored Algerian independence from France. That meant Muslim rule.

Jesus sat on a stool at the bar, facing the door. He said nothing. Wallace put on his friendliest face. The Englishman began a long, roundabout discourse in which he sought the answer to one question: What was going to happen in Algeria, particularly Algiers, if de Gaulle gave the country independence?

The question could hardly be put to a more crucial individual. Jesus was the number-one killer among scores of OAS gunmen. Few doubted that he and the others would mercilessly carry out the missions assigned to them. But there was always a question: If the situation looked hopeless, would they try to make a getaway rather than stand and perhaps die? It was well-known mercenary groups in other parts of Africa would welcome them. Ship passage was already assured. What would they do?

Wallace at last fell silent. Jesus ordered an anisette. Finally, he began with an explanation. The Europeans were determined to save Algeria and all of North Africa from communism. He asserted all of the FLN leadership was Communist. Jesus hoped that the United States would come to its senses and join this anticommunist crusade, but if they did not, the Europeans or French, as he put it, were prepared to fight and die for liberty and France.

Jesus said the French Algerians would stop at nothing to keep the country free. He claimed they were ready for a long siege. Elements of the French Army, including officers within France, would join them. The gunman said, if necessary, he and his compatriots would blow up the cities of Algiers and Oran as well as their harbor facilities. "This will be an all-out war," he concluded.

Several of Jesus' henchmen joined us. They ordered drinks all around and said we must tell their story to the world. After several more drinks and small talk, we were told our driver was ready. Jesus said it was our "duty" to report the truth, as he had reported it. He shook hands with both of us and proclaimed, "Long live French Algeria!"

Wallace and I didn't exchange thoughts on the ride back to our hotel. The last thing we needed on entering the Aletti was a drink, but both headed for the bar to compare notes. I told him I thought the whole affair was a propaganda show. Sure, we had to report what they said but I was not going to make it a long story. Wallace cautioned me. These were dangerous, desperate men. They were capable of almost anything. None had anything to lose. I should be careful. Their threats were real. I replied I would report the threats, but I didn't want to be used to promote their propaganda. We agreed to disagree.

On the following Sunday, I secretly spoke with Monsignor Leon-Etienne Duval, the Roman Catholic bishop of Algiers. Bishop Duval, a man of about 60 who had been born in France, was called "The Arab" by the OAS. The viewed him as a collaborator with the FLN and a traitor to France. I found

Duval to be a quiet, humble, soul-searching man. He was dedicated to the proposition that bloodshed must be halted if Frenchman and Arab, Christian and Muslim, were ever to live side by side in Algeria.

The Bishop made it clear he opposed those priests and lay Catholic in Algiers, Oran, and other parts of the country who actively participated in the OAS. He believed they compromised not only their faith and morality but the future of Christianity in North Africa. Duval was well aware of the defense expressed by these priests—they were required to remain with their flocks in these desperate hours. The bishop told them such loyalty could never justify the murders and other crimes sweeping the country.

Later, on a confidential basis, I told Wallace about my conversation with Duval. It was in repayment for allowing me to meet Jesus. The Englishman agreed Duval's remarks were significant since he would probably emerge as the most important Christian churchman in North Africa if the Muslims prevailed. He wasn't surprised by the split among the Catholic clergy but wondered what real effect it might have. He must get to know more clergy, fewer gunmen, and many fewer bartenders!

My relationship with Wallace was about to blow up. Every day for weeks, he wore the same blue blazer. Wallace was one of those Englishmen who forever had a cigarette dangling from his lips. The ashes were always falling on his jacket. In addition, because he ate heartily and in a hurry, the jacket was spotted with gravy, spaghetti sauce, and other stains. Yet the blazer was his trademark and wherever Wallace went the jacket was sure to go. I used to refer to it jokingly as Wallace's bloomin' blazer. He took this as good-natured kidding, until the afternoon I returned to the Aletti from a bombing and found Wallace pacing in the lobby. It was a most unlikely scene since he always did his ruminating in the bar. He had staked out the lobby so as not to miss me. Wallace loudly opened fire as soon as I entered.

"Well, here comes my great benefactor. The lad who's going

to clean up John Wallace. May I tell you, young man, that this blazer was here long before you ever came to Algeria and will remain long after you have departed. Go to blazes, Casserly!"

With that blast, he stormed into the bar. I was momentarily speechless. Quickly, I searched out other newsmen to find out why Wallace was angry. Corrado Pizzinelli, an Italian friend, had the answer.

"He's as mad as hell. I've never seen him so sore. The story is going around that you started a collection to buy Wallace a new blazer. I don't know who began the story but now everyone seems to believe it."

I could only quote Wallace's favorite phrase: "GAWD! GOOD GAWD!"

In the weeks that followed, no armistice could be arranged. I tried several intermediaries but Wallace was adamant. I was a turncoat, no longer his friend. He even refused an attempted apology. I tried to learn who started the rumor but failed. Meanwhile, the street murders and bombings increased. Several newsmen had close calls. Most of us were getting the shakes. I developed a nervous tick in my right eye.

Once, while Giorgetti was filming the body of an Arab shot dead in the street, two armed Europeans threatened to kill us if we didn't surrender the film. We did. On another occasion, at precisely noon near the radio station, shooting erupted all around me. When it was over, 12 Arabs lay in their own blood. The OAS had shot them as part of its campaign of psychological terror. A few days later, less than 20 minutes after I walked out of a pharmacy, an OAS bomb blew it up. Six innocent Muslim civilians died.

I did radio broadcasts to Paris for relay to the United States around noon most days. Several Frenchmen at the station warned me that I wasn't reporting to their satisfaction. One day, two young men in a car were waiting for me. Both were armed. They suggested I take a ride with them. Before dropping me off at the Aletti Hotel, they told me my broadcasts were being monitored. I was reporting too many OAS "atrocities." A word to the wise—atrocities were performed by Arabs, not them. Other correspondents received similar warnings. Presumably, if we continued these reports, we might be killed. I changed "atrocities" to "murdered."

We often heard gunfire and explosions in different parts of Algiers at night. The OAS was usually blowing up an army munitions depot or some building frequented by Muslims. At times, someone would knock on a hotel pipe—three short and two long clangs. That was the battle cry of the OAS and meant, *Algerie Francais*! (Algeria is French!) It was to remind reporters that the OAS was everywhere.

Perhaps the most dramatic night of the Algerian war for newsmen came when the hotel bar was suddenly invaded by four armed OAS terrorists. They were going to teach us what was going on in Algeria or kill us. I shall never forget Wallace and his British blazer. It was, as Churchill himself would have put it, their finest hour. As the four pointed their guns and threatened us, Wallace announced in his impeccable French, "I'm going to the pisser."

Their leader, who appeared to be Spanish, threatened to shoot the Englishman on the spot if he moved. John replied, before turning his back and walking out of the door of the bar, "I was going to the men's room before you were born."

He walked out in stunned silence.

The OAS crew recited to us, from behind cocked pistols and a machine gun, the same litany Wallace and I had heard from Jesus. They were the men fighting for freedom in the face of FLN communism.

After returning from the men's room, Wallace wouldn't permit them to slow down his drinking. He would grunt from time to time and sometimes muttered, *Merde*! (Shit!) after a gunman spoke.

After several hours of this, a French army captain in civilian clothes entered. He was followed by four men, all members of the OAS. The quartet aimed to enlist the captain in the terrorist organization, by reason or force.

For more than an hour, with arguments punctuated by threats and curses, the OAS men tried to convince the captain. Finally, the officer turned from his drink, waved his arms and shouted, "Shoot me, you bastards, if you have the courage!"

A Spaniard among the OAS, who was somewhat drunk, broke into tears. He placed his pistol next to the captain's drink and said, "No, my captain. If you will not join us, shoot me because then we are lost!"

The captain spoke. "I was fighting communism before any of you knew the meaning of the word. That, in itself, should tell you that you are insulting me. But to say to me, a French officer, that I must become a traitor and a coward, I say, no. No! No!"

Wallace put down his Scotch and applauded. "All, right, that's enough of this nonsense. Let's get down to some serious drinking."

With that, a dozen of us newsmen who had been sitting at tables in the bar nervously watching the trigger fingers, got up in a body and walked to the bar.

We started drinking again and the OAS men began to leave, but they shouted slogans supporting a French Algeria and epithets about our unwillingness to join their cause. I later walked up to Wallace, shook his hand, and congratulated him, "Good show, John." He looked at me and replied, "Does that mean you're buying?"

* * *

One bright April afternoon, after three-and-a-half months in Algiers, two men stopped me outside a cafe across the street from the Aletti. I was returning from a news briefing at the Prefecture. They suggested we have a drink inside. Seeing they were armed, I thought it was a good idea. The pair advised me the OAS considered my news broadcasts objectionable. Too much talk of European terrorism; therefore, I must leave the country within

24 hours or face the consequences. They downed their drinks and left.

I waited to tell our Paris office about the incident. Perhaps I could figure out some way to stay on. I wanted to be in Algiers when the peace treaty was signed and the expected confrontation came between the OAS and FLN. I mentioned the incident to Tom Lambert, a reporter for the *New York Herald-Tribune*, not thinking such a small matter could be a story. It was on the front page of the international edition of the *Trib* the following day and ABC Paris was upset because I hadn't told them. Lou Cioffi phoned saying they were sending another correspondent to Algiers the following day. Meantime, I was to fly to Tunis to cover the leaders of the FLN.

For the next five weeks, until the Algerian cease-fire on May 18, 1962, I covered FLN politics from Tunisia. *Time* magazine ran a piece mentioning my being thrown out of Algeria by the OAS. I became an instant hero to the FLN leadership and they gave me many stories.

I invited Joy to Tunis. She arrived on a Sunday and we drove out to the village of Sidi-bou-Said. The place had a quaint tea house, serving the most delicious tea we had ever tasted. It was made of local herbs, scented with mint. The scene could well have been in the year 1,000 since neither the Arabs, their dress, nor roaming donkeys or blind camels had changed a breath. We reminded one another that, not too many miles from the village, St. Monica had prayed at Carthage for her wayward son, Augustine. He was yet to become a saint. The Algerian war and, indeed, the 20th century was easily forgotten that afternoon because time had stopped at Sidi-bou-Said centuries earlier. The beauty of the place was its quiet forgetfulness of a busy but errant world.

After the peace treaty, I was assigned to Oran in hopes of interviewing Ben Bella. Algeria was in chaos. The OAS, instead of fighting, was on the run. Europeans poured out of the country on every available plane and ship. Some took as many belong-ings as they could carry by car to Tunisia. The new Muslim provisional government already showed signs of division, especially about the country's new leadership. Ben Bella, one of the original leaders of the revolution, had been released in France by President de Gaulle after years of imprisonment. He and his followers threatened to march on Algiers to establish power in the new government. Ben Bella was momentarily holed up in the small town of Tlemcen near Oran.

About 6:15 one morning, Giorgetti and I finally talked Ben Bella's cohorts into allowing us to meet with the Algerian revolutionary on the patio of a large villa they had taken over. Even at that early hour, Ben Bella conferred in one meeting after another with military and other advisers. We waited about an hour to see him. Ben Bella was a handsome young man who was brief and to the point: Algeria was on the road to a new socialism and no outsiders should interfere with its destiny.

In talking with other Algerians, I had the impression Ben Bella was not master of his own destiny. Although he was very popular with the masses, other Algerian leaders sought to wrest the top new government posts from his followers. Yet Ben Bella was to be reckoned with. He had spoken of himself in terms of three men—Tito, Nasser, and Castro. None was excess baggage in the Arab world of those days.

Ben Bella was a great admirer of Castro. In three different FLN army camps I had visited, photos of Ben Bella and Castro were side by side. Castro was seen as a pure socialist who had overcome great odds. That was how Ben Bella saw himself.

Nasser was a hero to most of the Arab world because of his bellicose attitude toward Israel. Ben Bella not only respected Nasser but, more importantly, feared him. Nasser was a man who attempted to make all enemies pay.

Despite the expectation, Ben Bella never really took over leadership of Algeria. He was undercut by his fellow revolutionaries who assumed command and placed him under house arrest. He was held there for many years. The country has witnessed considerable divisions among the Muslims ever since. Muslim fundamentalists, spurred by Iran, are now trying to capture control of the government from its more modern leaders.

During the war, Yugoslavia's Tito quietly furnished FLN units with doctors, medical equipment, and other assistance for years. The dictator's influence with Ben Bella and the other Algerian leadership was vastly underestimated by most countries.

I was meditating on all this as Giorgetti drove some 30 miles from Tlemcen to Sidi-bel-Abbes. It was as much a sentimental as a working trip since I wanted to see the longtime Legion headquarters. Sidi-bel-Abbes had been the home of the French Foreign Legion for more than a century. I hoped to see the legendary buildings and grounds. The Legion shrine, with its wooden hand of Captain Danjou who had died heroically in Mexico more than a century before, had been part of my boyhood reading.

How disappointing it was! The town, despite an impressive square and some fine buildings, was filthy. The Legion was housed in a massive complex of apartment buildings at the end of the town's central thoroughfare. It presented a great orange-yellow facade with high walls and a fence.

The commandant was not in, but an aide said the Legion was still present, mostly doing convoy duty for Europeans leaving the country. Despite reports to the contrary, the new Algerian leaders didn't wish to see all the skilled European farmers and technicians leave the country. The mostly untrained and often ill-disciplined Arabs desperately needed such assistance, at least for a transition period. At one point, some Europeans told the Legion, the Algerian army threatened to kill any French settlers trying to abandon their farms.

The officer cautiously explained the legionnaires would soon be leaving Sidi-bel-Abbes forever. Before they departed, the legionnaires would blow up the Sacred Way. The Way was little more than a mound of earth but, for decades, men had stood on the mound and accepted the Legion as mother, father, and flag.

Honor ceremonies were also held there. To legionnaires, it was like the altar of a cathedral. Before Legion service ended with a five-year enlistment, there were only two roads from that mound—death in the Legion or escape by desertion. The decision to blow up the shrine shocked me and, when I asked the reason, the officer explained, "Honor, my friend."

We watched and filmed as legionnaires formed a protective shield for some 20 French families and led them out of town to disappear in a cloud of dust. I was told about the Legion's sad, final departure a few months later. Before leaving their huge compound, the men fired their rifles in the air, a last gesture defying the decision of French President Charles de Gaulle to close the camp. They also blew up much of the headquarters, including their ammunition dumps. The legionnaires marched out of the compound in full uniform and colors with a band playing. They loudly chorused *Je Ne Regrette Rien* (I Regret Nothing), the lamentation of Edith Piaf, the "Little Sparrow" of French popular music. Units were transferred to Corsica or Pacific isles where the French were conducting atomic bomb tests.

The visit to Sidi-bel-Abbes tore the pages from my boyhood books that described so many Legion heroics and it crumpled them in my mind and along the dusty roadside back to Oran. I couldn't look back at the encampment. Giorgetti and I returned to the port city and watched Europeans leaving in ships departing for France and other parts of Europe.

We checked into a hotel for the night. I went to the bar in hopes of seeing some newsmen. John Wallace was there in his shirtsleeves. He saw me enter and shouted, "Oh, no. Not you again, Casserly. Is there no escape?"

I smiled. He relented and bought me a beer. I filled him in on our interview with Ben Bella—but not the important parts lest he scoop me on my own story—and our visit to Sidi-bel-Abbes.

Wallace wanted the answer to only one question, "Did you or did you not take up a collection to buy me a new blazer?"

"I did not!" I said. "On my honor."

"No fingers crossed?" Wallace insisted.

"No, John," I stressed. "I didn't do it."

"Casserly," he said with a grin, "you may make a good correspondent yet, even if you are a bloody Yank. I'll buy."

Giorgetti and I flew to Paris the following day. The Algerian war was over for both of us. But I knew Wallace's Union Jack, that British blazer, would fly again somewhere—perhaps at a bar in the midst of a new war.

Chapter 21

Journey of a Soul

FROM THE EARLY hours of May 31 to the evening of June 3, 1963, Pope John XXIII died in a slow but relentless agony lasting more than 80 hours. The papal death watch actually extended over a period of 14 days since the first signs of illness appeared on May 21. The final four days, before the Pope quietly closed his eyes and slipped into eternity, marked the man.

Pope John died of cancer. On November 3, 1962, seven months to the day before his death, Monsignor Loris Capovilla, the Pope's private secretary, told me confidentially that the Holy Father was suffering from cancer and wasn't expected to live more than six months. Five people knew of the papal illness but Pope John was not among them. The 81-year-old pontiff was never told of the cancer. He suspected it, however, and in subtle ways indicated he was aware of the terminal illness afflicting him. But the words *death* and *cancer* never passed his lips. That was typical of the man from the little farming town of Sotto Il Monte. He knew much more than he would mention.

Capovilla told me the story. One afternoon during these troubled months, while walking in the Vatican gardens with Monsignor Capovilla, the Pope noticed that his secretary appeared very sad. He asked his longtime assistant the reason. The slightly built aide, who weighed no more than 150 pounds, said he felt a bit tired. The Pope, recounting the physical exams, X rays, and other probing by his physicians, and the fact that his strength was ebbing, fenced with Capovilla and prodded him for a clearer response. A tear began to course down the secretary's face, but he quickly wiped it and hid his secret.

From that moment, knowing how deeply Capovilla cared about him, Pope John fully understood the seriousness of his illness. This was significant. It underscores how well the Pope hid his cancer from the outside world and those around him. He continued to work daily, carried out the physically grueling religious functions of the papacy, and, above all, maintained his commitment to the coming Ecumenical Council which he had called. Although his life was closing, John was opening the windows of the Roman Catholic Church to the winds of change. He did so with humility and quiet humor. Two stories come to mind. . . .

I had gone to Monsignor Capovilla in June of 1962 with an unusual proposal: that ABC be allowed to take its cameras inside the Vatican for three to six months to film a documentary in color about the inner workings of the Holy See. We wanted to shoot everything—the Pope's private apartment, his chapel while saying Mass, the Vatican's finest art and other treasures, including several days in the Sistine Chapel, the Swiss Guards at work and play, as well as informal chats with various Vatican workers, such as its gendarmes. No such undertaking had ever been approved by the Vatican although the Italian state television network, RAI, had requested such permission in the past. Pope John approved and, for the next six months, New York director Nick Webster, cameraman Edmondo Ricci, soundman Enrico Chini, Franco Bucarelli, and I roamed every part of the Vatican.

The climax came on January 4, 1963, when Pope John received us privately. It was my birthday and the first TV chat ever granted by a pope. The historic encounter was completely unprepared except for a brief message in French which His Holiness addressed to the American people. (The Pope never explained why he spoke French rather than Italian.) The Pope began by delivering his message to the Americans. It was a brief accolade and called on them to work for world peace.

The lines coming down the Pope's face were deep and his eyes appeared heavy. He was pale and his speech was somewhat labored. But he smiled roundly, shielding his fatigue, and his eyes twinkled momentarily.

I knelt on one knee to the Pope's left. I thanked him in Italian for allowing us to do a documentary inside the Vatican over the past six months. He replied, "Ah, but it was something of peace, not of war."

In the name of our crew, I congratulated him on being named Man of the Year by *Time* magazine. He laughed aloud saying, "But the Lord did all the work."

The Pontiff suddenly turned the tables and began interviewing me. "Tell me, what are the names of your children?"

"There is Kevin, Holy Father," I answered.

"Kevin? Kevin?" he asked. "But in Italian . . .?"

"The name doesn't exist," I said. "He's an Irish saint."

"But . . .?" the Pope still searched for Kevin's place in history.

"He's number two in Ireland, Your Holiness, after St. Patrick."

The Pope burst into laughter. "And the others?" he asked.

"Terence," I said, "whose name comes from the great Latin poet, Terentius."

John beamed. "A Latin poet!"

"And Jeffrey," I concluded. "Goffredo in Italian."

He smiled at the familiar name.

"They do not speak English," I told the Pope. "They converse only in Italian."

He laughed again, but said, "They must speak English and, of course, they will learn. Some day they will return to America."

The Pope perspired under the hot TV lights but continued. "My blessing to the boys and your wife. A blessing on your home. I must go now. I must go into the countryside today. There is much to do."

We needed a blessing for the American people so I asked the Pope to give us all a blessing. He replied, "Now? You wish a blessing now? Just tell me what to do. I am an obedient servant."

He imparted his blessing as cameraman Ricci recorded the moment. Then, he asked, *"Finito?"* (Finished?) John had turned and was leaving before anyone answered. He was gone before we knew it.

To the astonishment of Monsignor Capovilla and Monsignor Igino Cardinale, a prelate in the Vatican Secretariat of State who was also present, we began to dance around the papal library. Ricci yelled, *"Magnifico!"* I jumped almost three feet in the air. Franco was kissing me and Ricci embraced both of us. Soundman Chini was crying and kept repeating, "I don't believe it. I don't believe it. We've done it!"

We had scooped the world—an exclusive documentary on the Vatican with the Pope himself addressing the American people. No nation, no TV network had ever accomplished such a professional coup.

The credit, of course, belonged to Capovilla who won papal approval for the work. He had placed a lot of trust in me we would present the Vatican accurately. The monsignor came to me, handed me the original copy of the papal discourse in French, and we shook hands. Only the two of us would ever completely understand what that handshake meant. Each was fulfilling his promise. Quietly, I asked Capovilla, "Is he well?"

The secretary replied, "No, he's not."

On that sad note, we collected our television gear and marched out into St. Peter's Square where pilgrims shuffled into the Basilica to pray before some of the wonders of Christendom.

I saw the Pope next when he received Alexei Adjubei, then editor of the Soviet government newspaper *Izvestia*, and his wife, Rada, daughter of Soviet Premier Nikita Khrushchev.

His Holiness showed no weakness. He treated the Soviet couple graciously, indeed with great warmth, although relations between the Vatican and Moscow were still strained. John asked them about their children, told them of his interest in and admiration for the Soviet people and, in characteristic fashion, said he was very pleased to meet them.

I had been allowed to stand in an adjacent room and approached Rada, who spoke good English, after the Pope had departed. She said, "You know, he reminds me of my father." She was referring to them both as peasants. It was the impression of many the two farm boys would have gotten along famously if they had met. Both spoke the language of the soil. I was later told John would have received Khrushchev had the Soviet leader requested an audience, but he never did.

Khrushchev later freed Monsignor Josyf Slipyi, the Ukranian prelate who had spent 18 years in Soviet and Siberan labor camps. Khrushchev released the prelate despite opposition within the Kremlin. It had been a tradeoff—Slipyi's release for the papal audience.

These audiences reflected the last months of the Pope's life. His pain was excruciating. Painkilling drugs were sometimes administered so he could bear up to his public schedule, yet John never uttered a word of complaint. I learned this from Capovilla. Instead, he worked, talked, prayed, and smiled in apparent peace.

The strain began to show on Monsignor Capovilla. His weight slipped to about 115 pounds. His voice became a whisper. Every once in a while, he would send a brief note asking me to pray for him.

I often thought of Capovilla alone behind those high, leonine walls, of his nights without sleep at the Pope's bedside, listening as John breathed uncomfortably; of the nights when the Holy Father couldn't sleep, and the secret the two never discussed with one another.

During these months, I sometimes took our boys to St. Peter's Square on Sunday where they would see Pope John appear at his high apartment window and give his noon blessing. He usually had a few words in Italian for the crowd. I came to have great affection for his usual greeting: *Cari Figlioli* . . . (Dear Children . . .)

The boys liked to watch the Pope wave. They said he seemed to say to everyone, *Ciao! Ciao!*

On May 31, despite a Vatican announcement the Pope had rallied from a collapse, a prelate inside told me the Pontiff was close to death. Monsignor Capovilla never communicated with me during this final siege.

Meanwhile, I was living in the office and broadcasting around the clock. Minute by minute, hour by hour, the Pope was dying. He began to hemorrhage internally. Yet, the sturdy old man remained conscious, saying farewell to his cardinals one by one. They reported he was serene and smiled often. The Pope's stomach tumor was disintegrating with the cancerous tissue flowing through his body. Just before going into a coma, John said in Latin, *Ut unum sint.* (May they all be one.) He was calling for Christian unity. The Holy Father lost consciousness when his three brothers and a sister entered his bedroom.

Vatican Radio announced: "Pope John is in a state of agony. He is expiring."

Astonishingly, the Pope came out of the coma. He spoke with and blessed his brothers and sister. His doctors were unable to explain the change. But the rally failed and the 81-year-old pontiff began slipping away again. He would not surrender, however. At one point, he rose in his bed and said, "Jesus . . . Jesus . . . I am the Resurrection and the Life. With death, a new life begins. . . ." Then, he fell back again.

This was one of my broadcasts of June 2. It appeared to sum up the continuing agony:

"Step by step, John XXIII is still walking down the long road to join the popes of history. For one who has traveled so far—25 years as a foreign diplomat, visits to a score of countries, and some 150 trips outside the Vatican, breaking all previous precedent—this is perhaps his longest journey of all. The crisis is now approaching three full days and yet nothing is basically new. The Pope drifts between a peaceful coma and painful consciousness. Drugs are unable to quiet his wracking body but His Holiness still feebly lifts his hands in blessing. A cardinal has said that John is showing us how to die. Below in St. Peter's Square, the crowds of three days still kneel, weep, and pray. But on this long, heroic journey of his soul, John XXIII has never complained. He says: 'I observe my death step by step. My bags are packed and I am ready to go. Now I am gently moving toward the end.' It is the journey of a happy warrior."

Finally, the window shutters of the papal study were thrown open. I knew John was dead because the study adjoined the papal bedroom.

Vatican Radio mercifully flashed the end. After reading the official announcement on ABC Radio, I walked out of the small broadcasting studio in our office. Aldo Bisci, our office boy, handed me a bottle of beer. He trembled and tears flowed down his face. Aldo was a very gentle individual. He didn't drink but Aldo also took a bottle of beer. He raised it slightly and said,

"To Papa Giovanni."

I replied, "He died today, Aldo, but not in the hearts of millions. To quote him, here was a man, Aldo. A real man."

For the first time in my life, I walked downstairs to a barbershop and asked for a shave. It is a very strange feeling getting a barbershop shave for the first time—a little like turning 21 or casting your first vote. I looked in the mirror and wondered whether I had become a man.

On returning to the office, Aldo advised that ABC New York had requested one more broadcast on the Italian reaction to the Pope's death. After phoning Vatican prelates for more information, this was my last broadcast of June 3:

"One by one, they kissed his hands. Before the Augustinian brothers took away his body for final vesting in the raiment of a dead pope, they wanted to touch him. He had already touched them by the example of his life. The Vatican is now a small river of tears and it flows quietly among the little people, his people: Lieutenant Martelli of the gendarmes, the tall man who guarded him . . . Gustav, the Swiss Guard, who talked with him about life in the tiny Swiss village where he was born . . . Brother Federico, the small monk who always joked with him . . . Brother Vincenzo who bundled him against the cold . . . the handsome Gusso brothers who came with him from Venice, served his meals, and drove his papal limousine . . . Salvatore, that happy gardener out at Castelgandolfo who told him not to pull the power switch in the shed or 'Holy Father, the whole place will go up' . . . and Capovilla, his secretary of a decade, who now at last can go to sleep. These are his people, the unknowns, like the countless unknowns everywhere."

In the port of Genoa on June 4, the Soviet ship *Faleshty* lowered its flag to half-staff out of respect for the dead pontiff. Soviet Premier Khrushchev sent a long cable of condolences. Monsignor Slipyi, free from his Siberian prison camp, knelt and prayed in the Vatican. John F. Kennedy expressed the condolences of the American people.

If Pope John had a motto, it was perhaps this Latin phrase: *Per singulos dies.* (For each single day.) He took life day by day.

In the Pontiff's last will and testament, he wrote to his family: "As a result of this call (to the papacy), the name Roncalli was brought to the knowledge, the sympathy, and respect of the whole world. Behave well in maintaining yourself in humility, as I have tried to do myself, and not allow yourself to be taken in by the insinuations and loose talk of the world.

"The world only interests itself in making money, enjoying

life, and imposing itself at any cost even, unfortunately, through insolence."

The Pope explained why he had not conferred papal honors on his brothers, sister, and other relatives. He said their souls would be much richer by being blessed as simple farmers. He spoke of the gloriousness of poverty and the simple life. "This (poverty and simplicity) is and will be one of the most beautiful and appreciated titles of honor of Pope John and his Roncalli family."

Nearly two million people came to view the body of the peasant pope. Various Vatican authorities told me he may have been the most beloved pope since St. Peter. To John, that was nobility—to be loved.

I saw Monsignor Capovilla for the final time on a Sunday afternoon, our last in Rome. Joy and I drove to an orphanage located in a poor section on the eastern outskirts of the city near railroad tracks. Capovilla had moved from the papal apartments since the Pope's passing and occupied rooms on the top floor of the children's refuge. Our conversation lasted about four hours.

The monsignor, frail and trying to regain his strength, sat at his study desk working over some of Pope John's personal papers when we arrived. The Pope had left his secretary all his papers that did not pertain directly to papal affairs. There was no heat in the room. Capovilla wore a heavy sweater under his cassock. He told us he was outlining a book, to be called *Journal of a Soul*, that would contain many of the thoughts of the late pontiff over the life of his career. The work has since been published in many languages under Pope John's name.

We talked of the papal encyclicals, *Pacem in Terris* (Peace on Earth) and *Mater et Magistra* (Mother and Teacher). He explained Pope John used the Latin word *Terris* (earths) for a reason. He was considering the possibility of life on other planets.

As the afternoon faded into evening, Capovilla led us to an old desk. The wooden drawers were filled with old notebooks that a schoolboy would use. Scores of them, in various colors and sizes, were piled atop one another. Many were worn, perhaps 30 or 40 years old. The pages were yellowed with time. Some of the ink and pencil notes, all written in Italian, were barely legible.

"What are these?" I asked Capovilla.

He replied, "They are old diaries of the Holy Father."

Monsignor picked up one and began to read from it. The writings were meditation themes—love through suffering; love despite distance; the existence of love everywhere.

Pope John had written decades earlier of finding himself in the Middle East on his parents' wedding anniversary. Despite the miles and years away from his family, he wrote of his abiding affection for all of them. He said his father's farming was honest toil; his mother's advice was always right, and what he said to God about the two when he celebrated Mass that day.

In another entry, while in Istanbul, John related how he had come to recognize in his travels all people were basically the same. Men and women prized and sought love and goodness everywhere. Some, without knowing it, were searching for God. In all his diplomatic posts of Turkey, Greece, Bulgaria, and France, love was man's everyday, common language and goal.

In much of his writings, the Pope confessed his body was weak and he found it difficult to endure suffering. He offered his human frailty to God. Yet he must become a saint! How? To endure his own and the suffering of his friends and others in silence. To feel and be with others in their dark hours of physical and mental anguish. This was true love, he concluded—to be happy and even joyous while suffering with his fellows.

As we turned the pages of the notebooks, Capovilla mentioned that, in more than 50 years as a priest, the Pope missed saying Mass only twice. He never explained why. There were merely two blank pages in the notebooks.

As the light of the afternoon faded, I mentioned to Capovilla

Pope John was granted and happily withstood great physical suffering in his final weeks and days of life. In the final four days, God was to permit him the agony of a lifetime. His plea to be able to endure suffering was fulfilled. Angelo Giuseppe Roncalli had proved to be a man.

Chapter 22

November 22, 1963

IT WAS ABOUT 8:30 p.m. and we were just sitting down to our family dinner. The phone rang. Mark Richards, an ABC Radio news editor in New York, said "President Kennedy has been shot. Get back to the office. We need reaction." I grabbed my suit coat, and hollered to Joy that Kennedy was shot and I was returning to work. As I started our car, I yelled to her, "Call everybody on the staff. Tell them to come to the office."

Franco Bucarelli and I arrived about the same time. John F. Kennedy had already died in Dallas, Texas. Italian radio and television were carrying one news bulletin after another from Dallas and Washington. From our office windows above Piazza di Spagna, we would hear voices piercing the traffic below: *Kennedy e stato assassinato! Kennedy . . . assassinato!* (Kennedy has been assassinated!)

Soon everyone had arrived—camerman Joe Falletta, soundman Carlo Brillarelli, and Aldo Bisci who put more paper in our wire service machines. They eventually turned to me and asked the same question: "What do we do?"

"Phone the Pope," I said to Franco.

Everyone stared at me as if I had gone crazy. Falletta laughed. "The Pope? Who do ya think you are?" Falletta was a cynic and a perennial grouch. He believed in nothing and constantly tried to put people down.

Under the circumstances, I thought the idea might work. So I asked Franco again to call the Pope, meaning the papal secretary, Father Macchi. Bucarelli started dialing on one phone while I began calling Italian government officials on another to get their reactions. Meanwhile, I asked Aldo to book radio circuits to ABC in New York, one every half hour starting in 30 minutes. We actually got a circuit in about 15 minutes and I broadcast the Italian government reaction from our homemade office studio.

As I came out after the broadcast, Franco rushed up and said, "I got Father Macchi. He thought we were crazy. But I told him what you said: The American people would like to hear from the Pope when their president was shot. And that Kennedy was the first Catholic chief in the White House. He promised to ask the Pope and will call us back."

We waited anxiously for several minutes. The phone rang. Franco answered it. Father Macchi said with a note of surprise, "The Holy Father agrees. He's now writing out a statement in English. But you must be here in about 10 minutes. He has other things to do this evening. I will phone the Swiss Guards to let you in. Ten minutes. No more." Macchi hung up.

We frantically grabbed the television camera and other equipment and ran with it to Faletta's car where we stowed it in the trunk. Faletta and Brillarelli raced on in Joe's car while Franco and I followed them in Bucarelli's. The two cars tore through the streets and finally arrived at the open gate to the left of St. Peter's Basilica. The Swiss Guards knew Franco and me from the Vatican documentary and waved all of us through. We raced up to St. Damasus Courtyard, unloaded our gear, and took two elevators up to the papal library. Father Bruno, another assistant in the papal household, awaited us. We laid out our equipment in front of the Pope's reading desk. Father Macchi hurriedly arrived. How much time would we need to be ready? I said 10 more minutes. He seemed aghast but returned to Pope Paul. We couldn't find a frezzolite to light the Pope's face. Someone found it with a shout. Father Bruno was persuaded to help carry our empty work cases to a side wall. The Pope suddenly entered amid the bedlam. Brillarelli dropped a case with a crash. Everyone, including the Holy Father, was startled. Brillarelli kept saying it was empty.

Pope Paul, noting the confusion, nevertheless approached me and asked, "What about Mrs. Kennedy and their children?"

I replied Mrs. Kennedy hadn't been injured and was safe, but the children hadn't yet been told about their father. Faletta was still adjusting his camera as the Pope expressed shock and horror at the assassination. "How could something like this happen in a civilized country like the United States? It's incredible!" he said.

Father Macchi asked if we were ready. Faletta said we were. Brillarelli was the TV soundman and Bucarelli was recording on another machine for ABC Radio. Someone had to hold the frezzolite. Father Bruno was pressed into service and lifted the "frezzy" in his right hand. The stunned priest was now shining the light on the Pope's face.

Faletta had a problem: "Where's the Pope's mike?"

Brillarelli: "I got it. Wait a minute. I gotta put it around the Pope's neck."

The Pope's head snapped from side to side listening to the sharp questions and commands. Brillarelli began placing the mike around the Holy Father's white cassock and neck. He ran back to his sound equipment and fired back at the Pontiff, "Say something, Your Holiness."

Pope Paul: Say what?

Brillarelli: This is a test of your voice level. Say anything.

Paul read the first line from his statement.

Brillarelli: Good. That's fine. Keep it at that level.

Faletta: Wait a minute! I gotta get a meter reading on the light. Hold everything!

Both Faletta and Bucarelli converged on the Pope at the same time. Joe thrust his light meter near the Pope's forehead. Franco pushed a tape-recorder mike on top of the Pope's desk, just in front of his handwritten remarks.

I expected Father Macchi to start turning purple at this point and furtively glanced at him. He was chuckling. He had never seen such a circus. Turning to me, he seemed to be getting into the spirit of things and asked, "Would you like a picture of President Kennedy on the desk, the one he signed for the Holy Father when he visited last July?"

I nodded affirmatively. Father Macchi, getting even more into our mood, again asked: "How about the gold letter box with the presidential seal? President Kennedy also gave that to the Holy Father."

I nodded again. Father Macchi disappeared but quickly returned with the items. The Pope was now completely in our hands. Faletta moved in with his silent camera and began shooting cutaways to be used with our story. He continued what all of us had been doing—telling the Pope what to do. "Your Holiness, look at the picture of President Kennedy. That's it. Keep looking. I'm still shooting. That's right. Good!"

Faletta pointed to the other side of the Pope's desk. "Now, the letter box. Pick it up, please. That's right. Look at it. Keep looking. Fine. You can put it down now. OK, we're ready to shoot sound."

Casserly: Holy Father, we are almost ready for your remarks. Are you ready, Joe?

Faletta: No, I'm just getting the focus on him. All right, why don't you cue him? I'll start rolling now and you cue him in ten seconds.

Casserly: All right, Your Holiness, keep looking up. When I point to you with my right arm, start speaking.

I pointed and Pope Paul began to address the American people. "In this tragic hour for all of us . . ." The Pontiff spoke in English for about five minutes. When he finished, the Pope looked up and surprised us. "How was my English?"

Soundman Brillarelli responded for all of us. "Perfect, Your Holiness. We got every word."

The Pope smiled. We had forgotten Father Bruno, holding the frezzolite. He piped up. "Can I let my arm down now?"

All of us shouted, "Yes." We laughed.

Pope Paul slowly rose from his seat after Brillarelli removed his microphone. His Holiness came around his desk and into our midst. He did not speak but looked at us closely. Finally, searching my face, he said, "But you are American . . . ?"

Puzzled, I answered, "Yes, Your Holiness. Why?"

Then, it dawned on all of us. We had spoken only Italian in the Pope's presence. Not a word of English. The only person who had spoken English was the Pope.

Pope Paul was still studying us without speaking. I glanced around trying to understand what he was searching for. The awful truth quickly became obvious—our impromptu state of dress. Faletta wore a beaten-up sport jacket, a bright wool sport-shirt and no tie. Brillarelli had on an old turtleneck sweater. Bucarelli had on a bright sport jacket more suited to a Sunday soccer match. His yellow tie looked like a neon sign. I was dressed in a dark suit and tie, but that wasn't what the Pope was looking at. My shirt was hanging out in front and back. In carrying the equipment, I had come apart.

I began to apologize for our appearances. All joined me. We explained our rush and carrying the equipment. The Pope smiled but said nothing. Suddenly, he began handing each of us a memorial medal of his reign. He began to bless us and we knelt. Then Paul quickly disappeared. Fathers Macchi and Bruno remained behind and helped us carry out our equipment.

In the long hallway leading to the elevator, Monsignor Angelo Dell'Acqua, Undersecretary of State, awaited us. Dell'Acqua was half-dressed for bed. He was wearing an old-fashioned nightcap.

There was also a priest from Vatican Radio, a reporter from *L'Osservatore Romano*, the official Vatican newspaper, and Luciano Casimiri, chief of the Vatican Press Office. All began firing questions at us:

"How did you manage to get in? What did the Pope say? Can you give us the text?"

Monsignor Dell'Acqua, who knew me well, pulled me aside and asked, "How did you get in? Only Cardinal Cicognani, Secretary of State, sees the Holy Father at this late hour. Really, how did you do it?"

I shrugged and replied, "We phoned."

"You what?" Dell'Acqua asked incredulously.

"We called the papal apartment on the telephone," I answered.

Monsignor Dell'Acqua shook his head, sounded as if he were whispering some aspiration to himself, and wandered off still shaking his head.

The reporters from Vatican Radio, its newspaper, and Casimiri asked me for a copy of the Pope's statement. I didn't have a printed copy and didn't disclose we had it on tape for radio. I wasn't about to be scooped on my own story. Instead, I said they would have to get it from Macchi in the morning. In the meantime, we would have broadcast it on radio and TV a dozen times in the states.

We drove back to the office with the film and radio tape. ABC New York was astonished. Papal reaction in English only a few hours after the passing of President Kennedy, and no one else in the world had it! ABC-TV News was on the phone to us less than a minute after Radio alerted them we also had film. They advised me to have the film developed in Rome that night and send it via the relay satellite—to hell with cost—as soon as I could. Satellite transmission from Europe to the United States was in its early stages and prohibitively expensive but our dice were hot.

The Vatican was bombarded from the other U.S. television networks and radio-tv networks around the world for the radio tape and film. So was ABC New York. The Vatican referred all the callers to us. Through Italian state RAI Radio-TV, we made the Pope's statement available to stations on every continent. A priest at Vatican Radio told me. "It never happened before and will never happen again."

In all the excitement and work of covering the Kennedy story, no one at ABC New York congratulated us for our scoop. I didn't care. We had done it and no one could ever take the beat away from us. It was like climbing Mount Everest. No one saw you but you knew you had done something great.

A few months later, we scored another scoop with Pope Paul. I wrote him a letter and His Holiness agreed to deliver a special Easter message on world peace to the American people. We filmed him again and gave His Holiness similar TV direction. Monsignor Dell'Acqua again shook his head in disbelief. I am sure he concluded that not all the keys to the Vatican were in the hands of angels.

Chapter 23

A Puppet and a Mandolin

BEFORE THE FIRST buds of the Roman spring of 1964, a man came to our front door and said he was from the moving company. Kevin said he didn't look like Signor Gabrielli who used to transport us to the sea in summer time. Terry and little Jeff nodded their heads in agreement.

Joy invited the man inside. He explained it was necessary to place things in small boxes. These would later be placed in large crates. Everything must be secured to avoid damage. Kevin insisted the man had arrived early. He told the mover the mimosa tree had not yet bloomed and, therefore, we had time to wait for Anzio and the sea. The man replied he was talking about the Atlantic Ocean. We were shipping our household goods to America.

Kevin and his brothers didn't understand. They were going to Anzio, but it was too soon. The mimosa was not even yellow. After all, Kevin said proudly, The Way of the Mimosa was the name of our street.

The man took down the mandolin from atop our piano. Kevin told him it came from Naples. His brothers nodded this was indeed so. The mover placed the four double-stringed instrument on a couch. Kevin said mandolins had been making music for a very long time, since the 12th century. The man smiled and agreed.

Kevin explained this particular instrument had come from Via San Sebastiano in Naples. They had been making mandolins for three centuries there. But now, many of those small mandolin shops were being closed because few wanted to play the instrument. Most preferred the guitar. Franco had told him all that.

The mover took down our puppet from the piano top where it had been lying undisturbed for some time. Kevin said the puppet was Richard the Lion-hearted and came from Sicily. Richard fought against villains and other bad men. Kevin explained Don Riccardo, as we called him in our house, was a very special puppet. So he must be wrapped and boxed very carefully. The man agreed.

All puppets have a story, Kevin continued, like Pinocchio. He looked at me and said, "Papa has often told us the true story of Pinocchio."

I had said Pinocchio had truly lived. He wasn't just a wooden boy. The truth was actually revealed by Signora Giovanna Giannini, who lived in the little town of Castello near Florence, on her 90th birthday in 1963. She sat in a garden near her home and recalled, "My father was a gardener at the Villa Bel Riposo where Collodi lived. (Collodi was the pen name for Carlo Lorenzini who was the author of *Pinocchio* and many other children's tales.) I was a little blonde girl of only 12 when Collodi used to take me on his knee and ask me all sorts of questions.

"He would ask about life in our village, particularly the boys and their mischiefs. I soon began to realize that he was writing stories about these boys, only giving them other names.

"One day, Collodi told me he was writing a story about a puppet and would call him Pinocchio. Also, he was going to put me in his book. I would be the little fairy with the blue hair."

The signora said Pinocchio actually was a boy named Carlo.

Collodi used to see him from his window. Little Carlo was always in a neighbor's orchard. Collodi made it a point to meet Carlo and ask him questions. The youngster had a high, squeaky voice and, as the signora recalled, "He had a long nose and a mischievous smile. He always wore a small white cap on his head, just like Pinocchio."

The fox and the cat in the story were based on boy thieves Collodi saw in Florence. Geppetto, the woodmaker, used to repair furniture in the Lorenzini villa. The big oak was also there. That was where the fox and cat robbed Pinocchio of the golden coins.

The signora related Collodi would take supper to his room each evening. There, before his mirror, he would pretend to hold a conversation with her or little Carlo—with all the grimaces and gestures—and then hurriedly write down his impressions.

The little woman had become blind and her "blue hair" had turned to silver. Yet her memory remained. "My father and the other household workers soon learned of this because they could hear Collodi's voice. They began peeking through a keyhole to listen and watch him. So did I, but only once! How funny he was!"

I had told our boys Pinocchio first appeared in print about 1880, long before their mother or father was born. Also, his story had been translated into almost every language. I said, "He was a boy who was always a puppet and a puppet who was always a boy. Pinocchio is immortal."

The boys liked that. They knew that immortal meant Pinocchio would never die. "Nor will our mandolin or puppet ever die," I added.

The boys cheered.

I explained further, "It is just like Leondina who has taken care of all you boys since you were very small. She will never die. She and her husband, Angelo, will be with you as long as you live."

"Yes, that's right," the boys chorused.

I then explained we were leaving Italy. But our friends and Italy would never die. They would always remember Policarpo who came to fix our plumbing and other parts of our house. The boys nodded solemnly. And Signora Rossi who sewed clothes for their mother and stitched their shirts and pants. They nodded again. And Elena who helped dress them, cooked, and helped their mother with the washing and ironing. All three agreed. Franco, who worked with Papa, and his wife, Lucia, who brought them presents. Giulia, the portiere at our apartment building on Via Adelaide Ristori, who guarded them when they played in the garden and always knew where they were outside. Yes, the boys said. Elio Auticchio, Giulia's nephew who played with them for years. Indeed, they agreed. Bishop Primeau, Monsignor Landi, and Monsignor Joseph Howard, who baptized them. They nodded once more.

Caroline Tyndale, who came from England to watch over them and who would come to America with them. Dr. Giuseppe Ricci and Dr. Mario Mittiga who helped bring them into the world and took care of them. Like Pinocchio, the boys would never forget them. They nodded again.

The mover asked, "How long have you lived in Italy?"

"Seven years," I replied.

"Yes," he said, "you will remember Italy."

The man carefully put the puppet and mandolin to sleep in a box he sealed with wide tape. Our piano top was empty. Outside, the mimosa tree was still bare.

* * *

As I write these words, I can smell the roses in our Arizona garden. Our apple, apricot, plum, and Asian pear trees are full of fruit. Our Arizona cypress and Arizona locust stand old and tall in our front yard. A dozen flowering bushes surround the Prescott property. I look up into the hills, a mile high, and see thousands of alligator cedar, pine, manzanita, and scrub oak trees.

Sadly, there is no mimosa. But, in my study, our mandolin from Naples and our puppet, Don Riccardo from Sicily, live out their immortality. The puppet is resting his head on the side of the mandolin. His warrior's mask falls slightly over his eyes. Don Riccardo and his strings sleep in the long ago. And my eyes close with them.

Epilogue

ROME STRETCHED BEFORE us. The sun shone brightly and the hills were clear. It was like a dream. As we flew above the city, Joy said: "I can see St. Peter's Basilica." It was the ultimate confirmation. We had indeed returned after 27 years.

The taxi ride into the city from Leonardo da Vinci Airport weaved through new *borgate* (boroughs)—yellow, pink, red, and ochre palazzi that were laid like ugly slabs across the once-beautiful, open countryside. The artistry that marked the long growth of the Eternal City had been abandoned for large, faceless, crowded structures that rubbed against one another's flat, square shoulders. All of these compact apartment complexes had been built since we left Rome in 1964.

Little traffic moved this quiet November Saturday of 1991. The noonday sun warmed us from the chill of London. The taxi driver sped about 70 miles an hour until the outskirts of the city sprang up. He slowed further as we reached the Church of St. Paul Outside the Walls.

We recognized most of the piazzas although stores and other passing landmarks had disappeared. But the great monuments of the city—from the Vatican to Castel Sant' Angelo, the Campidoglio, the Coliseum, and Roman Forum—rose like old friends.

Traffic became heavier as we neared the *centro storico* (historic center) of Rome. I had noticed considerable scaffolding as we passed the Coliseum and asked the driver about it.

"Pollution," he said. "Chemicals and other smog from traffic and industrial waste dirty everything. Restoring and preserving the monuments has become an everyday job."

The gentleman, about 60, sighed. "But the air is worse. It's almost unbreathable at times. It's clean only on days like this when there's less traffic. Traffic is impossible. I can't make a living anymore unless I work 12 hours a day. And noise—traffic horns—it's like a rock concert."

We had arrived at our pensione, Trinita dei Monti, on Via Sistina near the Hassler Hotel. The cab ride was about $65 with tip. In our day, it had been about $15.

We stayed at the Trinita dei Monti because it was about $100 a day. The Hassler was more than $400 a day for a double room. In our time, the same Hassler room would have been about $70 a day.

We liked Via Sistina because we could walk to any part of the historic center and catch numerous buses or the underground metro nearby. It was at the top of the Spanish Steps looking down on the famous piazza and the chic shopping area of Via Condotti. Via Sistina was also an easy walk to the wide green lawns of Villa Borghese.

We met Corrado Pizzinelli and his wife, Maddelena, at their home before going to dinner. Corrado and I embraced and soon turned our thoughts to Algeria, the Middle East, and the old battles between the Christian Democrats and Communists. We also plowed deep into more current Italian politics.

In the booming 1980s, the Italian economy was the fastest growing in the industrialized world. But now public debt was soaring out of control and inflation was climbing. The country's inefficient government and high taxes, with nearly 20 percent of Italy's jobs mired in state political patronage, were crippling the economy. These state salaries added up to 60 percent of all public spending, putting Italy constantly in the midst of a budget crisis. It couldn't compete against other Common Market nations with such an economic albatross around the neck of its private sector. The collapse of the Soviet Union had put new pressure on the Christian Democrats and the government. Since Italy's Reds also had fallen into disrepute, the Christian Democrats could no longer use the country's large Communist party as an excuse for their failures. The Christian Democrats were still seen by the public as corrupt. The new national party, born of widespread frustration regarding political corruption, hadn't yet come to power.

I asked Corrado whether the government had made any progress in lifting southern Italy into modern Europe. He answered by citing the "Ancona Wall." Corrado also called it Italy's Berlin Wall. It was an invisible line running across the Italian boot from the Adriatic port of Ancona to just south of Rome. Below was the *Mezzogiorno*, sometimes called the "Latin America of Italy." The government had poured about $300 billion in development funds into southern Italy over more than four decades. Yet the region's income was still only a little more than half of that north of the Ancona-Rome line.

A revolutionary movement known as the Lombard League — centered in Milan and the rich, industrious province of Lombardy — startled the nation in 1990 by winning 20 percent of the vote in local elections up and down the boot. The League wanted to split Italy into a confederation like Switzerland. It was revolting against the inefficiency and tax burden of the government. Most said the South could keep Rome. They smiled and added: the Mafia, too. Despite great local and national efforts to wipe out the Mafia, it still ran much of the South.

As Corrado spoke, I returned to Montelepre, Sicily, and the grave of Turridu — Salvatore Giuliano, the Sicilian Robin Hood.

I could hear the boy's voice near the tombstone. "He's free. Turridu is now free."

I mentioned to Corrado and his wife that we had gone for a walk in the city that afternoon. We had passed my old INS office at 476 Via del Corso. Pietro Nenni was, of course, long dead but his Socialist party was still headquartered there. I asked a young policeman guarding the entrance who had succeeded the long-time Socialist leader.

"Nenni?" he replied. "Who's Nenni?"

I thanked the young man and looked across the street in search of my favorite coffee bar on the corner. It, too, had disappeared from the scene.

The fierce traffic, fumes, and noise of the old days also had passed away. Vehicles were now forbidden on Via del Corso except for ambulances, police cars, and, of course, government officials. I joked to Joy, "The *Onorevole* (the Honorable address for politics) will somehow circumvent the law."

We both laughed.

Of course, the men who parked my car on Via del Corso and at Piazza di Spagna were gone. No traffic was permitted in Piazza di Spagna either. But somehow, I could hear those long-ago voices directing parking:

Avanti, Dottore! (Forward, Doctor!) *Indietro, Avvocato!* (Back, Attorney!) *Fermate, Professore!* (Stop, Professor!) Their tips had ballooned with each bit of flattery to the drivers.

We sipped wine and talked of the Pizzinellis' life on the western outskirts of Rome. Corrado liked the tranquility of the countryside for writing. He had retired from his two newspapers. He received a journalist's pension and was now freelancing. Although Corrado was a well-established reporter and writer, life wasn't easy for them. Freelancing was difficult and Maddelena's monthly pay as a grade school teacher was only about $1,300. Many university professors earned only $1,600 a month. Yet Rome was one of the most expensive cities in Europe. For example, the average two-bedroom apartment cost about $208,000. Rent for the same apartment averaged $1,000 a month.

So how do Italians pay their bills? Maddelena said many families were three-income households: two jobs held by the husband and one by the wife. Italians had the lowest birth rate in Europe and were, in fact, below zero population growth.

Some were able to own apartments because they were passed down by their parents or grandparents. Others were still paying the mortgage on their parents' apartment. Others managed to beat the massive housing price increases of the last dozen years. But many scrimped and saved and were barely able to meet each month's mortgage or rent payment.

Romans call all this *L'arte d'arrangiarsi*—the art of arranging things. No matter how poor one may be, it's almost impossible to find an apartment in Rome for less than $500 a month. Many laborers have left the city for the Alban Hills and countryside outside Rome where they may find a small place for $300 or $400 a month. I spoke to a taxi driver who commuted by bus more than four hours each day. He said, some days in heavy traffic, the ride took more than five hours. The man worked 12 hours a day, six days a week.

Corrado drove us to a large restaurant a few miles from his home. It was a vast place that sat nearly 200 people. We arrived early, about 6:30 p.m., but the tables began to fill rapidly after 7:00 p.m.

I had forgotten about the elegance of Italian couples going to dinner on a Saturday evening. Every pin, every curl, every silk tie was in place. This was family *faccia*—face. No people express more gaity and laughter than Italians at dinner. An evening out is more than mere happy hours (often three at dinner); it is more like a *festa*—a big holiday.

The list of the *primi piatti*, the first plates, rambled on for two full mouth-watering pages in the menu, from *Spaghetti alle Vongole* (spaghetti with clams in the cook's own red sauce) to *Risotto alla Pescatora* (steamed rice with chunks of broiled fish usually in a cream sauce). This was followed by a long list of *secondi piatti* (main plates).

By 8:30 p.m., every seat in the restaurant was full. I couldn't take my eyes off the cheese table, even though it followed the meal. At least two dozen different cheeses clamored for my attention. It was enough to drive any cheese-lover crazy.

I had *Spaghetti alla Carbonara* (spaghetti with bacon smothered with a cream sauce) as a first plate, and *Abbacchio al Forno* (roast lamb) as the entrée—young lamb so tender it came close to melting in my mouth. The meal was topped with fresh mozzarella and espresso. I was full but the others had rich Italian rum cake to close out the evening. It reminded me of the Rome gas strike when we were forced to eat in a restaurant and our kids discovered rum cake.

Italians rarely dined on other cooking. The best French, Chinese, and other restaurants had a difficult time in Italy. Perhaps it was because the Italian menu was like the people's character— artistic, theatrical, irreverent, and very improvisational.

The family chatter around us had become a roar. Everybody was talking at once. Multitudes of children were squealing for food, dessert, and their parents' attention.

Our bill was about $300. That would have paid our onetime apartment rent in Rome for two months.

Corrado and Maddelena drove us back to our pensione. Few cars were on the streets because it was late and Rome was dark. The brief exchange with Corrado in his car summed up our meeting.

"It's not the old Rome of the fifties and sixties," he said.

"Yes," I responded, "I remember buying two beautiful oil paintings—copies of *Roma Sparita* (Disappeared Rome) from the 1800s—at the Flea Market at Porta Portese for $16. For me, most of the Old Rome is now antiquity. I feel lost."

We had arrived at our pensione. As Joy and I got out of the car, I said, "Long live the motor scooter!"

Corrado laughed and asked, "What do you mean by that?"

"I remember when the motor scooter was the king of Rome—family transportation—Mom, Pop, and maybe even two kids. That was my Rome."

"Amen," Corrado said.

All of us embraced.

We awoke early on Sunday morning and took the bus to St. Peter's Basilica. We were to meet Leondina, the children's one-time governess, about 1:00 p.m. at the Baptismal Font just inside the entrance to the left. Meantime, Pope John Paul II and thousands of Germans had taken over St. Peter's Square. The Pope was saying Mass and having a beatification ceremony for a German priest who had devoted his life to the poor of Cologne.

If Italy had changed, the Vatican had not. The giant square and the Basilica seemed exactly the same as the last time I had seen them. This was soon dramatically confirmed. Hundreds of pigeons swooped across the piazza on bombing runs. They blasted Joy and me several times. I said, "Just like old times."

Joy and Leondina wept on one another's shoulder. Leondina's hair had turned partly gray. Once a large woman, she had become much thinner, but her gentility and good heart had worn well with time. Leondina was the same dignified woman with soft, precise diction, and she still laughed with unabashed gusto. How I wished our boys were with us!

As we strolled through the streets surrounding the Vatican, I thought back to three popes—Pius XII, John XXIII, and Paul VI. Pius, courtly prince; John, the peasant, and Paul, the aristocratic diplomat. Also Pope John's secretary, now Archbishop Capovilla. How the Church had changed in the 27 years since then. There was now virtually no Latin, and a great loss of priests and nuns. A fierce internal fight was being made over birth control and other issues. Meantime, the Italian Curia in the Vatican had lost considerable power among the world's Catholics.

In the old days, no one in his wildest dreams could have conceived of such changes. The Church has been indeed, like Rome, transformed.

We found a modest trattoria and sat for lunch. Leondina recounted the years since we had seen her. She had continued working but had given up taking care of children as age slowed her. She had no children of her own. Her husband, Angelo, had unexpectedly passed away. Leondina lived in their two-bedroom apartment near Cinecitta (Italy's big movie studio lot) on the outskirts of the city.

We had a light lasagna with roast rabbit. Both were delicious. This was, as the dinner with Corrado and Maddelena, a few sweet hours of love and devotion. We spoke of family, friends, and acquaintances with the tenderness of long and faithful friendship. We had written each other faithfully through the years. Our loyalty had passed the test of time. We had survived. Perhaps that said everything. We were still here on earth to say hello after a very long time.

We began walking back to our pensione after lunch. A stream of cans and paper flowed in the Tiber River. Leondina said Italy was submerged in environmental problems. Perhaps the worst was the industrial and other wastes which had swamped the beaches of both the Mediterranean and Adriatic coasts.

Graffiti were splashed on houses. One said: "Get Drugs Out of Here!" Leondina explained official figures indicated as many as 200,000 Italians were addicted to cocaine and heroin. Drugs were everywhere.

Joy wanted to visit a church but we found the front doors locked. Leondina said most churches were now locked during the day since priests feared robberies. This was unknown in the old days.

We arrived at Piazza del Popolo which was as impressive as ever. The great Egyptian obelisk towered above the Sunday crowds. I could still hear party chief Palmiro Togliatti addressing his fellow Communists thronging the square. The roar of their approval dinned in my ears.

Canova's big coffee bar still attracted tourists and Italians alike. It was crowded with people drinking espresso and late-afternoon Italian brandy.

We walked up Via del Babuino past the beautiful furniture and other stores to Piazza di Spagna. The square was mobbed with tourists surrounding Bernini's fountains and taking the sun on the nearby steps. The young Italian men were still trying to pick up foreign girls with their old line, "Do you speak English?" If a girl said yes, they were off and running.

I searched most of the hundred or so steps that climbed up the Trinita dei Monti. I was looking back through the years again. It was here that I first met the *professore*, who painted the steps and square from virtually every angle. All his oils were small. Sometimes, he would do three or four in a day. I thought he did magnificent work and three of his works still hang on our walls.

On Monday, we took a bus to Piazza Navona. This was where we brought our boys each Christmas season to listen to the bagpipers from the Abruzzi Hills and eat roasted chestnuts. In the summer, the boys chorused for *tartufo gelato* (rich chocolate ice cream). The piazza had been a stadium for chariot races during ancient times. The outline of the track could still be seen in the oval street coursing around Bernini's famous water statues in the middle.

On that lovely sunny morning, we decided to have coffee and sat at a table watching a group of Italian schoolchildren and the tourists walk past. I choked when we got the bill for the two coffees—more than eight dollars! Yet, Bernini was worth it.

We visited the nearby Pantheon which had been the most important pagan basilica in ancient Rome. I was startled when a woman told me I could get a plenary indulgence by saying a few prayers and asking forgiveness for my sins. All my sins would be forgiven. I prayed like a man possessed!

One of Joy's most important missions in Rome was to buy five pair of leather gloves. The last of the five pair that she had purchased just before we left Rome in 1964 was finally splitting apart. After much searching, she bought five pair at a glove store with a few words of advice to a startled woman entering the shop: "Never skimp on what you pay for leather gloves, especially if you expect them to last for nearly 30 years!"

We had lunch and spent the rest of the day shopping for our children and grandchildren. I went to bed humming an old song made famous by actor Nino Manfredi, "Roma Non Fa La Stupida Sta Sera" (Rome Don't Be Stupid Tonight). I loved that song. It was so caustically Roman.

We bounced out of bed early Tuesday morning and took two rush-hour buses to our old neighborhood at Via Adelaide Ristori. Little appeared to have changed. The half-mile horseshoe street was still mostly covered by thick tree branches. Our old apartment building at Number 22 seemed virtually the same. Our onetime garden was rich with plants. Neighbors told us every family that had owned apartments in the building when we lived there had sold their places and moved away. Each apartment had gone for about $600,000. Our rent had been only about $150 a month.

Giulia, the house porter, was gone. So were the nieces and nephews who lived with her. We despaired at that because Giulia always knew everything. I also regretted that Elio Auticchio, her eldest nephew, had also moved. Elio was a brilliant youngster who was a part-time messenger for me. I eventually hired him to work in our office. We also inquired about our maid, Elena, but no one knew her. It was a very sad morning. I was upset that we couldn't find anyone we knew, especially Policarpo, the handyman. No one recalled him or his favorite phrase when looking at some new household crisis: "Funeral bells, folks!" How could we recapture the last 27 years in Rome without seeing these old friends?

We walked up to Piazza delle Muse, the magnificent vista looking north out of Rome. We could see the Italian foreign ministery and some of the stadiums built for the 1960 Olympics. The two coffee bars, which were there in our day, had expanded greatly. Not only were the bars themselves much larger, but the outside chairs had multiplied three and fourfold.

Joy's hairdresser, Lyda, had sold her business and retired. The same with Bruno, our auto mechanic. Gone, too, was the woman at the tobacco shop. But the *vinaio* (wine seller) was still there and he remembered us immediately. So did his wife. His store had disappeared, however, and they now owned a small grocery market. "The *supermercato* (supermarket)! The supermarket nearly killed all of us," he lamented, sweeping his hands in all directions. The butcher, bakery, and other small shops had long surrendered to the modern shopping giant.

Then the miracle happened. We struck up a conversation with the neighborhood gas-station owner. He knew Giulia's nephew, Elio, and promptly found his telephone number. I was trembling with excitement when I phoned his home. A young woman answered and I asked for Elio. She said he was at work. I told her I was an old American friend and gave her our phone number at the pensione. The woman said she was Elio's wife and promised to convey our message when her husband returned home that evening. She also said Giulia lived nearby. My mind and heart were racing when I hung up the phone. I turned to Joy and said, "That was Elio's wife. He's at work. And Giulia is still alive." A big smile brightened Joy's face.

We were still short of gifts for our children and took a bus to Piazza Fiume which was once filled with department and other large stores. It still was. For the next few hours, Joy spent us close to the poor house. She even found a beautiful suit for herself. Tired and aching, we took two buses back to our hotel. As the bus bumped along, I noticed a tall, gray-haired man clinging to a rail near the center door. It was Wilton Wynn! I rushed over but he didn't recognize me immediately. "I'm Jack Casserly, Wilton! Jack!"

Suddenly, he exploded, "Jack!"

The odds on such a meeting were perhaps a million to one. We embraced. I'm not sure it was Arab- or Italian-style. We had known one another in both the Middle East and Rome. He had been the Associated Press bureau chief in Cairo and later a correspondent and bureau chief for *Time* Magazine in Rome.

Joy now rushed over. "Wilton!" she exclaimed. He was getting off at Piazza Ungheria. There was no time to write anything. I asked him to call us at Trinita dei Monti which he knew well. We would have lunch together.

We arranged to have dinner with Franco Bucarelli, my longtime assistant, and his former wife, Lucia. The Neapolitan dandy and the hot-blooded Sicilian had divorced. They had two children, now grown and working.

We loved them both although each was volcanic. Lucia sometimes exploded like Sicily's Mount Etna and Franco erupted like Naples's Mount Vesuvius. Franco had had a string of girlfriends through the years but I knew Franco would never be happy with any of them. Lucia was too strong, too powerful a woman to forget. Franco needed great feeling in his life, someone who spoke, acted, and loved with the passion of a Sicilian. He married again, but soon divorced. He never met another Lucia and she never married again.

We agreed to meet in front of the Hassler Hotel about 7:00 p.m. Lucia saw us first and called to Joy from a distance. I recognized her immediately. Her great brown eyes still dominated her face. She had lost weight. Lucia was elegant in a light brown cashmere suit. She cried when she kissed Joy and they embraced for a long time. The last time that we had seen Lucia she was about 23 years old. Now she was now 50. I kissed her on the cheek. She was still crying.

Franco roared up in a $40,000 Alfa Romeo, chattering away on his car phone. His dark hair had turned completely white but his face was young and his eyes still quick. He still had the old razzmatazz: "Joy, my treasure. Dearest. The American princess."

No wonder girls and women fell so easily into his arms.

Franco gave me a bear hug. To Lucia, a wave and a Ciao.

We sped off to one of Franco's many haunts, but he was soon

back on his car phone. There had been some promotions at one of the government ministries. He was calling congratulations to the new chiefs. Those demoted were ignored. He laughed and said to me, "I'm doing what the Americans do—networking." Franco was now the radio correspondent of RAI, the state radio-TV monopoly, covering Italian President Franceso Cossiga. After leaving ABC, he had held various jobs at RAI—from correspondent to news producer. Cossiga met Franco and immediately determined here was a consummate politician. Franco would help make him a greater household name. The kid I knew in Naples was now traveling the world with Italy's ceremonial head of state.

We soon talked about Naples. Palazzo Reale, Castel Nuovo, the Galleria, the promenade along Via Carracciolo, Lucky Luciano, and Franco's parents. His mother had died years ago, and his father had passed away only a few months earlier. They were good people, hard working, and the old man had enjoyed life. He had an eye for the girls and good food. Franco was a chip off the old block.

I asked about Lombardi's pizzeria. Franco said it had moved but still operated near Santa Chiara Church. The family business was now nearly 500 years old.

Naples's traffic noise and polluted air were much worse. The metro area now had 1.5 million people. The city had declared one-fourth of Naples' apartment buildings and business offices to be unsafe. I asked Franco what the people said or did about it. He replied, "They just whistled." Whistling is a derisive jeer in Italy and the rest of Europe.

The *Camorra*, crime groups organized along the lines of the Mafia, still ran much of Naples. Small business and other shakedowns continued. A tremendous flow of contraband still made its way through the harbor and customs. Drugs from Sicily, the Middle East, and elsewhere were the hottest cargoes.

"But the Bay of Naples is still the most naturally beautiful harbor in the world," Lucia countered.

Franco added, "We're still the world's greatest individualists. We believe in nothing except the family. There's no community, no common good—only survival."

We spent about three hours at the restaurant talking of our children. Our Kevin had become a salesman and lived near San Francisco. Terry had graduated from college with a degree in math and worked for an electronics firm. Jeffrey had been a newspaperman but was then a press secretary for an Arizona congressman in Washington. Larry was a lieutenant in the U.S. Marine Corps and based at Tustin, an adjunct of El Toro, near Los Angeles.

Both of Franco and Lucia's children, a son and daughter, had joined the *carabinieri*.

All of our old friends at the Vatican had either retired or died. Franco said the place had become a "Polish principality" under Pope John Paul II, who came from Poland.

Retirement had also changed the face of virtually the entire Italian government and parliament. I knew only three people: Prime Minister Giulio Andreotti, Amintore Fanfani, who was in and out of government, and Togliatti's mistress who was still in parliament.

Franco laughed. "You still can't fire anyone in Italy. Not even a politician!"

Lucia was upset about the rise in crime and use of drugs. And laundry.

"Laundry?" Joy asked.

"Yes," Lucia said. "A new law says you can't hang it out a window as before. You've got to go up on the roof and hang it to the rear of the roof. Imagine what that means in Naples! Of course, most people ignore it."

She also lamented the loss of porters who used to guard the entrance to apartment buildings. "Apartment owners said porters were too costly so they were replaced by locked outside gates," Lucia said.

We talked a long time about car parking. Cars were now

parked everywhere—on sidewalks, lawns, everywhere. "You must have a car. Without one, you're nobody. Engines have replaced opera!" Lucia mused.

We drove back to our pensione. It was nearly midnight. Lucia talked of her job and the old days. She had retired from the Ministry of Treasury and now worked as the office manager for an insurance company. She recalled some of our picnics, walks in Villa Borghese, and trips together to Naples. She was crying.

I put my arms around Lucia when we said "Ciao!" It was a sad and final farewell—almost like a death in the family.

Another bear hug from Franco. I asked him if he remembered interviewing Mrs. Kennedy at Ravello outside Naples. He roared with laughter. Then we all said, "Ciao!" The parting was quick, like a gulp of espresso.

Joy and I went to bed and, on turning out the light, I said, "My only regret is that we won't go to Ponza. I'd like to sit on the docks and talk with the kids. Maybe a few still want to see America."

I turned out the light but could see those docks as clearly as sitting there 27 years ago.

* * *

Before meeting Wilton and Lila Wynn at their apartment near Piazza Ungheria, we stopped at San Roberto Bellarmino Church and lit a candle. I could still see the multicolored balloons at Sunday Mass many years before. As we left, three nuns pulled up in a car. I had never seen an Italian sister drive a car and was somewhat shocked.

Wilton had retired from *Time* magazine. His fondest memories were of covering Pope John Paul II and the Vatican. Wilton and Lila had become Roman Catholics. It was a big move for someone from Sicily Island, Louisiana, and a woman from Lebanon.

It was a nostalgic luncheon, talking about Cairo, Beirut, and other coverage of the Middle East. We lamented bitterly the destruction of Beirut, once one of the most beautiful cities in the world. Wilton had been a close friend of Egyptian President Gamal Abdel Nasser and his successor, Anwar Sadat. He wrote a book about Nasser and accompanied Sadat on his famous peace journey to Jerusalem. He had also written a book about the Catholic Church and the Vatican.

Wilton had become the total expatriate. Rome was his home. Neither he nor Lila could imagine living anywhere else. The soaring crime rate, horrendous traffic, and skyrocketing cost of living were merely bumps on the road. Life was Rome.

We had a very long and delicious lunch at a trattoria near Piazza Ungheria. It wasn't easy to stand after the five-course meal, and even more difficult to say farewell. How do you say good-bye to friends of more than 30 years, knowing in all likelihood you will never see one another again?

We got on the bus while Wilton and Lila stood silently on the sidewalk. We waved to one another until all had disappeared from each other's view. I turned to Joy and said, "I'm never coming back. It's too sad."

"Never say never," Joy replied.

Later, we took the underground metro to Leondina's apartment for dinner. Joy and Leondina went to a jewelry store where Joy bought 18-karat gold pieces for our children and grandchildren. Leondina got us a 10 percent discount because we were "one of the family."

The dinner with Leondina went as expected. We lamented the passing of her husband, Angelo. Joy showed her many photos of our children. We ate like gluttons because the lasagna and lamb were outstanding.

On returning to our hotel, I phoned Archbishop Capovilla, the former secretary of Pope John XXIII. It was a wonderful chat. He was living with the Sisters of the Poor at Sotto Il Monte, home of the late pontiff and his family. All of John's Vatican papers and other memorabilia were located in a small museum there.

I reminded Capovilla of my trip to the Roncalli farm with Bob Considine after John's election. The Pope's brothers had given us two bottles of their homemade red wine.

We talked of Venice, his old priestly province. An Italian business consortium and the Venice City Council had borrowed nearly $2 billion to install sea defenses and clean up the lagoon. The city's population had dropped from 150,000 to 80,000 since I had seen it. Meanwhile, 30,000 tourists poured into the region each summer day.

We laughed and said Ciao many times before finally hanging up our phones.

We had located Elena and, on the following morning, we met her at the apartment where she worked on Viale Parioli. She was the maid for a 90-year-old gentleman who was deaf. He was relatively well-off but needed considerable care.

Elena and Joy had a hugging session and, of course, exchanged photos of our children and her relatives. She had never married and had remained a maid through the years. Elena's shoulders were now more bent from the decades of the scrubbing and washing. She had begun work as a maid at the age of nine at Ancona near her village on the Adriatic coast. She was now about 60.

We walked to the outdoor market a few blocks away. Elena knew everyone. She was a queen and this was her kingdom. We bought three beautiful Italian sweaters and bantered with other merchants. Neither Joy nor I had forgotten our Italian despite not using it much for 27 years.

We had coffee at Piazza Ungheria. Elena reported she had purchased a small apartment at Piazza Leonardo da Vinci 22 near old Ciampino Airport on the outskirts of the city. It was for her retirement. She planned to retire in two years when she would receive a pension from the state. She's now retired there.

Elena insisted she should have gone to America when we returned there in 1964. It was never certain we could have gotten her a permanent visa although we tried. Elena's dream faded with each passing year.

She suggested we return to Rome and retire with her in her apartment. Joy said kindly, "Maybe we'll return here on another visit and have more time to spend with you."

The usual tears flowed as we boarded the bus back to our hotel. *Ciao! Ciao! Ci vediamo ancora!* (Goodbye! Goodbye! We'll see one another again!) Elena's brown eyes and dark brown hair disappeared in the distance. I said to Joy, "I'm just about drained."

Giulia, the porter, and her nephew, Elio, arrived with his wife and two children at the pensione about 8:00 p.m. They carried beautiful orchids and candy. I gave them a large box of chocolates. For the next hour, Joy learned all the gossip about our old apartment families on Via Adelaide Ristori. I spoke with Elio. He had risen to a manager's job in communications with the state railroad and worked out of Rome. We chatted until 11:00 p.m. It was time for Elio's children to go home to bed.

Our return to Rome was now almost over. We would leave for the United States about noon the following day. I looked out the hotel window and much of the city was still lit. The weather was mild and people still strolled on the sidewalks below. For a moment, one fleeting moment, nothing had changed in 27 years. Rome was again the elegant, pleasant, smiling city we had known as a family in the long ago. It was falling asleep in the soft light washing over the Coliseum and St. Peter's Basilica.

The memories flooded back. So many loving thoughts, filled with beauty and life. So many good friends. So many events that carried us to the far corners of Sicily, the Alps, and beyond. Such a magnificent city and country. And, *mamma mia*, the Italian people!

As for myself, I had never received greater honor than in the streets below. I could still hear the accolades from the parking guide as I shifted my car into reverse:

"*Lentamente!* (Slowly!) *Piano, piano!* (*Slow, slow!*) *Bravo,*

Commendatore, bravissimo! (Good, honored sir, very good!) *Commendatore, saluti alla famiglia!* (Honored sir, greetings to the family!)

What two greater words are there in the world—honor and family! Well, maybe one other, *l'amore!*